Make the Celebrations Last All Year

Need some inspiration in the kitchen? Look no further. From rehearsal dinners and Halloween movie nights to the Fourth of July, Thanksgiving, Easter and Christmas, this year's *Taste of Home Holiday & Celebrations* cookbook contains all the entertaining tips and tricks you'll need to impress loved ones. The stunning edition before you includes 252 recipes and 23 events, as well as helpful timelines, simple crafts and creative gift-giving ideas. No festivity is complete without a home cooked meal, and your guests won't be able to get enough of these fabulous dishes. Happy feasting!

SUBMIT YOUR RECIPE!

Would you like to see one of your family recipes featured in a *Taste of Home* collection?

Visit **tasteofhome.com/submit** to share your story and recipes.

ON THE COVER

ON THE FRONT COVER
BBQ Turkey Meatballs (p. 104); Marinated Mozzarella (p. 10); Ham & Cheese Biscuit Stacks (p. 10)

ON THE BACK COVER
Citrus Herb Turkey (p. 97); Blue Ribbon Red Velvet Cake (p. 184); Butter Cookies (p. 184); Watermelon Margaritas (p. 224); Lemon Basil Mojito Mocktails (p. 224); Fruity Chicken Salad Mini Sandwiches (p. 151); Spinach-Orzo Salad with Chickpeas (p. 147)

PAGE 49

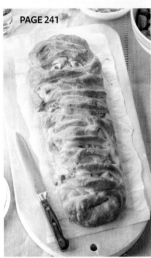

PAGE 241

PAGE 181

PAGE 127

PAGE 208

PAGE 29

Taste of Home.
HOLIDAY &
CELEBRATIONS

EDITORIAL
Vice President, Content Operations **Kerri Balliet**
Creative Director **Howard Greenberg**

Managing Editor/Print & Digital Books **Mark Hagen**
Associate Creative Director **Edwin Robles Jr.**

Editors **Amy Glander, Hazel Wheaton**
Associate Editor **Julie Kuczynski**
Art Director **Raeann Thompson**
Graphic Designer **Courtney Lovetere**
Copy Chief **Deb Warlaumont Mulvey**
Copy Editors **Dulcie Shoener (senior), Ronald Kovach,
Chris McLaughlin, Ellie Piper**
Editorial Services Manager **Kelly Madison-Liebe**
Editorial Production Coordinator **Jill Banks**
Editorial Intern **Stephanie Harte**

Content Director **Julie Blume Benedict**
Food Editors **James Schend; Peggy Woodward, RDN**
Recipe Editors **Sue Ryon (lead), Irene Yeh**

Culinary Director **Sarah Thompson**
Test Cooks **Nicholas Iverson (lead), Matthew Hass**
Food Stylists **Kathryn Conrad (lead), Lauren Knoelke, Shannon Roum**
Kitchen Operations Manager **Bethany Van Jacobson**
Culinary Assistant **Aria C. Thornton**
Food Buyer **Maria Petrella**

Photography Director **Stephanie Marchese**
Photographers **Dan Roberts, Jim Wieland**
Photographer/Set Stylist **Grace Natoli Sheldon**
Set Stylists **Melissa Franco (lead), Stacey Genaw, Dee Dee Schaefer**
Contributing Food Stylist **Sue Draheim**

Business Architect, Publishing Technologies **Amanda Harmatys**
Business Analysts, Publishing Technologies **Dena Ahlers, Kate Unger**
Junior Business Analyst, Publishing Technologies **Shannon Stroud**

Editorial Business Manager **Kristy Martin**
Editorial Business Associate **Andrea Meiers**
Rights & Permissions Assistant **Jill Godsey**

Editor, *Taste of Home* **Emily Betz Tyra**
Art Director, *Taste of Home* **Kristin Bowker**

BUSINESS
Publisher, *Taste of Home* **Donna Lindskog**
Strategic Partnerships Manager, Taste of Home Live **Jamie Piette Andrzejewski**

TRUSTED MEDIA BRANDS, INC.
President & Chief Executive Officer **Bonnie Kintzer**
Chief Financial Officer **Dean Durbin**
Chief Marketing Officer **C. Alec Casey**
Chief Revenue Officer **Richard Sutton**
Chief Digital Officer **Vince Errico**
Senior Vice President, Global HR & Communications
Phyllis E. Gebhardt, SPHR; SHRM-SCP
General Counsel **Mark Sirota**
Vice President, Product Marketing **Brian Kennedy**
Vice President, Consumer Acquisition **Heather Plant**
Vice President, Operations **Michael Garzone**
Vice President, Consumer Marketing Planning **Jim Woods**
Vice President, Digital Product & Technology **Nick Contardo**
Vice President, Digital Content & Audience Development **Kari Hodes**
Vice President, Financial Planning & Analysis **William Houston**

FRONT COVER PHOTOGRAPHY
Photographer **Grace Natoli Sheldon**
Food Stylist **Lauren Knoelke**
Set Stylist **Melissa Franco**

Table of Contents

'Tis the Season

Starters on a Stick 6

Holiday Comfort & Joy 16

White Elephant Party 28

Make-Ahead Holiday Sides 38

Feliz Navidad 48

Wine & Chocolate Party 58

Christmas Bars & Cookies 68

Holiday Breads 78

Giving Thanks

A Sentimental Thanksgiving. 90

Black Friday Slow Cooker Potluck 102

Gobble, Gobble Goodies. 112

Sugar & Spice Desserts. 122

Easter Gatherings

Food & Fellowship Potluck. 134

Easter Egg Luncheon. 144

5-Ingredient Easter Dinner. 154

Spring Staples 164

Special Celebrations

Seeing Red 176

Mother's Day Brunch. 186

Rehearsal Dinner 196

Low Country Boil 206

Rooftop Fireworks Party 216

Cheers for Cheese! 226

Scary Movie Night 236

Index 246

'TIS THE SEASON

A fine feast simmering on the kitchen stove might be today's version of chestnuts roasting on an open fire. What could be a warmer way to welcome the holiday season? Whether you're preparing a formal Christmas feast to impress the in-laws or a more casual white elephant party with friends, we've got you covered. These tasty tidbits, make-ahead sides, scrumptious sweets and more are guaranteed to make everyone jolly!

STARTERS ON A STICK 6

HOLIDAY COMFORT & JOY 16

WHITE ELEPHANT PARTY 28

MAKE-AHEAD HOLIDAY SIDES 38

FELIZ NAVIDAD 48

WINE & CHOCOLATE PARTY 58

CHRISTMAS BARS & COOKIES 68

HOLIDAY BREADS 78

Starters on a Stick

Ready to show off your glam side with a glittery holiday or New Year's Eve party? A lineup of tantalizingly tasty appetizers will certainly please a crowd, but if you want to pull out all the stops, try these fast and festive snacks on a stick.

The concept is simple and makes any combo of amazingly delish ingredients look like a work of art. Here you'll find a flavorful sampling of speared delectables, from simple finger foods like cheese cubes and sammies to heartier hot bites of the meatball and mini sausage variety. There are even sweet treats for dessert lovers.

Easy to hold and even more fun to eat, these no-fuss party faves will be the life of the party!

Marinated Mozzarella (p. 10) **Horseradish Meatballs** (p. 13)
Tortellini & Shrimp Skewers with Sun-Dried Tomato Sauce (p. 9)

GINGER-TUNA KABOBS

GINGER-TUNA KABOBS

My elegant one-bite appetizers will be the talk of the party. Ginger and tuna are a delicious flavor combination, and the wasabi sauce adds a nice zing. If desired, serve on a watercress-lined platter.
—Mary Beth Harris-Murphree, Tyler, TX

Prep: 25 min. + marinating • **Cook:** 5 min.
Makes: 16 kabobs

- 1 pound tuna steaks, cut into 16 cubes
- ¼ cup soy sauce
- 2 tablespoons rice vinegar
- 1 tablespoon sesame seeds
- 1 teaspoon pepper
- 2 tablespoons canola oil
- 16 pickled ginger slices
- 1 bunch watercress, optional
- ½ cup wasabi mayonnaise

1. Toss tuna with soy sauce and vinegar; refrigerate, covered, 30 minutes.
2. Drain tuna, discarding marinade; pat dry. Sprinkle tuna with sesame seeds and pepper. In a large skillet, sear tuna in oil until browned and center is medium rare or slightly pink; remove from skillet.
3. On each of 16 appetizer skewers, thread one ginger slice and one tuna cube. Serve with wasabi mayonnaise.

CARAMEL APPLE & BRIE SKEWERS

I'm a caterer, and these sweet treats rank among my best-sellers. Using prepared caramel makes them a snap to assemble. Who doesn't love a shortcut?
—Camille Ellis, Tampa, FL

Start to Finish: 10 min.
Makes: 6 skewers

- 2 medium apples, cubed
- 1 log (6 ounces) Brie cheese, cubed
- ½ cup hot caramel ice cream topping
- ½ cup finely chopped macadamia nuts
- 2 tablespoons dried cranberries

On each of six wooden appetizer skewers, alternately thread apple and cheese cubes; place on a serving plate. Drizzle with the caramel topping; sprinkle with macadamia nuts and cranberries.

TORTELLINI & SHRIMP SKEWERS WITH SUN-DRIED TOMATO SAUCE

TORTELLINI & SHRIMP SKEWERS WITH SUN-DRIED TOMATO SAUCE

These fresh-tasting skewers with a creamy sauce will have guests nibbling all night.
—Cacie Biddle, Bridgeport, WV

Prep: 30 min. • **Cook:** 15 min.
Makes: 32 appetizers

- 1 package (8 ounces) cream cheese, softened
- ½ cup sour cream
- ¼ cup fresh basil leaves
- ¼ cup oil-packed sun-dried tomatoes
- ¼ cup reduced-fat mayonnaise
- ¼ cup 2% milk
- 2 garlic cloves
- ½ teaspoon Louisiana-style hot sauce
- ¼ teaspoon salt
- ¼ teaspoon pepper

SKEWERS
- 1 package (9 ounces) refrigerated spinach tortellini
- 2 tablespoons olive oil
- 1 pound peeled and deveined cooked shrimp (31-40 per pound)
- 32 decorative or frilled toothpicks

1. Combine first 10 ingredients in a food processor; pulse until blended. Remove to a small bowl; refrigerate sauce, covered, until serving.
2. Cook tortellini according to package directions. Drain; rinse with cold water and drain again. Toss tortellini with oil. Thread tortellini and shrimp onto toothpicks. Serve with sauce.

MARINATED
MOZZARELLA

HAM & CHEESE BISCUIT STACKS

I serve these mini sandwiches at holiday parties, showers and tailgates. Honey and stone-ground mustard add a sweet and savory taste to every bite.
—Kelly Williams, Forked River, NJ

Prep: 1 hour • **Bake:** 10 min. + cooling
Makes: 40 appetizers

- 4 tubes (6 ounces each) small refrigerated flaky biscuits (5 count)
- ¼ cup stone-ground mustard

ASSEMBLY
- ½ cup butter, softened
- ¼ cup chopped green onions
- ½ cup stone-ground mustard
- ¼ cup mayonnaise
- ¼ cup honey
- 10 thick slices deli ham, quartered
- 10 slices Swiss cheese, quartered
- 2½ cups shredded romaine
- 40 decorative or frilled toothpicks
- 20 pitted ripe olives, drained and patted dry
- 20 pimiento-stuffed olives, drained and patted dry

1. Preheat oven to 400°. Cut biscuits in half to make half-circles; place 2 in. apart on ungreased baking sheets. Spread mustard over tops. Bake until golden brown, 8-10 minutes. Cool completely on wire racks.
2. Mix butter and green onions. In another bowl, mix mustard, mayonnaise and honey. Split each biscuit into two layers.
3. Spread biscuit bottoms with butter mixture; top with ham, cheese, romaine and biscuit tops. Spoon mustard mixture over tops. Thread one olive onto each toothpick; insert into stacks. Serve immediately.

DEEP-FRIED CANDY BARS ON A STICK

Why wait in a line at the State Fair for deep-fried candy bars when you can satisfy your curious taste buds in your own home? Be sure to make a lot—these novelties go fast!
—Taste of Home Test Kitchen

Prep: 20 min. • **Cook:** 5 min./batch
Makes: 2 dozen

- 1½ cups all-purpose flour
- 4½ teaspoons baking powder
- 1 tablespoon sugar
- 1 tablespoon brown sugar
- ⅛ teaspoon salt
- ⅛ teaspoon ground cinnamon
- 1 large egg
- ½ cup water
- ½ cup 2% milk
- ¼ teaspoon vanilla extract
- 24 fun-size Snickers and/or Milky Way candy bars, frozen
  Oil for deep-fat frying
  Wooden skewers
  Confectioners' sugar, optional

1. Whisk together first six ingredients. In another bowl, whisk together egg, water, milk and vanilla; add to dry ingredients, stirring just until moistened.
2. In an electric skillet or deep fryer, heat oil to 375°. Dip candy bars, a few at a time, into batter; fry until golden brown, about 30 seconds per side. Drain candy bars on paper towels.
3. Insert skewers into bars. If desired, dust with confectioners' sugar.

MARINATED MOZZARELLA

Cheese is irresistible on its own, but with a light marinade of herbs and spicy red pepper flakes, it's out of this world. Try bocconcini (small, semi-soft round balls of fresh mozzarella) in place of the cubed mozzarella if you'd like a different shape.
—Peggy Cairo, Kenosha, WI

Prep: 15 min. + marinating
Makes: 10 servings

- ⅓ cup olive oil
- 1 tablespoon chopped oil-packed sun-dried tomatoes
- 1 tablespoon minced fresh parsley
- 1 teaspoon crushed red pepper flakes
- 1 teaspoon dried basil
- 1 teaspoon minced chives
- ¼ teaspoon garlic powder
- 1 pound cubed part-skim mozzarella cheese

In a large resealable plastic bag, combine first seven ingredients; add cheese cubes. Seal bag and turn to coat; refrigerate at least 30 minutes.

HORSERADISH MEATBALLS

HORSERADISH MEATBALLS

Try my recipe if you're looking for a spicy twist on traditional meatballs. When I'm not entertaining, I enjoy them with hot cooked rice and a fresh salad for a more substantial meal.
—Joyce Benninger, Owen Sound, ON

Prep: 30 min. • **Bake:** 35 min.
Makes: 3 dozen

- 2 large eggs
- ½ cup dry bread crumbs
- ¼ cup chopped green onions
- 1 tablespoon prepared horseradish
- ½ teaspoon salt
- ¼ teaspoon pepper
- 1½ pounds lean ground beef (90% lean)
- ½ pound ground pork or turkey

SAUCE
- 1 small onion, finely chopped
- ½ cup water
- ½ cup chili sauce
- ½ cup ketchup
- ¼ cup packed brown sugar
- ¼ cup cider vinegar
- 1 tablespoon Worcestershire sauce
- 1 tablespoon prepared horseradish
- 1 garlic clove, minced
- 1 teaspoon ground mustard
- ¼ teaspoon hot pepper sauce

1. Preheat oven to 350°. Combine first six ingredients. Add beef and pork; mix lightly but thoroughly. Shape into 1½-in. balls. Place balls on a greased rack in a 15x10x1-in. pan. Bake until a thermometer reads 160° (165° if using ground turkey), 35-40 minutes.
2. Meanwhile, in a large saucepan, combine the sauce ingredients; bring to a boil, stirring frequently. Reduce heat; simmer, uncovered, 10 minutes. Gently stir in meatballs. Serve with decorative or frilled toothpicks.

CHEESE GRAPE APPETIZERS

CHEESE GRAPE APPETIZERS

These small bites are well worth the time. Serve them as part of an antipasto or cheese platter and alongside your favorite bottle of wine.
—Eleanor Grofvert, Kalamazoo, MI

Prep: 35 min. • **Bake:** 10 min. + cooling
Makes: about 5 dozen

- 4 ounces sliced almonds (about 1 cup)
- 1 package (8 ounces) cream cheese, softened
- 2 ounces crumbled blue cheese, room temperature
- 2 tablespoons minced fresh parsley
- 2 tablespoons heavy whipping cream, room temperature
- 1 to 1¼ pounds seedless red or green grapes, rinsed and patted dry
  Appetizer skewers or toothpicks

1. Preheat oven to 275°. Pulse almonds in a food processor until finely chopped (do not overprocess). Spread pieces in a 15x10x1-in. pan; bake until golden brown, 6-9 minutes, stirring occasionally. Transfer to a shallow bowl; cool slightly.
2. In another bowl, mix cream cheese, blue cheese, parsley and cream until blended. Insert a skewer into each grape. Roll grapes in cheese mixture, then in almonds; place on waxed paper-lined baking sheets. Refrigerate, covered, until ready to serve.

MARSHMALLOW POPS

Indulge your sweet tooth with fluffy chocolate-covered marshmallows. Kids can help decorate these cuties, and they're easily customizable to any holiday or occasion when rolled in coordinating colored toppings. Substitute vanilla baking chips for the semisweet chocolate chips if you like.
—Marcia Porch, Winter Park, FL

Prep: 30 min. + chilling
Makes: 20 servings

- 2 cups (12 ounces) semisweet chocolate chips
- 4½ teaspoons canola oil
- 40 large marshmallows
- 20 wooden pop sticks
  Toppings: assorted sprinkles, shredded coconut or finely chopped nuts

1. In a microwave, melt chocolate chips with oil; stir until smooth.
2. Thread two marshmallows on each pop stick. Dip marshmallows in melted chocolate, turning to coat; allow excess to drip off. Roll in toppings as desired. Place pops on waxed paper-lined baking sheets; refrigerate until set.

APRICOT WRAPS

COCONUT-RUM CAKE POPS

These coconut-coated cake pops with a hint of rum taste like paradise on a stick.
—*Taste of Home* Test Kitchen

Prep: 1½ hours + chilling
Makes: 4 dozen

- 1 package (16 ounces) angel food cake mix
- ¾ cup canned vanilla frosting
- 1 cup sweetened shredded coconut
- 1 teaspoon coconut extract
- ½ teaspoon rum extract
- 48 lollipop sticks
- 2½ pounds white candy coating, melted
  Lightly toasted sweetened shredded coconut

1. Prepare and bake cake mix according to package directions. Cool completely on a wire rack.
2. In a large bowl, mix frosting, coconut and extracts. Tear cake into pieces. In batches, pulse cake in a food processor until crumbs form. Stir crumbs into frosting mixture. Shape into 1-in. balls; place on baking sheets. Insert sticks. Freeze at least 2 hours or refrigerate at least 3 hours until firm.
3. Dip cake pops in melted candy coating, allowing excess to drip off. Roll in toasted coconut. Insert cake pops in a Styrofoam block; let stand until set.

APRICOT WRAPS

I'm proud of my large, diverse collection of recipes, many of which I accumulated in foreign countries during my husband's 25 years of service in the Air Force. We enjoy a variety of flavors, and these wraps are one of our favorites.
—Jane Ashworth, Beavercreek, OH

Prep: 20 min. • **Bake:** 20 min.
Makes: about 4½ dozen

- 1 pound bacon strips
- 3 cups dried apricots (about 14 ounces)
- ½ cup whole almonds
- ¼ cup plum preserves or apple jelly
- 2 tablespoons soy sauce

1. Preheat oven to 375°. Cut each bacon strip into thirds. Fold each apricot half around an almond; wrap each with a bacon strip and secure with a toothpick.
2. Place on two ungreased 15x10x1-in. pans. Bake until bacon is crisp, 10-13 minutes per side.
3. In a small saucepan, cook and stir preserves and soy sauce over low heat until blended and heated through. Drain wraps on paper towels. Serve with sauce.

SMOKED SAUSAGE APPETIZERS

A tangy sauce with a touch of currant jelly glazes these miniature sausages. They're an excellent party starter. Make a big batch because they won't last long!
—Kathryn Bainbridge
Pennsylvania Furnace, PA

Start to Finish: 25 min.
Makes: 6½ dozen

- ¾ cup red currant jelly
- ¾ cup barbecue sauce
- 3 tablespoons prepared mustard
- 1 package (28 ounces) miniature smoked sausages

In a large saucepan, combine jelly, barbecue sauce and mustard. Cook, uncovered, over medium heat until blended, 15-20 minutes, stirring occasionally. Stir in sausages; cook, covered, until heated through, about 5 minutes.

TOP TIP

Food Safety Tips

Appetizers left out for too long offer the perfect environment for bacteria to grow, so it's important to keep an eye on them. To avoid contamination, discard foods that have been left out for longer than 2 hours. Start by setting out small portions and replenish often. Store cold backup dishes in the fridge and hot backup dishes in a 200-250° oven.

Replenish foods with clean bowls and platters to avoid cross-contamination. Frequently check foods with a food thermometer. Hot foods should be held at 140° or warmer. Serve hot appetizers in chafing dishes, slow cookers and warming trays. Cold foods should be held at 40° or colder. Nestle dishes in bowls of ice to help keep them cold.

**COCONUT-RUM
CAKE POPS**

Holiday Comfort & Joy

There's so much joy and magic to soak in as the merry December days unfold to Christmas: family traditions, a perfectly lit tree, the coziness of a crackling fire when there's a storm raging outside. Your celebratory meal should be just as special.

This year enjoy a bountiful Christmas dinner combining elegance and rustic charm. Glazed beef tenderloin takes center stage along with fresh artichokes, buttery squash, a rich shrimp bisque, bread fragrant with caraway, and more. To further indulge the senses, enjoy chocolate cake, cheesecake and a classic Moscow Mule.

The best table is the one that brings together those you love. This year, welcome a joyful spirit and make the ordinary extraordinary.

Fresh Artichokes with Lemon-Yogurt Dip (p. 22) **Caraway Bread** (p. 20)
Bacon-Gruyere Smashed Potatoes (p. 25) **Bacon Beef Tenderloin with Cranberry Glaze** (p. 25)

'Tis the Season

Countdown to Christmas Dinner

Hang the wreath, bring out your finest china and whip up a batch of cheer. Invite loved ones over for an **elegant Christmas they won't soon forget.** There's enough smashed potatoes, beef tenderloin and creamy cheesecake for everyone. **You'll be the toast of the town!**

A FEW WEEKS BEFORE

☐ Prepare two grocery lists—one for nonperishable items to buy now and one for perishable items to buy a few days before Christmas.

TWO DAYS BEFORE

☐ Buy remaining grocery items.

☐ Bake the cake layers for the Three-Layer Chocolate Ganache Cake. Freeze or store in an airtight container.

☐ Wash china, stemware and table linens.

THE DAY BEFORE

☐ Prepare dough for Caraway Bread, letting it rise according to recipe directions. Bake bread. Cover or store in an airtight container.

☐ Mix together the dip ingredients for Fresh Artichokes with Lemon-Yogurt Dip. Refrigerate dip until serving.

☐ Prepare White Chocolate Cheesecake with Cranberry-Orange Compote. Refrigerate overnight.

☐ Combine beef and wine in sealed bag for the Bacon Beef Tenderloin with Cranberry Glaze. Refrigerate overnight to marinate.

☐ Set the table.

CHRISTMAS DAY

☐ About 5-6 hours before dinner, remove chocolate cake layers from the freezer. Prepare filling and ganache. Assemble cake and refrigerate at least 2 hours before serving.

☐ About 3-4 hours before dinner, place ingredients for Wine-Poached Pears in the slow cooker.

☐ About 3-4 hours before dinner, trim sprouts, then cook and dress Brussels Sprouts with Bacon Vinaigrette. Refrigerate salad for at least 3 hours before serving.

☐ About 2 hours before dinner, remove beef tenderloin from refrigerator. Prepare stuffing and fill center of roast. While beef is roasting, cook glaze. Keep roast warm until serving.

☐ About 1½ hours before dinner, prepare Bacon-Gruyere Smashed Potatoes and bake the Cranberry Roasted Squash. Keep dishes warm until serving.

☐ About 45 minutes before dinner, prepare Mushroom Shrimp Bisque. Keep warm until serving.

☐ About 45 minutes before dinner, trim and prepare artichokes. Serve with dip.

RIGHT BEFORE DINNER

☐ As guests arrive, prepare the Lemon-Herb Salmon Toasts and mix together ingredients for Moscow Mules. Serve immediately.

☐ Slice Caraway Bread into wedges and warm in the oven just before serving.

MUSHROOM SHRIMP BISQUE

This comforting recipe was born out of my family's love for seafood. For many years I tried to make a restaurant-quality bisque, and I finally got it right. Now it makes an appearance at every holiday.
—Deirdre Conley, Yorktown Heights, NY

Prep: 15 min. • **Cook:** 30 min.
Makes: 12 servings (3 quarts)

- ½ cup butter, cubed
- 1 pound medium fresh mushrooms, sliced
- 6 green onions, chopped
- 2 garlic cloves, thinly sliced
- ½ cup all-purpose flour
- ¼ teaspoon paprika
- 2 cartons (32 ounces each) chicken broth
- 2 cups half-and-half cream
- 1½ pounds uncooked shrimp (31-40 per pound), peeled and deveined
- ¼ cup chopped fresh parsley

1. In a 6-qt. stockpot, melt butter over medium-high heat. Add mushrooms and green onions; cook and stir 8-10 minutes or until mushrooms begin to brown. Add garlic; cook and stir 1 minute longer.

2. Stir in flour and paprika; cook and stir until well coated. Gradually stir in broth; bring to a boil. Reduce heat; simmer, uncovered, until thickened, stirring often. Gradually stir in cream and shrimp; cook 5 minutes longer or until shrimp turn pink. Sprinkle with parsley.

TOP TIP

Freeze Mushrooms For Longer Shelf Life

Fresh mushrooms should be used within a few days of purchase. If that's not possible, you can blanch or saute them, then freeze for up to 1 month for use in soups, sauces and casseroles. Freeze mushrooms in recipe-size portions for added convenience.

LEMON-HERB SALMON TOASTS

LEMON-HERB SALMON TOASTS

Quick, light and tasty, my salmon toasts make irresistible finger food.
—Christie Wells, Lake Villa, IL

Start to Finish: 20 min.
Makes: 2 dozen

- 1 package (8 ounces) cream cheese, softened
- 4 green onions, chopped
- 2 tablespoons snipped fresh dill or 2 teaspoons dill weed
- ¾ teaspoon sea salt
- ½ teaspoon pepper
- ¼ teaspoon cayenne pepper
- ¼ teaspoon grated lemon peel
- 2 teaspoons lemon juice
- 24 slices snack rye bread
- 8 ounces smoked salmon or lox
  Optional toppings: grated lemon peel, coarsely ground pepper and fresh dill sprigs

Preheat broiler. In a small bowl, beat the first eight ingredients. Place bread slices on baking sheets. Broil 4-5 in. from heat 1-2 minutes on each side or until lightly toasted. Spread with cream cheese mixture; top with salmon. Serve with toppings if desired.

CRANBERRY ROASTED SQUASH

I created this recipe one day when I wanted a warm, fragrant side dish. The aroma of the squash and cranberries cooking in the oven is just as heavenly as the taste itself.
—Jamillah Almutawakil, Superior, CO

Prep: 15 min. • **Bake:** 45 min.
Makes: 12 servings (¾ cup each)

- 1 medium butternut squash (5 to 6 pounds), peeled and cut into 1-inch cubes
- 1 medium acorn squash (about 1½ pounds), peeled and cut into 1-inch cubes
- ⅔ cup chopped fresh or frozen cranberries
- ¼ cup sugar
- 2 tablespoons olive oil
- 1 tablespoon butter, melted
- 1 tablespoon molasses
- 2 garlic cloves, minced
- 1½ teaspoons rubbed sage
- 1 teaspoon salt
- ½ teaspoon pepper

Preheat oven to 400°. In a large bowl, combine all ingredients. Transfer to two 15x10x1-in. baking pans. Roast 45-55 minutes or until tender, stirring and rotating pans halfway through cooking.

CARAWAY
BREAD

CARAWAY BREAD

A rustic round loaf of caraway bread is delicious eaten warm from the oven, as a base for sandwiches, alongside soup, or as toast. If you want to experiment, add sliced chives or sunflower seeds, or substitute other herbs for the caraway, such as dried rosemary or thyme.
—Frances Conklin, Cottonwood, ID

Prep: 20 min. + rising
Bake: 20 min. + cooling
Makes: 1 loaf (8 wedges)

    1   package (¼ ounce) active dry yeast
    1⅓ cups warm water (110° to 115°)
    2   to 3 teaspoons caraway seeds
    1   teaspoon salt
    1   teaspoon honey
    ¾   cup whole wheat flour
    2½ to 3 cups all-purpose flour
    2   teaspoons cornmeal

1. In a small bowl, dissolve yeast in warm water. In a large bowl, combine caraway seeds, salt, honey, yeast mixture, whole wheat flour and 1½ cups all-purpose flour; beat on medium speed until smooth. Stir in enough remaining flour to form a stiff dough (dough will be sticky).
2. Turn dough onto a floured surface; knead until smooth and elastic, about 6-8 minutes. Place in a greased bowl, turning once to grease the top. Cover with plastic wrap and let rise in a warm place until doubled, about 1 hour.
3. Grease a 15x10x1-in. baking pan; sprinkle with cornmeal. Punch down dough. Turn onto a lightly floured surface. Shape into a round loaf; place on prepared pan. Cover with greased plastic wrap and let rise in a warm place until almost doubled, about 30 minutes. Preheat oven to 425°.
4. Using a sharp knife, cut a large "X" in top of loaf. Bake on a lower oven rack 20-25 minutes or until golden brown. Remove from pan to a wire rack to cool.

MOSCOW MULE

Here's a retro cocktail that first became popular in the 1940s. It's traditionally served in a copper mug with plenty of ice and garnished with a lime slice. The recipe easily doubles to serve a crowd.
—*Taste of Home* Test Kitchen

Start to Finish: 5 min.
Makes: 6 servings

    2   cups ginger ale, chilled
    2   cups ginger beer, chilled
    ⅔   cup lime juice
    1¼ cups vodka
        Ice cubes
        Lime slices, optional

Combine the ginger ale, ginger beer, lime juice and vodka in a pitcher. Serve over ice. If desired, serve with lime slices.

WINE-POACHED PEARS

These pears look beautiful on a plate. The rosy color and wonderful flavor set the scene for a memorable holiday dinner.
—Patricia Stiehr, Eureka, MO

Prep: 10 min. • **Cook:** 3 hours
Makes: 12 servings

    2   cups port wine
    2   cups sugar
    1   teaspoon grated lemon peel
    6   medium Bosc pears, peeled

1. Place wine, sugar and lemon peel in a 5-qt. slow cooker; stir until sugar dissolves. Add pears.
2. Cook, covered, on low 3-4 hours or until pears are tender, turning pears halfway through cooking. Using a slotted spoon, remove pears; cut into slices (save cooking liquid for another use).

MOSCOW
MULE

BRUSSELS SPROUTS WITH BACON VINAIGRETTE

I'd never tried Brussels sprouts until I made this salad. It won me over and even charmed my family. Bacon and apples spruce up the flavor.
—Stephanie Gates, Waterloo, IA

Prep: 40 min. • **Cook:** 10 min. + chilling
Makes: 12 servings (1 cup each)

- 3 pounds fresh Brussels sprouts
- 10 bacon strips, chopped
- 1 medium red onion, halved and thinly sliced
- ⅔ cup white wine vinegar
- ⅓ cup honey
- ¼ cup Dijon mustard
- 2 medium apples, thinly sliced

1. Trim Brussels sprouts. Using a knife or the slicing blade on a food processor, thinly slice sprouts. Transfer sprouts to a large bowl. In a large skillet, cook bacon over medium heat until crisp, stirring occasionally. Remove with a slotted spoon; drain on paper towels. Discard drippings, reserving ¼ cup in pan.
2. Add onion to drippings; cook and stir over medium-high heat 3-5 minutes or until tender. Stir in vinegar, honey and mustard. Cook and stir 1 minute. Add bacon and apples to Brussels sprouts. Drizzle with onion mixture; toss to coat. Refrigerate at least 3 hours before serving.

FRESH ARTICHOKES WITH LEMON-YOGURT DIP

Artichokes are at their best when you prepare them simply, without a lot of fuss or seasonings to overdress them. Many people dip the petals in melted butter or mayonnaise, but I think you'll love my tangy lemon-yogurt dip.
—Jill Haapaniemi, Brooklyn, NY

Prep: 10 min. • **Cook:** 45 min.
Makes: 12 servings (1½ cups dip)

- 6 medium artichokes
- 3 tablespoons olive oil
  Sea salt and coarsely ground pepper to taste
- 1½ cups plain yogurt
- 1 teaspoon lemon juice
- ¼ teaspoon salt
- ¼ teaspoon pepper
  Lemon wedges

1. Using a sharp knife, cut 1 in. from top of each artichoke and trim stem so it will stand upright. Using kitchen scissors, cut off tips of outer leaves. Place artichokes upright in a Dutch oven; cover with water and bring to a boil. Reduce heat; simmer, covered, 35-40 minutes or until a leaf near the the center pulls out easily. Invert artichokes to drain. Cool slightly; cut each in half lengthwise. With a spoon, carefully scrape and remove the fuzzy center of each artichoke.
2. In a grill pan or large skillet, heat oil over medium-high heat. Place artichokes in pan, cut side down. Cook 5-7 minutes or until lightly browned. Sprinkle with salt and pepper. In a small bowl, mix yogurt, lemon juice, salt and pepper. Serve the artichokes with dip and lemon wedges.

FRESH ARTICHOKES WITH LEMON-YOGURT DIP

How to Cut an Artichoke Like a Pro

Artichokes are delicious hot or cold. Both the soft part of the outer petals and the heart are completely edible. Here's how to cut an artichoke prior to cooking and/or eating.

USING A SHARP KNIFE, cut 1 in. from top of each artichoke and trim the stem end so it will stand upright. Using a kitchen scissors, cut off the tips of the outer leaves.

CUT each in half lengthwise. With a spoon, carefully scrape and remove the fuzzy center; discard. Follow the recipe as directed or eat raw.

BACON BEEF TENDERLOIN
WITH CRANBERRY GLAZE

BACON BEEF TENDERLOIN WITH CRANBERRY GLAZE

I made this for Christmas one year and now people request it for every special event. Omit the jalapeno if you like.
—Rebecca Anderson, Driftwood, TX

Prep: 25 min. + marinating
Bake: 45 min. + standing
Makes: 12 servings

1 beef tenderloin (5 pounds)
2 cups port wine

RUB
2 tablespoons sea salt
2 tablespoons coarse sugar
1 tablespoon instant coffee granules

STUFFING
1 package (8 ounces) cream cheese, softened
8 slices crumbled cooked bacon
2 jalapeno peppers, seeded and finely chopped, optional

GLAZE
2 medium oranges
2 cups port wine
1 cup whole-berry cranberry sauce

1. In a large resealable plastic bag, combine beef and wine. Seal bag and turn to coat. Refrigerate 8 hours or overnight.
2. Preheat oven to 425°. Drain beef, discarding marinade. In a small bowl, combine salt, sugar and coffee granules; rub over beef. Cut lengthwise through the center of roast to within ½ in. of bottom.
3. In a small bowl, beat cream cheese, bacon and, if desired, jalapenos. Fill center of roast with the cream cheese mixture. Close roast and tie at 2-in. intervals with kitchen string.
4. Place on a rack in a roasting pan. Roast for 45-55 minutes or until meat reaches desired doneness (for medium-rare, a thermometer should read 135°; medium, 140°; medium-well, 145°). Meanwhile, finely grate peel from oranges. Cut oranges crosswise in half; squeeze juice from oranges. In a small saucepan, combine wine, cranberry sauce, orange peel and juice. Bring to a boil; cook 15-20 minutes or until liquid is reduced by half.
5. Remove roast from oven; tent with foil. Let stand for 15 minutes before slicing. Remove string. Serve roast with glaze.
Note: Wear disposable gloves when cutting hot peppers; the oils can burn skin. Avoid touching your face.

BACON-GRUYERE SMASHED POTATOES

BACON-GRUYERE SMASHED POTATOES

Gruyere cheese, bacon, sweet onions and herbs take smashed potatoes to a whole new level of amazing. This loaded side dish is so rich and satisfying, it could almost be eaten on its own!
—Lisa Speer, Palm Beach, FL

Prep: 20 min. • **Cook:** 1 hour
Makes: 16 servings (¾ cup each)

½ cup butter, divided
3 large sweet onions, halved and thinly sliced
1½ teaspoons salt, divided
¾ teaspoon pepper, divided
3 teaspoons minced fresh thyme or 1 teaspoon dried thyme
3½ pounds medium red potatoes, halved
1 cup 2% milk
10 slices bacon strips, cooked and crumbled
1 cup (4 ounces) shredded Gruyere or white cheddar cheese
Chopped fresh parsley, optional

1. In a large skillet, heat ¼ cup butter over medium-high heat. Add the onions, ¼ teaspoon salt and ⅛ teaspoon pepper; cook and stir 8-10 minutes or until softened. Reduce heat to medium-low; cook 40-50 minutes or until deep golden brown, stirring occasionally and stirring in thyme during last 5 minutes.
2. Place potatoes in a 6-qt stockpot; add water to cover. Bring to a boil. Reduce heat; cook, uncovered, 20-25 minutes or until tender. Drain; return to pan. Add milk and remaining butter, salt and pepper. Coarsely mash potatoes with a masher, leaving small chunks. Stir in bacon and onions; sprinkle with cheese. Let stand, covered, until cheese melts. If desired, sprinkle with parsley.

WHITE CHOCOLATE CHEESECAKE WITH CRANBERRY-ORANGE COMPOTE

From its creamy cheese texture to subtle orange flavor and tart cranberry topping, this dessert will steal the show at your holiday meal.
—Mary Richard, San Jose, CA

Prep: 30 min. • **Bake:** 55 min. + chilling
Makes: 12 servings

- 1½ cups chocolate wafer crumbs
- ¼ cup butter, melted
- 2 tablespoons sugar

FILLING
- 3 packages (8 ounces each) cream cheese, softened
- ¾ cup sugar
- 12 ounces white baking chocolate, chopped and melted
- ½ cup sour cream
- 1 tablespoon vanilla extract
- 3 large eggs, lightly beaten
- 2 teaspoons grated orange peel

CRANBERRY-ORANGE COMPOTE
- 1 package (12 ounces) fresh cranberries
- ¾ cup packed brown sugar
- ¾ cup orange juice
- 1 tablespoon grated orange peel
- ½ teaspoon ground ginger

GARNISH
- Sweetened whipped cream, optional

1. Preheat oven to 325°. Place a greased 9-in. springform pan on a double thickness of heavy-duty foil (about 18 in. square). Wrap foil securely around pan. Place on a baking sheet.
2. In a small bowl, mix wafer crumbs, butter and sugar. Press onto bottom of prepared pan. Bake 10 minutes. Cool on a wire rack.
3. In a large bowl, beat the cream cheese and sugar until smooth. Beat in the melted chocolate, sour cream and vanilla. Add eggs; beat on low speed just until blended. Fold in grated orange peel. Pour mixture over crust. Place springform pan in a large baking pan; add 1 in. of hot water to the larger pan to create a water bath.
4. Bake 55-65 minutes or until center is just set and top appears dull. Remove springform pan from water bath. Cool cheesecake on a wire rack for 10 minutes. Loosen sides from pan with a knife; remove foil. Cool 1 hour longer.
5. Meanwhile, for compote, in a large saucepan, combine compote ingredients. Cook over medium heat until berries pop, about 15 minutes. Cool mixture to room temperature. Spread over cheesecake. Allow cheesecake to cool completely. Cover and refrigerate overnight. When ready to serve, remove rim from pan. If desired, serve with whipped cream.

THREE-LAYER CHOCOLATE GANACHE CAKE

Prep: 30 min. • **Bake:** 30 min. + chilling
Makes: 16 servings

- 4 cups all-purpose flour
- 2¼ cups sugar
- ¾ cup baking cocoa
- 4 teaspoons baking soda
- 2¼ cups mayonnaise
- 2¼ cups cold brewed coffee
- 1½ teaspoons vanilla extract

FILLING
- 1 cup sugar
- 2 tablespoons cornstarch
- 1 cup 2% milk
- 2 teaspoons vanilla extract
- 1 cup butter, softened
- ¾ cup miniature semisweet chocolate chips

GANACHE
- 8 ounces semisweet chocolate, chopped
- 2 cups heavy whipping cream
- 1 teaspoon vanilla extract

GLAZE
- 8 ounces semisweet chocolate, chopped
- ¾ cup heavy whipping cream
- ¼ cup butter, cubed

1. Preheat oven to 350°. Line bottoms of three greased 9-in. round baking pans with waxed paper; grease paper. In a large bowl, whisk flour, sugar, cocoa and baking soda. Beat in mayonnaise, coffee and vanilla. Transfer batter to prepared pans. Bake 30-35 minutes or until a toothpick inserted in center comes out clean. Cool in pans 10 minutes before removing to wire racks; remove paper. Cool completely.
2. For filling, in a small heavy saucepan, mix sugar and cornstarch. Whisk in milk. Cook and stir over medium heat until thickened and bubbly. Reduce heat to low; cook and stir 2 minutes longer. Remove from heat; stir in vanilla. Cool completely. In a large bowl, cream butter. Gradually beat in cooled filling mixture. Stir in the chocolate chips.
3. For ganache, place chocolate in a large bowl. In a small saucepan, bring cream just to a boil. Pour over chocolate; let stand 5 minutes. Stir with a whisk until smooth. Stir in vanilla. Cool to room temperature, stirring occasionally. Refrigerate, covered, until cold. Beat ganache just until soft peaks form, about 15-30 seconds (do not overbeat mixture).
4. Place one cake layer on a serving plate; spread with half of the filling. Repeat layers. Top with remaining cake layer. Frost top and sides of cake with ganache. In a microwave-safe bowl, combine chocolate, cream and butter. Microwave at 50% power for 1-2 minutes or until smooth, stirring twice. Cool slightly, stirring occasionally. Drizzle over cake, allowing some to flow over sides. Refrigerate at least 2 hours before serving.

"This decadent triple-layer beauty is pure chocolate indulgence. The cake layers can be baked and frozen prior to final assembly; in fact, they're easier to work with when frozen."

—KATHLEEN SMITH, OVERLAND, MO

THREE-LAYER CHOCOLATE GANACHE CAKE

White Elephant Party

We've all heard the saying that one person's trash is another one's treasure, but at a White Elephant party, the lines between trash and treasure blur completely! Also known as Yankee Swap or Dirty Santa, the all-in-good-fun gift exchange has become a hot and happening holiday craze. (See rules on page 36.)

What would a White Elephant party be without white foods? As your guests are swapping, stealing and showing off their kitschy treasures, serve up a big helping of white-hued delights: creamy macaroni and cheese, slow-cooked chili, homemade eggnog, seasoned popcorn and white-frosted desserts, to name just a few.

Go ahead—eat, drink and be merry! Good times are in store.

Snow-Topped White Chocolate Macadamia Cookies (p. 35) **Slow-Cooked White Bean Chili** (p. 32)
Country White Bread (p. 32) **Appetizer Tortilla Pinwheels** (p. 31)

**WHITE CHEDDAR
MAC & CHEESE**

WHITE CHEDDAR MAC & CHEESE

My mac and cheese is simple and has lots of flavor from the cheeses and ground chipotle chile. I use Conchiglie Pasta because its large openings allow more melted cheese to pool inside. Yum!
—Colleen Delawder, Herndon, VA

Start to Finish: 25 min.
Makes: 8 servings

- 1 package (16 ounces) small pasta shells
- ½ cup butter, cubed
- ½ cup all-purpose flour
- ½ teaspoon onion powder
- ½ teaspoon ground chipotle pepper
- ½ teaspoon pepper
- ¼ teaspoon salt
- 4 cups 2% milk
- 2 cups shredded sharp white cheddar cheese
- 2 cups shredded Manchego or additional white cheddar cheese (about 8 ounces)

1. In a 6-qt. stockpot, cook pasta according to package directions. Drain; return to pot.
2. Meanwhile, in a large saucepan, melt butter over medium heat. Stir in flour and seasonings until smooth; gradually whisk in milk. Bring to a boil, stirring constantly; cook and stir until thickened, 6-8 minutes. Remove from heat; stir in cheeses until melted. Add to pasta; toss to coat.

TOP TIP

Mac & Cheese Redux

Give leftover mac and cheese new life by stirring in these tasty ingredients. Top with additional shredded white cheddar cheese if desired.

- For Taco Mac, stir in warm leftover taco meat, sauteed chopped sweet red pepper and whole kernel corn. Top with coarsely crushed tortilla chips for a little crunch.
- For Messy Mac, stir in warm leftover sloppy joe meat and a little bit of barbecue sauce.
- For Broccoli Mac, stir in steamed broccoli florets. Add cubed fully-cooked ham or crumbled bacon.

APPETIZER TORTILLA PINWHEELS

APPETIZER TORTILLA PINWHEELS

A friend gave me the recipe for this attractive and tasty appetizer. You can prepare the pinwheels in advance and slice just before serving to save time for other party preparations. It couldn't be more convenient!
—Pat Waymire, Yellow Springs, OH

Prep: 20 min. + chilling
Makes: about 4 dozen

- 1 package (8 ounces) cream cheese, softened
- 1 cup shredded cheddar cheese
- 1 cup (8 ounces) sour cream
- 1 can (4¼ ounces) chopped ripe olives
- 1 can (4 ounces) chopped green chilies, well drained
- ½ cup chopped green onions
  Garlic powder to taste
  Seasoned salt to taste
- 5 flour tortillas (10 inches)
  Salsa, optional

1. Beat cream cheese, cheese and sour cream until blended. Stir in olives, green chilies, green onions and seasonings.
2. Spread over tortillas; roll up tightly. Wrap each in plastic, twisting ends to seal; refrigerate several hours.
3. Unwrap. Cut into ½- to ¾-in. slices, using a serrated knife. If desired, serve with salsa.

HERBED DIP FOR VEGGIES

The herbs and seasonings in this dip blend beautifully, offering extra zip. It's perfect for dipping fresh veggies.
—Laurel Leslie, Sonora, CA

Prep: 15 min. + chilling
Makes: 1½ cups

- 1 cup mayonnaise
- ½ cup sour cream
- 1 tablespoon minced fresh chives
- 1 tablespoon grated onion
- 1 tablespoon capers, drained
- ½ teaspoon salt
- ½ teaspoon lemon juice
- ½ teaspoon Worcestershire sauce
- ¼ teaspoon dried parsley flakes
- ¼ teaspoon paprika
- ⅛ teaspoon curry powder
  Dash garlic salt
  Assorted fresh vegetables

In a small bowl, mix first 12 ingredients. Refrigerate, covered, 1 hour. Serve dip with vegetables.

SLOW-COOKED WHITE BEAN CHILI

SLOW-COOKED WHITE BEAN CHILI

My friend and I came up with an amazing chicken chili that simmers in the slow cooker. The Alfredo sauce base makes it stand apart from other white chilis. It's delicious served with warm homemade bread. Reduce the amount of cayenne pepper if you'd like less heat.
—Cindi Mitchell, St. Marys, KS

Prep: 15 min. • **Cook:** 3 hours
Makes: 12 servings (1 cup each)

- 3 cans (15½ ounces each) great northern beans, rinsed and drained
- 3 cups cubed cooked chicken breast
- 1 jar (15 ounces) Alfredo sauce
- 2 cups chicken broth
- 1½ cups frozen gold and white corn (about 8 ounces), thawed
- 1 cup shredded Monterey Jack cheese
- 1 cup shredded pepper jack cheese
- 1 cup sour cream
- 1 small sweet yellow pepper, chopped
- 1 small onion, chopped
- 1 to 2 cans (4 ounces each) chopped green chilies
- 3 garlic cloves, minced
- 3 teaspoons ground cumin
- 1½ teaspoons white pepper
- 1 to 1½ teaspoons cayenne pepper Salsa verde and chopped fresh cilantro, optional

In a 5- or 6-qt. slow cooker, combine all ingredients except salsa and cilantro. Cook, covered, on low until vegetables are tender and flavors are blended, 3-4 hours, stirring once. If desired, serve with salsa and cilantro.

THREE-HERB POPCORN

Try this seasoned treat for a tasty twist on plain popcorn. Mixed nuts add crunch and flavor but are optional. The next time you have creamed soup or chili, sprinkle a small handful over individual servings.
—Flo Burtnett, Gage, OK

Start to Finish: 15 min.
Makes: about 6 quarts

- 6 quarts (24 cups) popped popcorn (about ¾ cup unpopped kernels)
- ½ cup butter, cubed
- 1 teaspoon dried basil
- 1 teaspoon dried chervil
- ½ teaspoon dried thyme
- 1 can (12 ounces) mixed nuts, optional Salt to taste

1. Place popcorn in a large bowl or roasting pan. In a small saucepan, melt butter over medium heat. Remove from heat; stir in herbs. Drizzle over popcorn and toss to coat.
2. If desired, stir in nuts. Add salt to taste.

COUNTRY WHITE BREAD

Everyone loves a good slice of homemade bread, especially when it's spread with butter or jam. These loaves are especially nice because the crust stays tender. My husband makes most of the bread at our house, and this recipe is his favorite.
—Joanne Shew Chuk, St. Benedict, SK

Prep: 20 min. + rising
Bake: 25 min. + cooling
Makes: 2 loaves (16 slices each)

- 2 packages (¼ ounce each) active dry yeast
- 2 cups warm water (110° to 115°)
- ½ cup sugar
- 2 teaspoons salt
- 2 large eggs
- ¼ cup canola oil
- 6½ to 7 cups all-purpose flour

1. In a large bowl, dissolve yeast in warm water. Add sugar, salt, eggs, oil and 3 cups flour; beat on medium speed until smooth. Stir in enough remaining flour to form a soft dough.
2. Turn dough onto a floured surface; knead until smooth and elastic, about 6-8 minutes. Place in a greased bowl, turning once to grease the top. Cover with plastic wrap and let rise in a warm place until doubled, about 1 hour.
3. Punch down dough. Divide in half and shape into loaves. Place in two greased 9x5-in. loaf pans. Cover with kitchen towels; let rise in a warm place until doubled, about 1 hour. Preheat the oven to 375°.
4. Bake until golden brown, for 25-30 minutes. Remove from pans to wire racks to cool.

TOP TIP

Proofing Yeast

To make sure active dry yeast (not quick-rise yeast) is alive and active, you may first want to proof it. Try this easy method:

Dissolve one package of yeast and 1 teaspoon sugar in ¼ cup warm water (110° to 115°). Let stand for 5 to 10 minutes. If the mixture foams up, the yeast mixture can be used because the yeast is doing its job. If it does not foam, discard it.

**COUNTRY
WHITE BREAD**

LAYERED CANDY
CANE DESSERT

LAYERED CANDY CANE DESSERT

This fabulous dessert has the magical flavor of candy canes plus the bonus of an Oreo cookie crust. And it looks like a winter wonderland.
—Dawn Kreuser, Green Bay, WI

Prep: 25 min. + chilling
Makes: 24 servings

- 1 package (14.30 ounces) Oreo cookies
- 6 tablespoons butter, melted
- 1 package (8 ounces) cream cheese, softened
- ¼ cup sugar
- 2 tablespoons 2% milk
- 1 carton (12 ounces) frozen whipped topping, thawed, divided
- ¾ cup crushed candy canes (about 7 regular size), divided
- 2 packages (3.3 ounces each) instant white chocolate pudding mix
- 2¾ cups cold 2% milk

1. Pulse the cookies in a food processor until fine crumbs form. Add melted butter; pulse just until combined. Press crumbs onto bottom of a 13x9-in. dish. Refrigerate while preparing filling.
2. Beat cream cheese, sugar and milk until smooth. Fold in 1 cup of the whipped topping and ½ cup of the crushed candies. Spread over crust.
3. Whisk pudding mix and milk 2 minutes; spread over cream cheese layer. Spread with the remaining whipped topping. Refrigerate, covered, 4 hours. Sprinkle with remaining candies just before serving.

SNOW-TOPPED WHITE CHOCOLATE MACADAMIA COOKIES

Just like snowflakes, these fluffy cookies will melt in your mouth. Include them as part of your cookie platter or serve them in decorative cupcake lines for extra visual appeal. See photo on page 29.
—*Taste of Home* Test Kitchen

Prep: 35 min.
Bake: 15 min./batch + cooling
Makes: about 3 dozen

- 1 tube (16½ ounces) refrigerated sugar cookie dough
- ⅓ cup all-purpose flour
- ½ teaspoon vanilla extract
- ¾ cup white baking chips
- ½ cup finely chopped macadamia nuts, toasted

GLAZE
- 1½ cups confectioners' sugar
- 3 tablespoons 2% milk
- ½ teaspoon lemon extract
- 1½ cups sweetened shredded coconut

1. Preheat oven to 350°. Place cookie dough in a large bowl; let stand at room temperature 5-10 minutes to soften.
2. Add flour and vanilla to dough; beat until blended (dough will be slightly crumbly). Stir in baking chips and nuts. Shape level tablespoons of dough into balls; place 2 in. apart on parchment paper-lined baking sheets.
3. Bake until bottoms are lightly browned, 12-14 minutes. Remove to wire racks to cool completely.
4. For glaze, mix confectioners' sugar, milk and extract until smooth. Dip tops of cookies in glaze. Sprinkle with coconut, patting gently to adhere. Let cookies stand until frosting is set.
Note: To toast nuts, bake in a shallow pan in a 350° oven for 5-10 minutes or cook nuts in a skillet over low heat until lightly browned, stirring occasionally.

HOMEMADE EGGNOG

After one sip, folks will know this smooth and creamy holiday staple is homemade, not a store-bought variety. If desired, add a half cup rum or brandy.
—Pat Waymire, Yellow Springs, OH

Prep: 15 min. • **Cook:** 30 min. + chilling
Makes: about 3½ quarts

- 12 large eggs
- 1½ cups sugar
- ½ teaspoon salt
- 8 cups whole milk, divided
- 2 tablespoons vanilla extract
- 1 teaspoon ground nutmeg
- 2 cups heavy whipping cream
  Additional nutmeg, optional

1. In a heavy saucepan, whisk together eggs, sugar and salt. Gradually add 4 cups milk; cook and stir over low heat until a thermometer reads 160°-170°, about 30-35 minutes. Do not allow to boil. Immediately transfer to a large bowl.
2. Stir in vanilla, nutmeg and remaining milk. Place bowl in an ice-water bath, stirring until mixture is cool. (If mixture separates, process in a blender until smooth.) Refrigerate mixture, covered, until cold, at least 3 hours.
3. To serve, beat cream until soft peaks form. Whisk gently into cooled milk mixture. If desired, sprinkle with additional nutmeg before serving.
Note: Eggnog may be stored, covered, in the refrigerator for several days. Whisk before serving.

WHITE CHRISTMAS CAKE

Prep: 35 min. + cooling
Bake: 25 min. + cooling
Makes: 16 servings

- 4 large eggs, separated
- ½ cup water
- 4 ounces chopped white candy coating or white baking chips
- 1 cup butter, softened
- 2 cups sugar
- 1 tablespoon vanilla extract
- 2½ cups all-purpose flour
- ½ teaspoon baking powder
- ½ teaspoon baking soda
- 1 cup buttermilk
- 1 cup sweetened shredded coconut
- 1 cup chopped pecans

FROSTING
- 1 package (8 ounces) cream cheese, softened
- ½ cup butter, softened
- 3¾ cups confectioners' sugar
- 1 tablespoon 2% milk
- 1 teaspoon vanilla extract

OPTIONAL DECORATIONS
- White candy coating or white chocolate chips, melted
- Fresh cranberries

1. Place egg whites in a large bowl; let stand at room temperature 30 minutes. In a small saucepan, bring water to a boil. Remove from heat; stir in candy coating until blended. Cool 20 minutes.
2. Preheat oven to 350°. Line bottoms of three greased 8-in. square or 9-in. round baking pans with parchment paper; grease parchment paper.
3. Cream butter and sugar until light and fluffy. Beat in egg yolks and vanilla. Beat in candy coating mixture. In another bowl, whisk together flour, baking powder and baking soda; add to creamed mixture alternately with buttermilk, beating after each addition. Fold in coconut and pecans. With clean beaters, beat egg whites on medium speed until stiff peaks form; fold into batter.
4. Transfer batter to prepared pans. Bake until a toothpick inserted in center comes out clean, 25-30 minutes. Cool in pans 10 minutes before removing to wire racks; remove paper. Cool completely.
5. For frosting, beat cream cheese and butter until smooth. Beat in confectioners' sugar, milk and vanilla. Spread frosting between layers and over the top and sides of cake.
6. If desired, pipe holly leaves with melted candy coating onto a waxed paper-lined baking sheet. Refrigerate designs until set. Decorate cake with cranberries and leaf designs. Refrigerate leftovers.

APRICOT WHITE FUDGE

This fudge is a family favorite and a nice variation from typical dark or milk chocolate fudge. The luscious blend of flavors and stained-glass look are hard to beat. It makes great Christmas gifts.
—Debbie Purdue, Westland, MI

Prep: 20 min. • **Cook:** 10 min. + chilling
Makes: about 2 pounds (81 pieces)

- 1½ teaspoons plus ½ cup butter, divided
- 2 cups sugar
- ¾ cup sour cream
- 12 ounces white baking chocolate, chopped
- 1 jar (7 ounces) marshmallow creme
- ¾ cup chopped dried apricots
- ¾ cup chopped walnuts

1. Line a 9-in. square pan with foil; grease foil with 1½ teaspoons butter.
2. In a heavy saucepan, combine sugar, sour cream and remaining butter. Bring to a boil over medium heat, stirring mixture constantly. Cook and stir until a candy thermometer reads 234° (soft-ball stage), about 5½ minutes. Remove from the heat.
3. Stir in chocolate until melted. Stir in marshmallow creme until blended. Stir in apricots and walnuts. Immediately spread mixture into prepared pan. Refrigerate, covered, overnight.
4. Using foil, lift fudge out of pan. Remove foil; cut fudge into 1-in. squares.
Note: We recommend that you test your candy thermometer before each use by bringing water to a boil; the thermometer should read 212°. Adjust the temperature up or down based on your test.

WHITE ELEPHANT EXCHANGE RULES

Whether it's an office party or a gathering of friends, the white elephant has become a favorite holiday tradition. The rules can be whatever you want them to be, but the goal is to spark friendly competition and have a great time!

There are variations galore, but here's a rundown of the most widely accepted way to play:

- Every guest brings a wrapped gift. Set guidelines for gifts before the party. Put all the wrapped gifts in a central spot.

- Put numbered slips of paper—one for each participant—in a basket.

- Each guest draws a number from the basket. Guest #1 goes first, selects a gift from the table and opens it. Oohs and aahs all around!

- Guest #2 either selects a gift from the table and unwraps it or steals #1's gift. If #2 chooses to steal, guest #1 chooses another gift from the table and opens it.

- Guest #3 can either select a gift from the table and open it or steal a gift from either #1 or #2. Guests who have their gifts stolen will always choose a replacement gift—either from the table or stolen from another guest. (They can't directly steal their own gifts back in the same turn.)

- After a maximum of three swaps, the turn ends.

- After all players have taken a turn, guest #1 has a chance to steal a gift, making a direct swap with another guest. That guest can steal, and so on. There is no limit to the number of steals on the last turn—the exchange ends when a guest decides to keep the gift instead of stealing another guest's.

"Wow! is the reaction from family and guests when they see and taste this lovely three-layer cake. White chocolate, coconut and pecans make the cake so delicious."

—NANCY REICHERT, THOMASVILLE, GA

Make-Ahead Holiday Sides

The turkey or ham may be the star of Christmas dinner, but it's the colorful salads and savory side dishes that put the finishing touch on a fabulous holiday meal. Here's a lineup of festive accompaniments that are *extra* special—because each one can be prepped in advance, saving you precious time on the day of the party.

There's something for everyone in this delicious mix of palate-pleasing sides, whether it's a delectable slow-cooked dressing, a chunky veggie soup, cozy butternut squash or a refreshing salad.

Time to break out the happy dance! With these tasty time-saving recipes as part of your holiday dinner game plan, hosting the big event just got easier!

Make-Ahead Mashed Potatoes (p. 40) **Slow-Cooked Sausage Dressing** (p. 44) **Seasoned Garlic Gravy** (p. 40)

SEASONED
GARLIC GRAVY

MAKE-AHEAD MASHED POTATOES

Used to whipping up potatoes at the last minute? Never again! These are the most delicious mashed spuds we've ever tasted—but best of all, you can make them the day before the big feast. See photo on page 38.
—Marion Lowery, Medford, OR

Prep: 40 min. + chilling • **Cook:** 15 min.
Makes: 12 servings (¾ cup each)

- 4 pounds medium potatoes (about 12), peeled and quartered
- 1 package (8 ounces) cream cheese, softened
- ⅓ cup sour cream
- ⅓ cup butter, softened
- 1¼ teaspoons salt
- 1 teaspoon paprika
- ½ teaspoon pepper
- ¼ cup minced fresh chives, optional
- 2 tablespoons 2% milk

1. Place potatoes in a large saucepan; add water to cover and bring to a boil. Reduce heat; cook, uncovered, until tender, 15-20 minutes. Drain.
2. In a large bowl, beat cream cheese and sour cream until smooth. Add potatoes; beat until light and fluffy. Beat in butter, seasonings and, if desired, chives. Transfer to a greased 2½-qt. microwave-safe dish. Refrigerate, covered, overnight.
3. Remove from refrigerator 30 minutes before heating. Microwave, uncovered, on high 10 minutes, stirring once. Stir in milk. Microwave until heated through, about 5 minutes.

Note: This recipe was tested in a 1,100-watt microwave.

SEASONED GARLIC GRAVY

Poultry seasoning perks up this simple yet tasty no-mess gravy that's perfect for turkey as well as over mashed potatoes.
—Hannah Thompson, Scotts Valley, CA

Start to Finish: 15 min.
Makes: 2 cups

- 3 tablespoons butter
- 1 teaspoon minced garlic
- ¼ cup all-purpose flour
- ½ teaspoon poultry seasoning
- ⅛ teaspoon pepper
- 2 cups chicken broth

In a small saucepan, heat the butter over medium heat. Add garlic; cook and stir 1 minute. Stir in flour, poultry seasoning and pepper until smooth; gradually whisk in broth. Bring to a boil, stirring constantly; cook and stir until thickened, 1-2 minutes.

PERFECT WINTER SALAD

This is my most-requested salad recipe. It's delicious as a side salad or even as a main dish with grilled chicken breast. I think it's so good, I sometimes eat it at the end of the meal, instead of dessert!
—DeNae Shewmake, Burnsville, MN

Start to Finish: 20 min.
Makes: 12 servings (1 cup each)

- ¼ cup reduced-fat mayonnaise
- ¼ cup maple syrup
- 3 tablespoons white wine vinegar
- 2 tablespoons minced shallot
- 2 teaspoons sugar
- ½ cup canola oil
- 2 packages (5 ounces each) spring mix salad greens
- 2 medium tart apples, thinly sliced
- 1 cup dried cherries
- 1 cup pecan halves
- ¼ cup thinly sliced red onion

1. In a small bowl, mix the first five ingredients; gradually whisk in oil until blended. Refrigerate dressing, covered, until serving.
2. To serve, place remaining ingredients in a large bowl; toss with dressing.

TOP TIP

How Many Potatoes?

Generally, three medium russet potatoes or eight to 10 small new white potatoes equal 1 pound. If you usually purchase the same type of potatoes, weigh them in the produce section of your grocery store so you know exactly what 1 pound of your favorite variety is.

PERFECT
WINTER
SALAD

SLOW COOKER
PINEAPPLE
SWEET POTATOES

SLOW COOKER PINEAPPLE SWEET POTATOES

Pineapple and pecans make a pretty topping for this versatile side dish. It's light, tasty and not too sweet, and making it in the slow cooker leaves extra space in the oven for other dishes.

—Bette Fulcher, Lexington, TX

....

Prep: 15 min. • **Cook:** 4 hours
Makes: 12 servings

    4 large eggs, lightly beaten
    6 to 6½ cups mashed sweet potatoes
       (without added milk or butter)
    1 cup 2% milk
    ½ cup butter, melted
    1 teaspoon salt
    1 teaspoon ground cinnamon
    1 teaspoon vanilla extract
    ½ teaspoon ground nutmeg
    ½ teaspoon lemon extract
    1 can (8 ounces) sliced pineapple,
       drained
    ¼ cup chopped pecans

1. In a large bowl, mix the first nine ingredients. Transfer mixture to a greased 3-qt. slow cooker. Top with the pineapple and pecans.
2. Cook mixture, covered, on low until a thermometer reads 160°, 4-5 hours.

CRANBERRY-NUT COUSCOUS SALAD

If you're looking for something fun and unique for a holiday dinner, try this salad featuring couscous, dried cranberries and almonds. It's easy to make and good for you, too!

—Jean Ecos, Hartland, WI

....

Prep: 25 min. + chilling
Makes: 10 servings

    1 package (10 ounces) plain couscous
    1 cup dried cranberries
    ¾ cup chopped green onions
    ¾ cup chopped sweet yellow or red
       pepper
    ¾ cup slivered almonds, toasted
DRESSING
    ⅓ cup lemon juice
    ¼ cup olive oil
    ½ teaspoon paprika
    ¼ teaspoon salt
    ⅛ teaspoon pepper

1. Prepare couscous according to the package directions using water and olive oil. Fluff with a fork; transfer to a large bowl. Refrigerate couscous until cold, about 30 minutes.
2. Add cranberries, green onions, yellow pepper and almonds to couscous. In a small bowl, whisk together the dressing ingredients; toss with salad. Refrigerate, covered, until serving.
Note: To toast nuts, bake in a shallow pan in a 350° oven for 5-10 minutes, or cook nuts in a skillet over low heat until lightly browned, stirring occasionally.

EGGNOG MOLDED SALAD

This gelatin looks so lovely on a platter, and the delicious fruit is made all the better with a hint of eggnog flavor. It's refreshing as part of any meal.

—Alice Ceresa, Rochester, NY

....

Prep: 35 min. + chilling
Makes: 12 servings

    1 teaspoon unflavored gelatin
    1 can (15¼ ounces) sliced pears
    1 package (6 ounces) lemon gelatin
    1 cup (8 ounces) sour cream
    ¾ cup eggnog
    1 can (11 ounces) mandarin oranges,
       drained
       Orange slices, maraschino cherries
       and mint leaves, optional

1. In a small bowl, sprinkle unflavored gelatin over ¼ cup cold water; let stand 1 minute.
2. Drain pears over a 2-cup measuring cup, reserving syrup. Add enough water to the syrup to measure 2 cups; pour into a saucepan. Bring to a boil; remove from heat. Add lemon gelatin and unflavored gelatin mixture; stir 2 minutes to dissolve completely. Cool 15 minutes.
3. Stir in sour cream and eggnog until well blended. Refrigerate until partially set.
4. Cut oranges and drained pears into chunks; stir into gelatin mixture. Pour into a 6-cup ring mold coated with cooking spray. Refrigerate, covered, until firm. If desired, serve salad with oranges, cherries and mint.

SLOW-COOKED
SAUSAGE DRESSING

MAPLE-ALMOND BUTTERNUT SQUASH

My heartwarming squash is a cinch to prepare and is especially good on a chilly day. It's a great choice for a weeknight but impressive enough for company, too.
—Judy Lawson, Chelsea, MI

....

Prep: 20 min. • **Cook:** 5¼ hours
Makes: 10 servings

- ½ cup maple syrup
- ½ cup butter, melted
- 4 garlic cloves, minced
- 1 teaspoon salt
- ½ teaspoon pepper
- 1 medium butternut squash (about 4 pounds), peeled and cut into 2-inch pieces
- ½ cup heavy whipping cream
- ¼ cup sliced almonds
- ¼ cup shredded Parmesan cheese

1. Mix first five ingredients. Place squash in a 4-qt. slow cooker; toss with syrup mixture. Cook, covered, until squash is tender, 5-6 hours.
2. Stir in cream; cook, covered, on low until heated through, 15-30 minutes. Top with almonds and cheese.

SLOW-COOKED SAUSAGE DRESSING

This dressing is so good, and it's lower in fat than traditional recipes. It's super convenient to make it in the slow cooker.
—Raquel Haggard, Edmond, OK

....

Prep: 20 min. • **Cook:** 3 hours
Makes: 12 servings (⅔ cup each)

- 7 cups seasoned stuffing cubes
- 1 medium tart apple, chopped
- ⅓ cup chopped pecans
- 1½ teaspoons rubbed sage
- ½ teaspoon pepper
- ½ pound reduced-fat bulk pork sausage
- 1 large onion, chopped
- 2 celery ribs, chopped
- 1 can (14½ ounces) reduced-sodium chicken broth
- 2 tablespoons reduced-fat butter, melted

1. Place first five ingredients in a large bowl. In a large nonstick skillet, cook and crumble sausage with onion and celery over medium-high heat until no longer pink, 4-5 minutes; drain. Add to stuffing mixture; stir in broth and butter. Transfer to a greased 5-qt. slow cooker.
2. Cook, covered, on low until heated through and apple is tender, 3-4 hours, stirring once.
Note: This recipe was tested with Land O'Lakes light stick butter.

HEARTY VEGETABLE SOUP

A friend gave me the idea to use V8 juice in soup because it yields a more robust flavor. This hot, chunky classic makes a great first course.
—Janice Steinmetz, Somers, CT

....

Prep: 25 min. • **Cook:** 1 hour 20 min.
Makes: 16 servings (4 quarts)

- 1 tablespoon olive oil
- 8 medium carrots, sliced
- 2 large onions, chopped
- 4 celery ribs, chopped
- 1 large green pepper, seeded and chopped
- 1 garlic clove, minced
- 2 cups chopped cabbage
- 2 cups frozen cut green beans (about 8 ounces)
- 2 cups frozen peas (about 8 ounces)
- 1 cup frozen corn (about 5 ounces)
- 1 can (15 ounces) garbanzo beans or chickpeas, rinsed and drained
- 1 bay leaf
- 2 teaspoons chicken bouillon granules
- 1½ teaspoons dried parsley flakes
- 1 teaspoon salt
- 1 teaspoon dried marjoram
- 1 teaspoon dried thyme
- ½ teaspoon dried basil
- ¼ teaspoon pepper
- 4 cups water
- 1 can (28 ounces) diced tomatoes, undrained
- 2 cups V8 juice

1. In a stockpot, heat oil over medium-high heat; saute carrots, onions, celery and green pepper until crisp-tender. Add garlic; cook and stir 1 minute. Stir in remaining ingredients; bring to a boil.
2. Reduce heat; simmer, covered, until vegetables are tender, 1 to 1½ hours. Remove bay leaf.

HEARTY
VEGETABLE
SOUP

LEMON RICE SALAD

This brightly flavored salad with a light burst of citrus has a pleasing combination of textures. Weeknight meals turn into special occasions when you serve it.
—Margery Richmond, Lacombe, AB

Prep: 25 min. + chilling
Makes: 16 servings (¾ cup each)

- 1 cup olive oil
- ⅓ cup white wine vinegar
- 1 garlic clove, minced
- 1 to 2 teaspoons grated lemon peel
- 2 teaspoons sugar
- 1 teaspoon Dijon mustard
- ½ teaspoon salt
- 6 cups cooked long grain rice
- 2 cup cooked wild rice
- 2 cups diced seeded cucumbers
- ⅔ cup thinly sliced green onions
- ¼ cup minced fresh parsley
- ¼ cup minced fresh basil or
  1 tablespoon dried basil
- ½ teaspoon pepper
- ½ cup chopped pecans, toasted

1. For dressing, place the first seven ingredients in a jar with a tight-fitting lid; shake well. In a large bowl, toss long grain rice and wild rice with the dressing. Refrigerate, covered, overnight.

2. Stir cucumbers, green onions, parsley, basil and pepper into the rice mixture. Refrigerate, covered, 2 hours. Stir in pecans just before serving.

Note: To toast nuts, bake in a shallow pan in a 350° oven for 5-10 minutes, or cook nuts in a skillet over low heat until lightly browned, stirring occasionally.

TOP TIP

Grated Citrus Peels

The peel from citrus fruit adds a burst of flavor to recipes and color to garnishes.

Citrus peel, also called zest, can be grated into fine shreds with a Microplane grater. For slightly thicker and longer shreds, use a zester; for long, continuous strips, use a stripper. Remove only the colored portion of the peel, not the bitter white pith.

LEMON RICE SALAD

BARLEY, GREENS & SWEET POTATO SALAD

Chock-full of whole grains and fresh vegetables, this pretty dish can be served as a side or as a meal on its own.
—Kim Van Dunk, Caldwell, NJ

Prep: 25 min. • **Cook:** 45 min.
Makes: 12 servings (¾ cup each)

- 5 cups water
- 1 cup medium pearl barley
- 2 medium sweet potatoes, peeled and cut into ¼-inch cubes
- ¾ cup chopped walnuts, toasted
- 2 cups frozen peas (about 8 ounces), thawed
- 1 medium red onion, finely chopped
- 1 cup finely chopped fresh kale
- 1 cup finely chopped fresh baby spinach
- ½ cup finely chopped fresh arugula

DRESSING

- ⅓ cup balsamic vinegar
- ⅓ cup olive oil
- 1 tablespoon honey
- ¾ teaspoon salt
- ¼ teaspoon pepper

1. In a large saucepan, bring water to a boil. Stir in barley. Reduce heat; simmer, covered, until tender, 45-50 minutes. Transfer to a large bowl; cool slightly.
2. Place sweet potatoes in a large saucepan; add water to cover. Bring to a boil. Reduce heat; cook, uncovered, just until tender, 5-7 minutes. Drain.
3. Add walnuts and remaining vegetables to barley; gently stir in sweet potatoes. In a small bowl, whisk together dressing ingredients; toss with salad. Serve at room temperature or refrigerate, covered, and serve cold.

Note: To toast nuts, bake in a shallow pan in a 350° oven for 5-10 minutes, or cook nuts in a skillet over low heat until lightly browned, stirring occasionally.

FREEZE & BAKE ROLLS

These homemade rolls are fancy enough for a feast but handy enough for almost any occasion. Keep them in the freezer for Sunday meals and company dinners; they always taste fresh.
—Jayne Duce, Raymond, AB

Prep: 40 min. + rising
Bake: 15 min. + freezing
Makes: 4 dozen

- 2 packages (¼ ounce each) active dry yeast
- 2 teaspoons plus ½ cup sugar, divided
- 1½ cups warm water (110° to 115°)
- 1½ cups warm whole milk (110° to 115°)
- ¼ cup canola oil
- 4 teaspoons salt
- 7½ to 8½ cups all-purpose flour
  Butter, melted

1. In a large bowl, dissolve yeast and 2 teaspoons sugar in warm water; let stand 5 minutes. Add warm milk, oil, salt and remaining sugar. Stir in enough flour to form a stiff dough.
2. Turn dough onto a floured surface; knead until smooth and elastic, about 6-8 minutes. Place in a greased bowl, turning once to grease the top. Cover with plastic wrap and let rise in a warm place until doubled, about 1½ hours.
3. Punch down dough. Turn onto a lightly floured surface; divide into four portions. Divide and shape each portion into 12 balls. Roll each ball into a 10-in. rope; tie into a loose knot, pinching together ends. Place 2 in. apart on greased baking sheets. Cover with kitchen towels; let rise in a warm place until doubled, 20-30 minutes. Preheat oven to 300°.
4. Brush rolls with melted butter. Bake 15 minutes to parbake. Cool completely on a wire rack. Freeze in resealable plastic freezer bags.
5. When ready to use, preheat oven to 375°. Bake frozen rolls on baking sheets until browned and heated through, for 12-15 minutes.

Feliz Navidad

What would Christmas be without traditions? For many, tradition comes wrapped in a big batch of tamales—bundles of masa (corn dough) stuffed with meat and other savory or sweet fillings and steamed in their corn husk wrappers.

Tamales have been a classic in Mexican and Latino kitchens for centuries, and making them is just as much a part of the holiday experience as eating them. Folks will often gather for a *tamalada*, a day-long tamale-making party, in preparation for the holiday feast.

This year, serve the traditional wrapped beauties alongside a zesty lineup of stuffed peppers, pinto beans, rice, sangria, tres leches cake and more. It will be a flavor fiesta like none other. Deliciosa!

Topsy-Turvy Sangria (p. 56) **Southwestern Rice** (p. 52)
Chicken Tamales (p. 55) **Homemade Guacamole** (p. 51)

**CANTINA
PINTO BEANS**

CANTINA PINTO BEANS

Cumin, cilantro and red pepper flakes lend Southwestern flair to tender pinto beans in this dish, which was inspired by one we had at a restaurant in Dallas. The chef added chunks of ham, but my version is meatless. It makes a great Tex-Mex side or a filling lunch when you serve it with warm corn bread.
—L.R. Larson, Sioux Falls, SD

Prep: 15 min. + standing • **Cook:** 1½ hours
Makes: 10 servings

- 2 cups dried pinto beans (about ¾ pound)
- 2 cans (14½ ounces each) reduced-sodium chicken broth
- 2 celery ribs, diced
- ¼ cup diced onion
- ¼ cup diced green pepper
- 1 garlic clove, minced
- 2 bay leaves
- 1 teaspoon ground cumin
- ½ teaspoon rubbed sage
- ¼ teaspoon crushed red pepper flakes
- 2 cans (14½ ounces each) Mexican diced tomatoes, undrained
- ½ teaspoon salt
  Chopped fresh cilantro

1. Sort and rinse beans with cold water. Place beans in a Dutch oven; add water to cover by 2 in. Bring to a boil; boil for 2 minutes. Remove from heat; let stand, covered, 1 hour.
2. Drain and rinse beans, discarding liquid. Return beans to pan. Stir in broth, celery, onion, green pepper, garlic and seasonings; bring to a boil. Reduce heat; simmer, uncovered, until beans are very tender, about 1 hour.
3. Discard bay leaves. Stir in tomatoes and salt. Simmer, uncovered, until mixture is heated through, 25-30 minutes, stirring occasionally. Serve with cilantro.

CHILE RELLENO SQUARES

HOMEMADE GUACAMOLE

Nothing is better than freshly made guacamole when you're eating something spicy. It's easy to whip together in a matter of minutes, and it quickly tames anything that's too hot. See photo on page 49.
—Joan Hallford, North Richland Hills, TX

Start to Finish: 10 min.
Makes: 2 cups

- 3 medium ripe avocados, peeled and cubed
- 1 garlic clove, minced
- ¼ to ½ teaspoon salt
- 2 medium tomatoes, seeded and chopped, optional
- 1 small onion, finely chopped
- ¼ cup mayonnaise, optional
- 1 to 2 tablespoons lime juice
- 1 tablespoon minced fresh cilantro

Mash avocados with garlic and salt. Stir in remaining ingredients.

CHILE RELLENO SQUARES

A friend gave me this recipe for a simple variation of chile rellenos, and now my family requests it often. It makes a tasty appetizer or flavorful complement to a Mexican-style meal.
—Fran Carll, Long Beach, CA

Prep: 10 min. • **Bake:** 25 min.
Makes: 16 servings

- 3 cups shredded Monterey Jack cheese
- 1½ cups shredded cheddar cheese
- 2 cans (4 ounces each) chopped green chilies, drained
- 2 large eggs
- 2 tablespoons whole milk
- 1 tablespoon all-purpose flour

1. Preheat oven to 375°. Sprinkle half of each of the cheeses onto bottom of a greased 8-in. square baking dish. Layer with chilies and remaining cheeses.
2. Whisk together eggs, milk and flour; pour over top. Bake, uncovered, until set, 25-30 minutes. Cool casserole 15 minutes before cutting.

SOUTHWESTERN RICE

MEXICAN STUFFED PEPPERS

My stuffed peppers make a nutritious and economical meal. I top them with sour cream and serve tortilla chips and salsa on the side. Replace the ground beef with lean ground turkey if you want to cut fat.
—Kim Coleman, Columbia, SC

Prep: 25 min. • **Bake:** 30 min.
Makes: 8 servings

- 1 pound lean ground beef (90% lean)
- 1 can (14½ ounces) diced tomatoes and green chilies, undrained
- 1 envelope (5.4 ounces) Mexican-style rice and pasta mix
- 1½ cups water
- 8 medium sweet peppers
- 2 cups shredded Mexican cheese blend, divided

1. Preheat oven to 375°. In a large skillet, cook and crumble beef over medium heat until no longer pink, 5-7 minutes; drain. Stir in tomatoes, rice mix and water; bring to a boil. Reduce heat; simmer, covered, until liquid is absorbed, 6-8 minutes.
2. Cut and discard tops from peppers; remove seeds. Place peppers in a greased 13x9-in. baking dish. Place ⅓ cup beef mixture in each pepper; sprinkle each with 2 tablespoons cheese. Top with remaining rice mixture. Bake, covered, 25 minutes.
3. Sprinkle with remaining cheese. Bake, uncovered, until cheese is melted and peppers are crisp-tender, 5-10 minutes.

SOUTHWESTERN RICE

I created this zippy rice dish after trying something similar at a restaurant. It's a colorful addition to meals when you want to bring the Southwest to your table. Add cubes of grilled chicken to make it a meal.
—Michelle Dennis, Clarks Hill, IN

Start to Finish: 30 min.
Makes: 8 servings

- 1 tablespoon olive oil
- 1 medium green pepper, diced
- 1 medium onion, chopped
- 2 garlic cloves, minced
- 1 cup uncooked long grain rice
- ½ teaspoon ground cumin
- ⅛ teaspoon ground turmeric
- 1 can (14½ ounces) reduced-sodium chicken broth
- 2 cups frozen corn (about 10 ounces), thawed
- 1 can (15 ounces) black beans, rinsed and drained
- 1 can (10 ounces) diced tomatoes and green chilies, undrained

1. In a large nonstick skillet, heat oil over medium-high heat; saute pepper and onion 3 minutes. Add garlic; cook and stir 1 minute.
2. Stir in rice, spices and broth; bring to a boil. Reduce heat; simmer, covered, until rice is tender, about 15 minutes. Stir in remaining ingredients; cook, covered, until heated through.

JICAMA ROMAINE SALAD

We're big fans of jicama, also known as the Mexican yam bean or Mexican turnip. With a flavor similar to that of an apple, the root vegetable adds some crunch, sweetness and feisty flair to this salad.
—Stephanie Homme, Baton Rouge, LA

Start to Finish: 15 min.
Makes: 8 servings

- 4 cups torn romaine
- 4 cups julienned peeled jicama
- 2 medium tomatoes, cut into thin wedges
- ½ cup shredded reduced-fat cheddar cheese

DRESSING
- ¼ cup chopped green chilies
- 2 tablespoons fat-free mayonnaise
- 1 tablespoon fat-free milk
- 1 tablespoon sour cream
- 1 garlic clove, minced
- 1 teaspoon dried oregano
- ½ teaspoon ground cumin
- ⅛ teaspoon hot pepper sauce

Combine first four ingredients. In a small bowl, mix dressing ingredients. Toss gently with salad. Serve immediately.

TOP TIP

Freeze Summer Bell Peppers for Use Later

Stuffed peppers are my specialty for fall and winter potlucks. So in the summer, when bell peppers are abundant, I collect as many as I can and freeze them. To prepare the peppers for freezing, wash well; remove seeds and stems. Blanch for 3 minutes; drain well and freeze on a waxed paper-lined baking sheet. Once frozen, place the peppers in resealable plastic freezer bags for long-term storage. Then enjoy throughout the fall and winter.
—Ruth J., Albuquerque, NM

CHICKEN
TAMALES

CHICKEN TAMALES

I love making tamales from scratch for my husband and our four children.
—Cindy Pruitt, Grove, OK

Prep: 2½ hours + soaking • **Cook:** 50 min.
Makes: 20 tamales

- 24 **dried corn husks**
- 1 **broiler/fryer chicken (3 to 4 pounds), cut up**
- 3 **quarts water**
- 1 **medium onion, quartered**
- 2 **teaspoons salt**
- 1 **garlic clove, crushed**

DOUGH
- 1 **cup shortening**
- 3 **cups masa harina**

CHICKEN FILLING
- 6 **tablespoons canola oil**
- 6 **tablespoons all-purpose flour**
- ¾ **cup chili powder**
- ½ **teaspoon salt**
- ¼ **teaspoon garlic powder**
- ¼ **teaspoon pepper**
- 2 **cans (2¼ ounces each) sliced ripe olives, drained**

1. Place corn husks in a large bowl; cover with cold water and soak until softened, at least 2 hours (image 1).
2. Place chicken, water, onion, salt and garlic in a 6-qt. stockpot; bring to a boil. Reduce heat; simmer, covered, until chicken is tender, 45-60 minutes. Remove chicken from broth; cool slightly. Remove bones and skin; shred chicken. Strain and skim fat from stock; reserve 6 cups stock for dough and filling.
3. For dough, in a large bowl, beat shortening until light and fluffy, about 1 minute. In small amounts, beat in masa harina alternately with 2 cups stock. Drop a small amount of dough into a cup of cold water; dough should float to the top. If dough does not float, continue beating until it becomes light enough to float (image 2).
4. In a Dutch oven, heat oil; stir in flour until blended. Cook and stir over medium heat until lightly browned, 7-9 minutes. Stir in seasonings, chicken and 4 cups stock; bring to a boil. Reduce the heat; simmer, uncovered, until thickened, about 45 minutes, stirring occasionally.
5. Drain corn husks; tear four of the husks to make 20 strips for tying tamales. On the wide end of each remaining husk, spread

HOW-TO
How to Make Tamales

Refer to these photos when following the steps for prepping, wrapping and steaming tamales. Feel free to mix up the filling ingredients to appeal to various palates.

3 tablespoons dough to within ½ in. of side edges; top each with 2 tablespoons chicken mixture and 2 teaspoons olives (image 3). Fold long sides of husk over filling, overlapping slightly (image 4). Fold over narrow end of husk; tie with a strip of husk to secure (image 5).
6. Place a large steamer basket in a 6-qt. stockpot over 1 in. of water; place tamales upright in steamer (image 6). Bring to a boil; steam, covered, until dough peels away from husk, about 45 minutes, adding additional hot water to pot as needed.

Note: Fresh masa (dough made from stone-ground corn flour, called masa harina) is the foundation of a perfect tamale. You can find masa harina and dried corn husks in your supermarket's ethnic food aisle or online.

TOPSY-TURVY
SANGRIA

FRIED ICE CREAM

Refrigerated pie crust sprinkled with cinnamon sugar makes short work of this popular Mexican restaurant-style treat. Top scoops with honey, caramel ice cream topping or sweetened whipped cream.
—*Taste of Home* Test Kitchen

Prep: 30 min. + freezing
Makes: 8 servings

- 1 sheet refrigerated pie pastry
- 1½ teaspoons sugar
- 1 teaspoon ground cinnamon
- 1 quart vanilla ice cream
  Oil for deep-fat frying
- ½ cup honey

1. Preheat oven to 400°. Unroll pastry onto an ungreased baking sheet. Mix sugar and cinnamon; sprinkle over pastry. Prick thoroughly with a fork. Bake until golden brown, 10-12 minutes. Cool completely on a wire rack.

2. Place baked pastry in a large resealable plastic bag; crush to form coarse crumbs. Transfer crumbs to a shallow bowl. Using a ½-cup ice cream scoop, drop a scoop of ice cream into crumbs; roll quickly to coat and shape into a ball. Transfer to a wax paper-lined baking sheet; place in freezer. Repeat with seven additional scoops of ice cream; freeze until firm, 1-2 hours.

3. To serve, heat oil to 375° in an electric skillet or deep-fat fryer. Fry ice cream balls until golden, 8-10 seconds. Drain on paper towels. Serve immediately in chilled dishes. Drizzle with honey.

TOPSY-TURVY SANGRIA

A friend gave me this recipe a few years ago. It's perfect for relaxed get-togethers. It tastes best when you make it the night before and let the flavors steep. But be careful—it goes down easy!
—*Tracy Field, Bremerton, WA*

Start to Finish: 10 min.
Makes: 10 servings (¾ cup each)

- 1 bottle (750 milliliters) merlot
- 1 cup sugar
- 1 cup orange liqueur
- ½ to 1 cup brandy
- 3 cups cold lemon-lime soda
- 1 cup sliced fresh strawberries
- 1 medium orange, sliced
- 1 medium lemon, sliced
- 1 medium peach, sliced
  Ice cubes

In a pitcher, stir first four ingredients until sugar is dissolved. Stir in soda and fruit. Serve over ice.

CLASSIC TRES LECHES CAKE

Prep: 45 min. • **Bake:** 20 min. + chilling
Makes: 10 servings

- 4 large eggs, separated
- ⅔ cup sugar, divided
- ⅔ cup cake flour
  Dash salt
- ¾ cup heavy whipping cream
- ¾ cup evaporated milk
- ¾ cup sweetened condensed milk
- 2 teaspoons vanilla extract
- ¼ teaspoon rum extract

TOPPING
- 1¼ cups heavy whipping cream
- 3 tablespoons sugar
  Sliced fresh strawberries and dulce de leche, optional

1. Place egg whites in a large bowl; let stand at room temperature 30 minutes. Line bottom of a 9-in. springform pan with parchment paper; grease paper.

2. Meanwhile, preheat oven to 350°. In another large bowl, beat egg yolks until slightly thickened. Gradually add ⅓ cup sugar, beating on high speed until thick and lemon-colored. Fold in flour, a third at a time.

3. Add salt to egg whites; with clean beaters, beat on medium until soft peaks form. Gradually add remaining sugar, 1 tablespoon at a time, beating on high after each addition until sugar is dissolved. Continue beating until soft glossy peaks form. Fold a third of the whites into batter, then fold in remaining whites. Gently spread into prepared pan.

4. Bake until top springs back when lightly touched, 20-25 minutes. Cool 10 minutes before removing from pan to a wire rack to cool completely.

5. Place cake on a rimmed serving plate. Poke holes in top with a skewer. In a small bowl, mix the cream, evaporated milk, sweetened condensed milk and extracts; brush slowly over cake. Refrigerate, covered, 2 hours.

6. For topping, beat cream until it begins to thicken. Add sugar; beat until peaks form. Spread over top of cake. If desired, top with strawberries and dulce de leche just before serving.

"This cake gets its name from the three types of milk—evaporated, sweetened condensed and heavy whipping cream—used to create a moist and tender texture."

—*TASTE OF HOME* TEST KITCHEN

CLASSIC TRES LECHES CAKE

Wine & Chocolate Party

Some things are just *meant to be*, and wine and chocolate are a culinary match made in heaven. You love them both—and your friends, too!—so bring them all together for the ultimate tasting experience with a holiday wine and chocolate party.

Here you'll find a sweet lineup of chocolatly indulgences that pair with your favorite reds and whites. Fall in love with truffles, biscotti, fondue, mousse, cheesecake and other blissful morsels, each one featuring a different kind of chocolate. And if you're new to pairing or want to try something different, see our suggestions on page 66.

So go ahead—mix and match to your heart's content, and toast to good friendship, good dessert and good wine!

Cashew Clusters (p. 60) **Chocolate Truffles** (p.65)

CASHEW
CLUSTERS

CHOCOLATE PISTACHIO BISCOTTI

Chocolate, pistachios and cranberries unite in this recipe. Biscotti are sometimes dipped in or served with sweet dessert wine, a tradition that has roots in Italy.
—Gilda Lester, Millsboro, DE

Prep: 30 min. • **Bake:** 30 min. + cooling
Makes: 40 cookies

⅓ cup butter, softened
1 cup plus 1 tablespoon sugar, divided
3 large eggs
2 teaspoons vanilla extract
2¾ cups all-purpose flour
⅓ cup baking cocoa
2½ teaspoons baking powder
½ teaspoon ground cinnamon
1 cup (6 ounces) semisweet chocolate chips
½ cup pistachios
½ cup dried cranberries

1. Preheat oven to 350°. In a large bowl, cream butter and 1 cup sugar until light and fluffy. Add eggs, one at a time, beating well after each addition. Beat in the vanilla. Mix the flour, cocoa, baking powder and cinnamon; add to the creamed mixture and mix well (the dough will be sticky). Stir in the chocolate chips, pistachios and cranberries.
2. Divide dough into four portions. On ungreased baking sheets, shape portions into 10x2½-in. rectangles. Sprinkle with remaining sugar. Bake 20-25 minutes or until set. Carefully remove to wire racks; cool 5 minutes.
3. Transfer to a cutting board; cut each rectangle into 10 slices. Place cut side down on ungreased baking sheets. Bake 5-8 minutes on each side or until lightly browned. Remove to wire racks to cool. Store in an airtight container.

CASHEW CLUSTERS

I make these treats for the many bake sales at the local community college where I work. I'm proud to say that they are always the first to sell out!
—Betsy Grantier, Charlottesville, VA

Prep: 20 min. + standing • **Cook:** 5 min.
Makes: about 6 dozen

1 pound white candy coating, coarsely chopped
1 cup (6 ounces) semisweet chocolate chips
4 ounces German sweet chocolate, chopped
⅓ cup milk chocolate chips
2 cups salted whole cashews (about 9 ounces)
2 cups salted cashew halves and pieces (about 9 ounces)

1. Place first the four ingredients in a large microwave-safe bowl; microwave, covered, at 50% power until melted, 5-6 minutes, stirring every 30 seconds. Stir in the cashews.
2. Drop mixture by tablespoonfuls onto waxed paper-lined pans; let stand until set. Store in an airtight container.
Note: This recipe was tested in a 1,100-watt microwave.

SPICY CHOCOLATE BARK

Warm hearts and heat up the holidays with this melt-in-your-mouth confection. With just four ingredients, it's an easy-to-make gift. And those who have a penchant for spicy foods may put it at the top of their holiday wish lists!
—Taste of Home Test Kitchen

Prep: 10 min. + chilling • **Cook:** 5 min.
Makes: about 1½ pounds

1 pound milk chocolate candy coating, coarsely chopped
½ teaspoon cayenne pepper
½ cup chopped cashews, toasted
½ cup chopped pecans, toasted

1. In a microwave, melt candy coating; stir until smooth. Stir in remaining ingredients. Spread onto a waxed paper-lined pan. Refrigerate until set, about 20 minutes.
2. Break bark into small pieces. Store in an airtight container in the refrigerator.
Note: To toast nuts, bake in a shallow pan in a 350° oven for 5-10 minutes, or cook nuts in a skillet over low heat until lightly browned, stirring occasionally.

CHOCOLATE
PISTACHIO BISCOTTI

ORANGE CHOCOLATE FONDUE

Invite your friends and family to try this luscious fondue during the holiday season. For other creative dippers, consider fruit, cubed angel food cake, shortbread cookies, biscotti, marshmallows and pretzels. Good fruit options include dried apricots, cantaloupe chunks, orange segments and drained pineapple chunks. If you don't have fondue forks, use regular forks or wooden skewers.
—Mary Jean DeVries, Grandville, MI

Start to Finish: 15 min.
Makes: 1⅓ cups

- ½ cup milk chocolate chips
- 3 ounces bittersweet chocolate, chopped
- ½ cup heavy whipping cream
- 3 tablespoons thawed orange juice concentrate
- 1 frozen pound cake (16 ounces), thawed and cubed
  Assorted fresh fruit

In a heavy saucepan, combine both chocolates and cream (image 1); cook and stir over low heat until smooth. Stir in orange juice concentrate (image 2); keep warm. Serve with dippers (image 3).

DOUBLE CHOCOLATE FUDGE

If you love fudge, this recipe is sure to satisfy your deepest chocolate craving. The rich treat is a favorite all year long, especially at Christmas.
—Marilyn Jordan, Hoosick Falls, NY

Prep: 25 min. + chilling
Makes: 5 pounds (150 pieces)

- 1½ teaspoons plus 2 tablespoons butter, divided
- 4½ cups sugar
- 1 can (12 ounces) evaporated milk
  Pinch salt
- 1 jar (7 ounces) marshmallow creme
- 12 ounces German's sweet chocolate, chopped
- 2 cups (12 ounces) semisweet chocolate chips
- 2 cups chopped walnuts, optional

1. Line a 15x10x1-in. pan with foil; grease foil with 1½ teaspoons butter.

2. In a heavy large saucepan, combine sugar, milk, salt and remaining butter. Bring to a rapid boil over medium heat, stirring constantly. Cook 5 minutes, stirring constantly. Remove from heat.
3. Stir in marshmallow creme until melted. Stir in both chocolates until melted. If desired, stir in walnuts. Immediately spread into prepared pan. Refrigerate until firm.
4. Using foil, lift fudge from pan. Remove foil; cut fudge into 1-in. squares. Store between layers of waxed paper in airtight containers in the refrigerator.

CHOCOLATE MOLTEN CAKES

Be prepared to swoon once you dip into this indulgent flourless cake and warm chocolate oozes from its center. It was one of the favorite desserts on the menu at La Boucherie restaurant. Try it, and you'll understand why!
—Matthew Lawrence, Vashon, WA

Start to Finish: 30 min.
Makes: 6 servings

- 2 teaspoons plus 1 cup butter, cubed, divided
- 6 teaspoons plus ¼ cup sugar, divided
- 1¼ pounds semisweet chocolate, chopped
- 2 large eggs
- 6 large egg yolks

1. Preheat oven to 350°. Grease six 6-oz. ramekins or custard cups with 2 teaspoons butter. Sprinkle sides and bottoms of each ramekin with 1 teaspoon sugar; set aside.
2. In a double boiler or metal bowl over hot water, melt chocolate and remaining butter; stir until smooth. Remove from heat. In a large bowl, beat eggs, egg yolks and remaining sugar until thick and lemon-colored. With a spatula, fold half of the egg mixture into chocolate mixture just until blended. Fold in the remaining egg mixture.
3. Transfer to prepared ramekins. Place ramekins on a baking sheet. Bake 17-20 minutes or until a thermometer inserted in the center reads 160° and sides of the cakes are set.
4. Remove from the oven; let stand for 1 minute. Run a knife around sides of the ramekins; invert cakes onto dessert plates. Serve immediately.

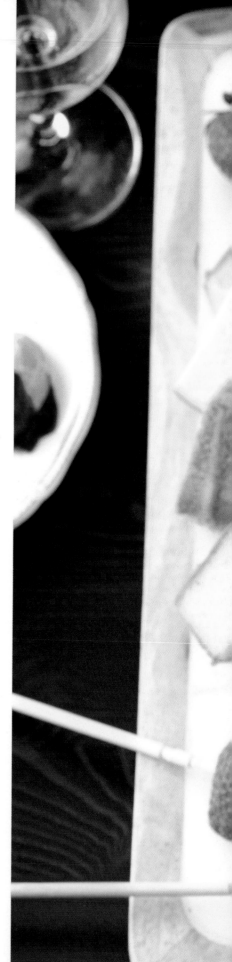

ORANGE
CHOCOLATE
FONDUE

How To Make Chocolate Fondue

To serve a smooth and delicious chocolate fondue, follow these easy steps.

COMBINE chocolates and cream in a heavy saucepan. Cook and stir over low heat until smooth.

STIR in orange juice concentrate. Keep mixture warm.

SERVE with fruit, cake cubes or other dippers.

ELEGANT
WHITE CHOCOLATE
MOUSSE

ELEGANT WHITE CHOCOLATE MOUSSE

"Simply elegant" is a fitting description for this smooth treat. Whipped cream teams up with white chocolate to make this easy recipe extra special.
—Laurinda Johnston, Belchertown, MA

Prep: 20 min. + chilling
Makes: 8 servings

- 12 ounces white baking chocolate, coarsely chopped
- 2 cups heavy whipping cream, divided
- 1 tablespoon confectioners' sugar
- 1 teaspoon vanilla extract

1. In a small heavy saucepan, combine chocolate and ⅔ cup cream; cook and stir over medium-low heat until smooth. Transfer to a large bowl; cool to room temperature.
2. In a small bowl, beat the remaining cream until it begins to thicken. Add the confectioners' sugar and vanilla; beat until soft peaks form. Fold ¼ cup of the whipped cream into chocolate mixture, then fold in remaining whipped cream.
3. Spoon into dessert dishes. Refrigerate, covered, at least 2 hours.

MOCHA SHORTBREAD

My coffee-flavored shortbread is delicious on its own, but if you want to add a touch of sweetness, serve with ice cream and strawberry sauce. I take the crispy wedges to community events and give some away as Christmas gifts.
—Caronlyn Van Boening, Blue Springs, NE

Prep: 15 min. • **Bake:** 25 min. + cooling
Makes: 16 cookies

- 1¼ cups all-purpose flour
- ⅓ cup sugar
- 2 tablespoons baking cocoa
- 1 teaspoon instant coffee granules, finely crushed
- ½ cup cold butter

1. Preheat oven to 325°. In a bowl, mix flour, sugar, cocoa and coffee; cut in the butter until the mixture resembles fine crumbs. Gather crumbs into a ball; knead 2 minutes.
2. On an ungreased baking sheet, pat dough into a 7½-in. circle. Cut into 16 wedges, but do not separate. Prick each wedge several times with a fork. Bake 25-30 minutes.
3. Remove from oven; recut into wedges. Cool 5 minutes; remove from pan to a wire rack to cool completely.

CHOCOLATE TRUFFLES

You may be tempted to save this recipe for a special occasion since these smooth, creamy chocolates are divine. But with just a few ingredients, they're easy to make any time. See photo on page 59.
—Darlene Wiese-Appleby, Creston, OH

Prep: 20 min. + chilling
Makes: about 4 dozen

- 3 cups (18 ounces) semisweet chocolate chips
- 1 can (14 ounces) sweetened condensed milk
- 1 tablespoon vanilla extract
  Optional coatings: chocolate sprinkles, Dutch-processed cocoa, espresso powder and cocoa nibs

1. In a microwave-safe bowl, melt the chocolate chips with the milk; stir until smooth. Stir in vanilla. Refrigerate, covered, 2 hours or until firm enough to roll into balls.
2. Shape into 1-in. balls. Roll balls in coatings as desired.

CHOCOLATE-DIPPED MACAROONS

Macaroons are small, pretty and delicate. They can be tricky to make, but these chocolate-dipped beauties are worth the time and effort.
—Joylyn Trickel, Helendale, CA

Prep: 45 min.
Bake: 25 min./batch + chilling
Makes: 5 dozen

- 5 large egg whites
- ½ teaspoon vanilla extract
- 1⅓ cups sugar
- 4 cups sweetened shredded coconut, toasted
- ¾ cup ground almonds
- 12 ounces bittersweet or semisweet chocolate, melted

1. Place egg whites in a large bowl; let stand at room temperature 30 minutes. Preheat oven to 275°.
2. Add vanilla to egg whites; beat on medium speed until soft peaks form. Gradually add sugar, about 2 tablespoons at a time, beating on high until stiff glossy peaks form and the sugar is dissolved. Gradually fold in coconut and almonds, about ½ cup at a time.
3. Drop egg white mixture by rounded tablespoonfuls onto parchment paper-lined baking sheets, 2 in. apart. Bake until firm to the touch, about 25 minutes. Remove to wire racks to cool completely.
4. Dip bottoms of cookies in melted chocolate; allow excess to drip off. Place on waxed paper-lined baking sheets. Refrigerate 1 hour or until set. Store in airtight containers.
Note: To toast coconut, bake in a shallow pan in a 350° oven for 5-10 minutes or cook in a skillet over low heat until golden brown, stirring occasionally.

TOP TIP

Soft Peaks

Dessert recipes often call for beating egg whites until soft peaks form. Beat room temperature egg whites with an electric mixer on medium speed until the peaks curl down when the beaters are lifted up. To ensure the egg whites reach full volume, make sure the bowl and beaters are free from oil and the egg whites contain no specks of yolk.

BITTERSWEET CHOCOLATE CHEESECAKE

While it's common for one generation to pass a cherished recipe down to the next, sometimes there's one that's so good it goes the other way! That's the case here: I'm a great-grandmother, and I received this recipe from my niece. My entire family enjoys this velvety cheesecake.
—Amelia Gregory, Omemee, ON

Prep: 20 min. + chilling
Bake: 1 hour + cooling
Makes: 16 servings

- 1 cup chocolate wafer crumbs
- ½ cup finely chopped hazelnuts, toasted
- ⅓ cup butter, melted
- 3 packages (8 ounces each) cream cheese, softened
- 1 cup sugar
- 12 ounces bittersweet chocolate, melted and cooled
- 1 cup (8 ounces) sour cream
- 1½ teaspoons vanilla extract
- ½ teaspoon almond extract
  Dash salt
- 3 large eggs, lightly beaten

GLAZE
- 4 ounces bittersweet chocolate, chopped
- ¼ cup heavy whipping cream
- 1 teaspoon vanilla extract
  Whipped cream and additional toasted hazelnuts, optional

1. Preheat oven to 350°. Mix wafer crumbs, hazelnuts and melted butter; press onto bottom of an ungreased 9-in. springform pan.
2. Beat cream cheese and sugar until smooth. Beat in cooled chocolate, then sour cream, extracts and salt. Add eggs; beat on low speed just until blended. Pour over crust. Place pan on a baking sheet.
3. Bake until center is almost set, 60-65 minutes. Cool on a wire rack 10 minutes. Loosen sides from pan with a knife; cool 1 hour longer. Refrigerate 3 hours.
4. For glaze, in a microwave, melt chocolate with cream; stir until smooth. Stir in vanilla. Spread over cheesecake. Refrigerate, covered, overnight. Remove rim from pan. If desired, served with whipped cream and additional hazelnuts.

ALL COUPLED UP

Play Cupid with your sips and sweets by trying these perfect-match pairings.

MOSCATO D'ASTI
Light and sweet, with a hint of bubbles and a slight orange flavor

Pairs well with
White chocolate, orange-flavored chocolate, orange candy or kumquats dipped in semisweet chocolate

CRANBERRY WINE
Both sweet and tart with intense cranberry flavor

Pairs well with
Rich, buttery dark chocolate truffles (the darker the better)

BRACHETTO D'ACQUI
Chocolate pairing all-star; slightly sweet and effervescent, with strawberry and red fruit flavors

Pairs well with
Sampler of assorted chocolates; strawberries dipped in chocolate

ASTI SPUMANTE
Sweet and sparkling, with aromas of flowers and ripe summer fruits

Pairs well with
Dried apricots or pretzels dipped in bittersweet chocolate; sea foam candy

TAWNY PORT
Caramelly and nutty with hints of cinnamon and clove

Pairs well with
Chocolate hazelnut truffles, chocolate cashew clusters, chocolate cheese (from the cheese case)

Christmas Bars & Cookies

For any Christmas celebration, big or small, there's nothing like a freshly baked cookie, a scrumptious homemade brownie or a pretty layered bar to make the moment memorable.

Here you'll find the best sweet treats to fill your holiday cookie platter. Discover rich, chocolaty brownies sprinkled with crushed candies; old-fashioned drop cookies studded with nuts; tangy fruit-filled bars and other merry morsels.

Whether you whip up your Christmas goodies to give as gifts, swap in a cookie exchange or stack high on a dessert tray, let these be your inspiration. And then, let the holiday baking begin!

Chocolate-Strawberry Pretzel Cookies (p. 77)

**CANDY CANE
SHORTBREAD
BARS**

CANDY CANE SHORTBREAD BARS

I created these bars for my daughter, who loves peppermint. The delicate, buttery shortbread melts in your mouth. They're a hit wherever I take them.
—Susan Ciuffreda, Huntersville, NC

Prep: 30 min. • **Bake:** 20 min. + cooling
Makes: 2 dozen

- 1 cup butter, softened
- 1 cup packed brown sugar
- 1 large egg yolk
- 1½ teaspoons peppermint extract
- 2 cups all-purpose flour

BUTTERCREAM

- 2 cups confectioners' sugar
- ¼ cup butter, melted
- 2 tablespoons 2% milk
- ½ teaspoon peppermint extract
- 2 drops red food coloring, optional

TOPPING

- 9 ounces white baking chocolate, melted and cooled slightly
- ¾ cup crushed candy canes (about 10 regular)

1. Preheat oven to 350°. Line a 13x9-in. baking pan with parchment paper, letting ends extend up sides.
2. In a large bowl, cream butter and brown sugar until light and fluffy. Beat in egg yolk and extract. Gradually beat in flour. Press evenly into prepared pan.
3. Bake 16-19 minutes or until the edges are brown. Cool completely in pan on a wire rack.
4. In a bowl, combine buttercream ingredients; beat until smooth. Spread over shortbread. Carefully spread white chocolate over top. Sprinkle with candy canes; let stand until set.
5. Lifting with parchment paper, remove shortbread from pan. Cut into bars.

CRANBERRY EGGNOG CHEESECAKE BARS

CRANBERRY EGGNOG CHEESECAKE BARS

My family loves cheesecake in all of its incarnations. These bars combine tart cranberries and rich cream cheese, and taste even better when chilled overnight.
—Carmell Childs, Ferron, UT

Prep: 20 min. • **Bake:** 50 min. + chilling
Makes: 2 dozen

- 1 package spice cake mix (regular size)
- 2½ cups old-fashioned oats
- ¾ cup butter, melted
- 2 packages (8 ounces each) cream cheese, softened
- ½ cup sugar
- ⅛ teaspoon ground nutmeg
- ½ cup eggnog
- 2 tablespoons all-purpose flour
- 3 large eggs
- 1 can (14 ounces) whole-berry cranberry sauce
- 2 tablespoons cornstarch

1. Preheat oven to 350°. Line a 13x9-in. baking pan with parchment paper, letting ends extend up sides; grease paper.
2. In a large bowl, combine cake mix and oats; stir in melted butter. Reserve 1⅓ cups crumb mixture for topping; press remaining mixture onto the bottom of prepared pan.
3. In a large bowl, beat cream cheese, sugar and nutmeg until smooth. Gradually beat in eggnog and flour. Add eggs; beat on low speed just until blended. Pour cream cheese mixture over crust.
4. In a small bowl, mix cranberry sauce and cornstarch until blended; spoon over cheesecake layer. Sprinkle with reserved crumb mixture. Bake 50-55 minutes or until edges are brown and the center is almost set.
5. Cool 1 hour on a wire rack. Refrigerate at least 2 hours. Lifting with parchment paper, remove cheesecake from pan. Cut into bars.

Note: This recipe was tested with commercially prepared eggnog.

FRUITCAKE CHRISTMAS COOKIES

My rich fruit-and-nut filled drop cookies are a deliciously fun take on traditional fruitcake. They make great gifts for folks who love the old-fashioned treat. Their flavor actually gets better over time!
—Julia Funkhouser, Carson, IA

Prep: 25 min. • **Bake:** 15 min./batch
Makes: about 3½ dozen

- 1 cup butter, softened
- ¾ cup packed brown sugar
- 1 large egg
- ½ teaspoon vanilla extract
- 1⅔ cups all-purpose flour
- ½ teaspoon baking soda
- ¼ teaspoon salt
- 1½ cups dates, finely chopped
- 4 ounces red candied cherries, halved
- 4 ounces candied pineapple, diced
- ½ cup whole hazelnuts, toasted
- ½ cup coarsely chopped pecans
- ½ cup coarsely chopped walnuts

1. Preheat oven to 325°. In a large bowl, cream butter and brown sugar until light and fluffy. Beat in the egg and vanilla. In another bowl, whisk together flour, baking soda and salt; gradually beat into creamed mixture. Stir in remaining ingredients.

2. Drop dough by teaspoonfuls onto greased baking sheets. Bake until golden brown, about 15 minutes. Store in an airtight container. (Cookies are best after a few days.)

Note: To toast whole hazelnuts, bake in a shallow pan in a 350° oven 7-10 minutes or until fragrant and lightly browned, stirring occasionally. To remove skins, wrap hazelnuts in a tea towel; rub with towel to loosen skins.

FRUITCAKE CHRISTMAS COOKIES

HONEY PECAN TRIANGLES

I've been stirring up batches of these tasty bar cookies for years, and they're always one of the first to disappear from my tray. They have the goodness of pecan pie and are so easy to serve to a crowd.
—Debbie Fogel, East Berne, NY

Prep: 20 min. • **Bake:** 45 min. + cooling
Makes: 4 dozen

- 2 teaspoons plus ½ cup butter, softened, divided
- ½ cup packed brown sugar
- 1 large egg yolk
- 1½ cups all-purpose flour

TOPPING
- 1 cup packed brown sugar
- ½ cup butter, cubed
- ¼ cup honey
- ½ cup heavy whipping cream
- 4 cups chopped pecans

1. Preheat oven to 350°. Line a 13x9-in. baking pan with foil, letting ends extend up sides; grease foil with 2 teaspoons butter.
2. In a large bowl, cream remaining butter and brown sugar until light and fluffy; beat in egg yolk. Gradually beat in flour. Press into prepared pan. Bake crust until golden brown, about 15 minutes.
3. Meanwhile, in a large saucepan, combine brown sugar, butter and honey. Bring to a boil over medium heat, stirring constantly; cook and stir 3 minutes. Remove from heat; stir in cream and pecans. Pour over crust. Bake until hot and bubbly, about 30 minutes. Cool completely on a wire rack.
4. Lifting with foil, remove from pan. Cut into 24 squares. Cut squares diagonally into triangles.

MAPLE-GLAZED CINNAMON CHIP BARS

Whenever I make these, the kitchen smells like Christmas. The cinnamon chips are a pleasant suprise, and the maple glaze adds a fancy touch and fabulous flavor.
—Lyndi Pilch, Springfield, MO

Prep: 20 min. • **Bake:** 20 min.
Makes: 2 dozen

- 1 cup butter, softened
- 2 cups packed brown sugar
- 2 teaspoons vanilla extract
- 2 large eggs
- 2⅔ cups all-purpose flour
- 2 teaspoons baking powder
- 1 teaspoon salt
- ¾ cup cinnamon baking chips
- 1 tablespoon cinnamon sugar

GLAZE
- ½ cup confectioners' sugar
- 3 tablespoons maple syrup
- ½ teaspoon vanilla extract

1. Preheat oven to 350°. In a large bowl, cream butter and brown sugar until well blended. Beat in vanilla and eggs, one at a time. In another bowl, whisk together flour, baking powder and salt; gradually beat into the creamed mixture. Stir in cinnamon chips. Spread into a greased 13x9-in. baking pan. Sprinkle with cinnamon sugar.
2. Bake until golden brown and a toothpick inserted in center comes out clean, 20-25 minutes. Cool completely in pan on a wire rack.
3. In a small bowl, mix all glaze ingredients until smooth; drizzle over top. Cut into bars. Store in an airtight container.

TOP TIP
Cutting Brownies & Bars

For basic bars and brownies (those without soft fillings or toppings), line the pan with foil before baking. When cool, lift foil from the pan. Trim the edges of the bars or brownies, then cut into bars, squares or diamonds.

For perfectly sized bars, lay a clean ruler on top and make cut marks with the point of a knife. Use the edge of the ruler as a cutting guide, and cut with a gentle sawing motion. Remove the corner piece first.

How many pieces? An 8-inch square pan will yield 16 pieces when cut four rows by four rows. A 13x9-inch pan will yield 48 pieces when cut six rows by eight rows.

**PISTACHIO
BROWNIE
TOFFEE BARS**

1. Preheat oven to 350°. Whisk together flour and baking powder.
2. In a large bowl, mix the brown sugar, melted butter and maple flavoring. Beat in eggs, one at a time, mixing well after each addition. Stir in flour mixture and walnuts. Spread batter into a greased 9-in. square baking pan.
3. Bake until a toothpick inserted in center comes out clean, 27-32 minutes. Cool completely in pan on a wire rack. If desired, dust with confectioners' sugar. Cut into bars.

MERRY GRINCHMAS COOKIES

Baking cookies around the holidays is a big deal in our house. This one is simple, delicious and fun to make with kids. Whip up a batch while watching your favorite Christmas movies.
—Angela Lemoine, Howell, NJ

Prep: 20 min. + chilling
Bake: 15 min. + cooling
Makes: about 4 dozen

- ½ cup butter, softened
- 1 package (8 ounces) cream cheese, softened
- 1¼ cups sugar
- 2 teaspoons vanilla extract
- 1 teaspoon green food coloring
- 2 large eggs
- 3 cups all-purpose flour
- 2 teaspoons baking powder
- ¼ teaspoon salt
- 1 cup confectioners' sugar
- 48 heart-shaped gumdrops

1. In a large bowl, beat butter, cream cheese and sugar until smooth. Beat in vanilla, food coloring and eggs, one at a time, beating well after each addition. In another bowl, whisk together flour, baking powder and salt; gradually beat into creamed mixture. Refrigerate, covered, 1 hour or until firm enough to shape.
2. Preheat oven to 350°. Shape dough into 1½-in. balls; roll in confectioners' sugar. Place 2 in. apart on ungreased baking sheets.
3. Bake until tops are cracked and edges are set, 12-15 minutes. Immediately press a gumdrop into each cookie. Cool cookies 5 minutes before removing to wire racks to cool.

PISTACHIO BROWNIE TOFFEE BARS

These brownie bars have a homespun appeal and the surprise of pistachios. They've been a sought-after staple on Christmas cookie trays for years.
—Matt Shaw, Warrenton, OR

Prep: 20 min. • **Bake:** 30 min. + cooling
Makes: 3 dozen

- ¾ cup butter, softened
- ¾ cup packed brown sugar
- 1 large egg yolk
- ¾ teaspoon vanilla extract
- 1½ cups all-purpose flour

FILLING
- 1 package fudge brownie mix (13x9-inch pan size)
- ⅓ cup water
- ⅓ cup canola oil
- 1 large egg

TOPPING
- 1 package (11½ ounces) milk chocolate chips, melted
- ¾ cup chopped salted roasted pistachios

1. Preheat oven to 350°. In a large bowl, cream butter and brown sugar until light and fluffy. Beat in egg yolk and vanilla. Gradually beat in flour, mixing well. Press onto bottom of a greased 15x10x1-in. baking pan.

2. Bake until golden brown, 12-14 minutes. Meanwhile, in a large bowl, combine brownie mix, water, oil and egg until blended.
3. Spread brownie batter over hot crust. Bake until center is set, 14-16 minutes. Cool completely in pan on a wire rack.
4. Spread melted chocolate over top; sprinkle with pistachios. Let stand until set. Cut into bars.

MAPLE BUTTERSCOTCH BROWNIES

I often make a double batch of these brownies—they go fast no matter where I take them! I've baked them for family dinners and church suppers, and I always come back with an empty pan. They're easy to make and freeze well.
—Grace Vonhold, Rochester, NY

Prep: 15 min.
Bake: 30 min. + cooling
Makes: 16 brownies

- 1½ cups all-purpose flour
- 1 teaspoon baking powder
- 1¼ cups packed brown sugar
- ½ cup butter, melted
- 1½ teaspoons maple flavoring
- 2 large eggs
- 1 cup chopped walnuts
  Confectioners' sugar, optional

PISTACHIO BROWNIE TOFFEE BARS

PEPPERMINT
BROWNIES

PEPPERMINT BROWNIES

My grandmother encouraged me to enter these brownies in the county fair—where they earned top honors! With crushed peppermint candies, they're a pretty treat to serve during the holidays.
—Marcy Greenblatt, Redding, CA

Prep: 15 min. • **Bake:** 35 min.
Makes: 2 dozen

- 1⅓ cups all-purpose flour
- 1 cup baking cocoa
- 1 teaspoon salt
- 1 teaspoon baking powder
- ¾ cup canola oil
- 2 cups sugar
- 2 teaspoons vanilla extract
- 4 large eggs
- ⅔ cup crushed peppermint candies

GLAZE
- 1 cup (6 ounces) semisweet chocolate chips
- 1 tablespoon shortening
- 2 tablespoons crushed peppermint candies

1. Preheat oven to 350°. Line a 13x9-in. baking pan with foil; grease foil.
2. In a bowl, whisk together the first four ingredients. In a large bowl, beat oil and sugar until blended. Beat in vanilla and eggs, one at a time, beating well after each addition. Gradually add flour mixture; stir in peppermint candies. Spread mixture into prepared pan.
3. Bake until a toothpick inserted in the center comes out clean, 35-40 minutes. Cool in pan on a wire rack.
4. In a microwave, melt chocolate chips and shortening; stir until smooth. Spread over brownies; sprinkle with candies.

TOP TIP

Storage Tips for Brownies & Bars

Cover a pan of uncut brownies or bars with foil. (If made with perishable ingredients, like cream cheese, they should be covered and refrigerated.) Once the bars are cut, store them in an airtight container. Most bars freeze well for up to 3 months. To freeze a pan of uncut bars, place in an airtight container or resealable plastic bag. Or wrap individual bars in plastic wrap and stack in an airtight container.

CHOCOLATE-STRAWBERRY PRETZEL COOKIES

Every year I try to come up with a new recipe for my cookie tray, and this one has become a favorite. Who ever would guess how good pretzels are in cookies? See photo on page 69.
—Isabel Minunni, Poughkeepsie, NY

Prep: 30 min. + chilling
Bake: 10 min./batch + cooling
Makes: about 1 dozen

- 1 cup unsalted butter, softened
- ½ cup sugar
- 2 large eggs
- 1½ cups finely ground pretzels (about 6 ounces)
- 1 cup all-purpose flour
- 1 teaspoon baking powder
- ⅔ cup semisweet chocolate chips, melted
- ⅓ cup seedless strawberry jam
   Confectioners' sugar

1. In a large bowl, cream butter and sugar until light and fluffy. Add eggs, one at a time, beating well after each addition. In another bowl, mix ground pretzels, flour and baking powder; gradually beat into creamed mixture. Divide dough in half. Shape each into a disk; wrap in plastic. Refrigerate until firm enough to roll, about 1 hour.
2. Preheat oven to 350°. On a lightly floured surface, roll each portion of dough to ¼-in. thickness. Cut with a floured 3½-in. tree-shaped cookie cutter. Using a floured 1¾-in. tree-shaped cookie cutter, cut out the centers of half of the cookies. Place solid and window cookies 1 in. apart on ungreased baking sheets.
3. Bake 8-10 minutes or until edges are light brown. Remove from pans to wire racks to cool completely.
4. Spread melted chocolate onto bottoms of solid cookies; let stand until firm. Spread jam over cooled chocolate; top with window cookies. Dust lightly with confectioners' sugar.

Freeze option: Freeze undecorated cookies in freezer containers. To use, thaw in covered containers and decorate as directed.

SUGARED RAISIN PEAR DIAMONDS

With their tender golden crust and tempting pear and raisin filling, these fabulous bars stand out on any buffet table. Substitute apples for the pears; you'll still get yummy results!
—Jeanne Allen, Rye, CO

Prep: 20 min. + cooling
Bake: 45 min. + cooling
Makes: about 2 dozen

- 5 cups plus 1 tablespoon all-purpose flour, divided
- ½ cup plus 6 tablespoons sugar, divided
- 1 teaspoon salt
- 1 teaspoon grated lemon peel
- 1½ cups cold butter, cubed
- 1 cup half-and-half cream
- 6 cups diced peeled ripe pears (about 7 medium)
- 1 cup golden raisins
- 2 tablespoons lemon juice
- ¼ teaspoon ground cinnamon
- 1 large egg, lightly beaten
   Additional sugar

1. Preheat oven to 350°. In a large bowl, mix 5 cups flour, ½ cup sugar, salt and lemon peel; cut in butter until crumbly. Gradually add cream, tossing with a fork until a dough is formed. Divide the dough in half.
2. On a large piece of lightly floured waxed paper, roll one half of dough to a 17x12-in. rectangle. Transfer to an ungreased 15x10x1-in. baking pan; press onto bottom and up sides of pan.
3. Bake until lightly browned, about 20 minutes. Cool on a wire rack. Increase oven setting to 400°.
4. In a large bowl, toss pears with raisins, lemon juice, cinnamon and the remaining flour and sugar. Spread over crust. Roll remaining dough to a 16x11-in. rectangle; place over filling, trimming edges if necessary. Brush top with beaten egg; sprinkle with additional sugar.
5. Bake until golden brown, 25-30 minutes. Cool on a wire rack. Cut into diamond-shaped bars.

Holiday Breads

Nothing delights friends and family like a holiday gift made especially for them. The blissful, homey comfort of breads, muffins, biscuits, scones and other warm-from-the-oven specialities is the perfect way to show them how much you care.

Here you'll find the right baked beauty to give as a heartwarming gift or to accompany your own meals at home. Some are sweet, some are savory, but each one is guaranteed to leave hungry tummies more than satisfied.

Share the love this season with a gift from your hands and your heart.

Cherry Pull-Apart Bread (p. 83)

JALAPENO CHEESE BREAD

Cheddar cheese and jalapenos give this savory bread a spicy Southwestern flair. It makes a great accompaniment to chilis and stews. Top it with sweet cream butter and watch it disappear.

—Julie Delisle, Sainte-Sabine, QC

Prep: 25 min. + rising
Bake: 30 min. + cooling
Makes: 2 loaves (12 slices each)

- 1 package active dry yeast (¼ ounce)
- 1 cup warm water (110° to 115°)
- ¼ cup sugar
- 2 tablespoons canola oil
- ½ teaspoon salt
- 3 to 3½ cups all-purpose flour
- 2 cups shredded cheddar cheese
- ½ cup finely chopped seeded jalapeno peppers

1. Dissolve yeast in warm water. In a large bowl, combine the sugar, oil, salt, yeast mixture and 2 cups flour. Beat on medium speed until smooth. Stir in enough of the remaining flour to form a stiff dough. Stir in cheese and jalapenos.
2. Turn dough onto a floured surface; knead until smooth and elastic, about 6-8 minutes. Place in a greased bowl, turning once to grease the top. Cover with plastic wrap and let rise in a warm place until doubled, about 1 hour.
3. Punch dough down. Divide in half and shape into loaves. Place in two greased 8x4-in. loaf pans. Cover with kitchen towels; let rise in a warm place until almost doubled, about 40 minutes. Preheat oven to 350°.
4. Bake until golden brown, 30-35 minutes. Remove from pans to wire racks to cool.

Note: Wear disposable gloves when cutting hot peppers; the oils can burn skin. Avoid touching your face.

BEST CINNAMON ROLLS

Surprise a neighbor with a batch of oven-fresh cinnamon rolls slathered in cream cheese frosting. These breakfast treats make Christmas morning or any special occasion even more memorable.

—Shenai Fisher, Topeka, KS

Prep: 40 min. + rising
Bake: 20 min. + cooling
Makes: 16 rolls

- 1 package (¼ ounce) active dry yeast
- 1 cup warm whole milk (110° to 115°)
- ½ cup sugar
- ⅓ cup butter, melted
- 2 large eggs
- 1 teaspoon salt
- 4 to 4½ cups all-purpose flour

FILLING
- ¾ cup packed brown sugar
- 2 tablespoons ground cinnamon
- ¼ cup butter, melted, divided

FROSTING
- ½ cup butter, softened
- ¼ cup cream cheese, softened
- ½ teaspoon vanilla extract
- ⅛ teaspoon salt
- 1½ cups confectioners' sugar

1. Dissolve yeast in warm milk. In another bowl, combine sugar, butter, eggs, salt, yeast mixture and 2 cups flour; beat on medium speed until smooth. Stir in enough remaining flour to form a soft dough (dough will be sticky).
2. Turn dough onto a floured surface; knead until smooth and elastic, about 6-8 minutes. Place in a greased bowl, turning once to grease the top. Cover with plastic wrap and let rise in a warm place until doubled, about 1 hour.
3. Mix brown sugar and cinnamon. Punch down dough; divide in half. On a lightly floured surface, roll one portion of dough into an 11x8-in. rectangle. Brush with 2 tablespoons butter; sprinkle with half of the brown sugar mixture to within ½ in. of edges. Roll up jelly-roll style, starting with a long side; pinch seam to seal. Cut into eight slices; place in a greased 13x9-in. pan, cut side down. Cover with a kitchen towel. Repeat steps with remaining dough and filling. Let dough rise in a warm place until doubled, about 1 hour. Preheat oven to 350°.
4. Bake until golden brown, 20-25 minutes. Cool on wire racks.
5. For frosting, beat butter, cream cheese, vanilla and salt until blended; gradually beat in confectioners' sugar. Spread over tops. Refrigerate leftovers.

BASIL PARMESAN BREAD

The combination of basil, Parmesan cheese and sun-dried tomatoes give this hearty bread a flavor that will take you right to Tuscany!

—Sherry Hulsman, Elkton, FL

Prep: 25 min. + rising • **Bake:** 25 min.
Makes: 2 loaves (16 slices each)

- 1 package (¼ ounce) active dry yeast
- 1½ cups warm water (110° to 115°)
- ½ cup warm 2% milk (110° to 115°)
- 3 tablespoons sugar
- 3 tablespoons olive oil
- 2 teaspoons salt
- 5 to 6 cups bread flour
- 1 cup shredded Parmesan cheese
- ¼ cup chopped oil-packed sun-dried tomatoes
- 3 teaspoons dried basil
- 1 teaspoon hot pepper sauce

1. In a large bowl, dissolve yeast in warm water. Add milk, sugar, oil, salt and 4 cups flour. Beat on medium speed until smooth. Stir in cheese, tomatoes, basil, pepper sauce and enough remaining flour to form a soft dough (dough will be sticky).
2. Turn dough onto a floured surface; knead until smooth and elastic, about 6-8 minutes. Place in a greased bowl, turning once to grease the top. Cover with plastic wrap and let rise in a warm place until doubled, about 1½ hours.
3. Punch down dough. Divide in half and shape into loaves. Place in two greased 9x5-in. loaf pans. Cover pans with kitchen towels; let dough rise in a warm place until doubled, about 1 hour. Preheat the oven to 375°.
4. Bake until golden brown, 25-30 minutes. Remove from pans to wire racks to cool.

BASIL PARMESAN BREAD

S'MORES MONKEY
BREAD MUFFINS

S'MORES MONKEY BREAD MUFFINS

When it comes to mini versions of anything, I'm sold. These muffins are ooey-gooey individual-size monkey breads made with frozen dinner rolls, graham cracker crumbs, chocolate chips, and mini marshmallows. They couldn't be easier to make, and kids love them.
—Tina Butler, Royse City, TX

....

Prep: 35 min. • **Bake:** 15 min.
Makes: 1 dozen

- 15 frozen bread dough dinner rolls, thawed but still cold
- 6 tablespoons butter, cubed
- 1⅓ cups graham cracker crumbs
- ½ cup sugar
- 1 cup miniature semisweet chocolate chips, divided
- ¾ cup miniature marshmallows

ICING
- 1 cup confectioners' sugar
- ½ teaspoon butter, softened
- 1 to 2 tablespoons 2% milk

1. Preheat oven to 375°. Line 12 muffin cups with foil liners.
2. Using a sharp knife, cut each dinner roll into four pieces. In a shallow bowl, mix cracker crumbs and sugar. In a large microwave-safe bowl, microwave butter until melted. Dip three pieces of dough in butter, then roll in crumb mixture to coat; place in a prepared muffin cup. Repeat until all muffin cups are filled. Sprinkle muffin tops with ¾ cup chocolate chips and marshmallows.
3. Toss remaining dough pieces with remaining butter, rewarming butter if necessary. Place two additional dough pieces into each cup; sprinkle with the remaining chocolate chips.
4. Bake until golden brown, 15-20 minutes. Cool 5 minutes before removing muffins from pan to a wire rack. Mix icing ingredients; spoon over tops. Serve warm.

CHERRY PULL-APART BREAD

CHERRY PULL-APART BREAD

Every year I make a huge batch of my cherry bread—some goes to friends as a special treat, and the rest we enjoy as part of our Christmas breakfast. Refrigerated biscuits give the texture of scones to a pretty loaf that's much quicker than yeast bread made from scratch.
—Beverly Batty, Forest Lake, MN

....

Prep: 35 min. • **Bake:** 35 min. + cooling
Makes: 1 loaf (8 servings)

- ¼ cup all-purpose flour
- 2 tablespoons sugar
- ¼ cup cold butter, cubed
- ¼ cup slivered almonds, toasted and finely chopped
- 2 tablespoons maraschino cherries, drained and finely chopped
- ½ teaspoon almond extract
- 1 tube (16.3 ounces) large refrigerated flaky biscuits (8 count)

ICING
- ½ cup confectioners' sugar
- 1 teaspoon butter, softened
- ¼ teaspoon almond extract
- 2 to 3 teaspoons water
- 2 tablespoons slivered almonds, toasted and chopped
- 1 tablespoon maraschino cherries, drained and chopped

1. Preheat oven to 350°. In a small bowl, mix flour and sugar; cut in butter until crumbly. Stir in almonds, cherries and extract until crumbly and well blended.
2. Split biscuits horizontally in half. Line the bottom of a greased 8x4-in. loaf pan with three biscuit halves. Sprinkle 2 tablespoons crumb mixture over biscuits; press gently into dough.
3. Place remaining biscuit halves on a lightly floured surface. Top each with remaining crumb mixture; press gently to adhere. Stack seven of the topped biscuits; place stack sideways at one end of the pan, facing crumb sides inward. Repeat with remaining six biscuits, placing stack at opposite end of pan, again facing crumb sides inward.
4. Bake until golden brown, 35-40 minutes. Cover loosely with foil if top browns too quickly. Cool in pan 10 minutes before removing to a serving plate.
5. For icing, mix confectioners' sugar, butter, extract and enough water to reach a drizzling consistency. Spoon over warm bread. Top with almonds and cherries.

HEAVENLY CHEESE DANISH

This tempting cheese danish is baked to flaky perfection and made to shine with a simple egg wash gloss. It tastes just as decadent as any breakfast pastry you'd find in a bakery or coffee shop.
—Josephine Triton, Lakewood, OH

Prep: 50 min. + chilling
Bake: 15 min. + cooling
Makes: 16 rolls

- 2 packages (¼ ounce each) active dry yeast
- ½ cup warm water (110° to 115°)
- 4 cups all-purpose flour
- ⅓ cup sugar
- 2 teaspoons salt
- 1 cup cold butter, cubed
- 1 cup 2% milk
- 4 large egg yolks

ASSEMBLY
- 3 teaspoons ground cinnamon, divided
- 12 ounces cream cheese, softened
- ⅓ cup sugar
- 1 large egg, separated
- 1 tablespoon water
- 2 tablespoons maple syrup

1. Dissolve yeast in warm water. In another bowl, mix flour, sugar and salt; cut in butter until crumbly. Add milk, egg yolks and yeast mixture; stir to form a soft dough (dough will be sticky). Cover with plastic wrap; refrigerate 8-24 hours.
2. To assemble, punch down dough; divide into four portions. On a lightly floured surface, pat each portion into a 9x4-in. rectangle; sprinkle each with ¾ teaspoon cinnamon. Cut each rectangle lengthwise into four 9x1-in. strips. Twist each strip, then loosely wrap strip around itself to form a coil; tuck under end and pinch to seal. Place 3 in. apart on greased baking sheets.
3. Beat cream cheese, sugar and egg yolk until smooth. Press an indentation in center of each roll; fill with 1 rounded tablespoon cream cheese mixture. Cover with greased plastic wrap; let dough rise in a warm place until doubled, for about 45 minutes. Preheat oven to 350°.
4. Whisk egg white with water; brush over rolls. Bake until golden brown, 15-20 minutes. Remove to wire racks; brush with syrup. Serve warm. Refrigerate leftovers.

PUMPKIN CRANBERRY BREAD

The favorite flavors of the season come together in this easy-to-make quick bread. The mellow sweetness of the pumpkin is beautifully balanced by the tart tang of the cranberries.
—Kristen Dinsmore, Fort Polk, LA

Prep: 15 min. • **Bake:** 1 hour + cooling
Makes: 2 loaves (16 slices each)

- 3 cups all-purpose flour
- 3 cups sugar
- 5 teaspoons pumpkin pie spice
- 2 teaspoons baking soda
- 1½ teaspoons salt
- 4 large eggs
- 1 can (15 ounces) pumpkin
- 1 cup canola oil
- ½ cup orange juice
- 1 cup dried cranberries

1. Preheat oven to 350°. Whisk together first five ingredients. In another bowl, whisk together eggs, pumpkin, oil and orange juice; add to flour mixture, stirring just until moistened. Fold in cranberries.
2. Transfer to two greased 9x5-in. loaf pans. Bake until a toothpick inserted in center comes out clean, 60-65 minutes. Cool in pans 10 minutes before removing to wire racks to cool.

ORANGE BISCUITS WITH HONEY BUTTER

Traditional biscuits get a sweet, citrusy spin in this heavenly version. They're perfect for a morning treat or as a side when serving a spicy chili or stew.
—Patricia Overley, Chino Hills, CA

Prep: 25 min. • **Bake:** 10 min.
Makes: about 1 dozen (½ cup butter)

- 2 cups all-purpose flour
- 3 teaspoons baking powder
- 1 teaspoon sugar
- 1 teaspoon salt
- ½ cup cold butter, cubed
- ¾ cup 2% milk
- 1 tablespoon grated orange peel
- 3 tablespoons orange juice

ORANGE HONEY BUTTER
- ½ cup butter, softened
- ½ cup honey
- 2 teaspoons grated orange peel

1. Preheat oven to 450°. Whisk together first four ingredients; cut in butter until mixture resembles coarse crumbs. Mix milk, orange peel and orange juice; stir into dry ingredients just until moistened.
2. Turn onto a floured surface; knead gently 8-10 times. Pat or roll dough to ½-in. thickness; cut with a floured 2½-in. biscuit cutter. Place 1 in. apart on an ungreased baking sheet. Bake until golden brown, 8-12 minutes.
3. For honey butter, beat butter until softened; beat in honey and orange peel. Serve with warm biscuits.

APPLE CIDER DOUGHNUT HOLES

Their light, tender texture and apple cider flavor make these small bites a big hit! My mom made them every year as soon as the weather turned cool. I carry on the tradition, and the aroma always brings back cherished memories.
—Rebecca Baird, Salt Lake City, UT

Prep: 20 min. • **Cook:** 5 min./batch
Makes: about 3 dozen

- ½ cup sugar
- 3 teaspoons ground cinnamon
- ⅛ teaspoon ground nutmeg, optional

DOUGHNUTS
- ½ cup sugar
- 2 tablespoons shortening
- 2 large eggs
- 2 cups all-purpose flour
- 2 teaspoons baking powder
- ½ teaspoon salt
- ½ cup apple cider or juice
  Oil for deep-fat frying

1. In a small bowl, mix sugar, cinnamon and, if desired, nutmeg.
2. In a large bowl, beat the sugar and shortening until crumbly. Add eggs, one at a time, beating well after each addition. In another bowl, whisk together flour, baking powder and salt; add to the sugar mixture alternately with cider.
3. In an electric skillet or deep fryer, heat oil to 350°. Carefully drop batter by tablespoonfuls, a few at a time, into hot oil. Fry until dark golden brown, about 2 minutes per side. Drain on paper towels; cool 5 minutes. Toss in spiced sugar.
Note: Doughnuts can be tossed with confectioners' sugar instead of spiced sugar; cool 10 minutes before coating.

**APPLE CIDER
DOUGHNUT HOLES**

BANANA NUT BREAD

I always have ripe bananas on hand so I can make this tasty quick bread—my family adores it! I bet your family will love this nutty bread as much as we do.
—Susan Jones, La Grange Park, IL

Prep: 10 min. • **Bake:** 50 min. + cooling
Makes: 1 loaf (16 slices)

- ¼ cup butter, softened
- ¾ cup sugar
- 2 large eggs
- ¾ cup mashed ripe banana (about 1 large)
- ½ cup sour cream
- 2¼ cups all-purpose flour
- 1 teaspoon ground cinnamon
- ¾ teaspoon baking soda
- ½ teaspoon salt
- ½ cup chopped walnuts
  Additional walnuts, semisweet chocolate chips or coarse sugar, optional

1. Preheat oven to 350°. Beat butter and sugar until blended. Add the eggs, one at a time, beating well after each addition. Stir in banana and sour cream. Whisk together flour, cinnamon, baking soda and salt. Add to mixture, stirring just until moistened. Fold in ½ cup walnuts.
2. Transfer to a greased 9x5-in. loaf pan. If desired, sprinkle with additional walnuts.
3. Bake until a toothpick inserted in center comes out clean, 50-60 minutes. Cool in pan 10 minutes before removing to a wire rack to cool.

ALL-STAR MUFFIN MIX

I keep this mix handy in my pantry or cupboard, so I'm always ready to whip up muffins quickly for dinner or just in case a friend stops by for coffee.
—Nancy Mackey, Madison, OH

Prep: 20 min. • **Bake:** 20 min.
Makes: 4 batches (12 per batch)

- 8 cups all-purpose flour
- 3 cups sugar
- 3 tablespoons baking powder
- 2 teaspoons salt
- 2 teaspoons ground cinnamon
- 2 teaspoons ground nutmeg

ADDITIONAL INGREDIENTS
- 1 large egg
- 1 cup 2% milk
- ½ cup butter, melted

In a large bowl, whisk first six ingredients until well blended. Store in airtight containers in a cool dry place or in the freezer up to 6 months. When ready to use, follow the basic instructions for Plain Muffins, incorporating one of the eight flavor variations if desired. **Yield:** 4 batches (11 cups mix).

Plain Muffins Preheat oven to 400°. Whisk together egg, milk and melted butter. Add 2¾ cups muffin mix, stirring just until moistened. Fill paper-lined muffin cups three-fourths full. Bake until a toothpick inserted in center comes out clean, 18-21 minutes. Cool 5 minutes before removing from pan to a wire rack. Serve warm.

Blueberry Muffins Prepare muffins as directed, folding 1 cup fresh or frozen blueberries into prepared batter.

Rhubarb-Orange Muffins Prepare muffins as directed, adding ⅓ cup orange marmalade to egg mixture and folding ¾ cup diced fresh or frozen rhubarb into prepared batter.

Banana Muffins Prepare muffins as directed, adding 1 cup mashed ripe bananas to egg mixture.

Cranberry-Pecan Muffins Prepare muffins as directed, tossing 1 cup chopped fresh or frozen cranberries, ½ cup chopped pecans and 3 tablespoons sugar with muffin mix before adding to egg mixture.

Apricot-Cherry Muffins Prepare muffins as directed, tossing ½ cup each chopped dried apricots and dried cherries with muffin mix before adding to egg mixture.

Cappuccino Muffins Prepare muffins as directed, tossing 1 cup miniature semisweet chocolate chips and 2 teaspoons instant coffee granules with muffin mix before adding to egg mixture.

Carrot-Raisin Muffins Prepare muffins as directed, tossing ¾ cup shredded carrots and ⅓ cup golden raisins with muffin mix before adding to egg mixture.

Apple-Cheese Muffins Prepare muffins as directed, tossing ½ cup each shredded peeled apple and shredded Colby-Monterey Jack cheese with muffin mix before adding to egg mixture.

BANANA NUT BREAD

HAZELNUT CHOCOLATE CHIP SCONES

Chocolate, hazelnuts and the tangy taste of buttermilk—these delicious scones are easy to make, come together fast, and taste so good with your morning coffee.
—Trisha Kruse, Eagle, ID

Prep: 20 min. • **Bake:** 15 min.
Makes: 8 scones

  2   cups all-purpose flour
 ¼   cup packed brown sugar
1½   teaspoons baking powder
 ½   teaspoon baking soda
 ½   teaspoon salt
 ½   cup cold butter, cubed
  1   large egg
 ½   cup buttermilk
1½   teaspoons vanilla extract
  1   cup semisweet chocolate chips
  1   cup hazelnuts, coarsely chopped

1. Preheat oven to 400°. Whisk together first five ingredients; cut in butter until mixture resembles coarse crumbs. In another bowl, whisk together the egg, buttermilk and vanilla; stir into crumb mixture just until moistened. Stir in the chocolate chips and hazelnuts.
2. Turn onto a lightly floured surface; knead gently eight times. Pat dough into a 6-in. circle. Cut into eight wedges; place on a greased baking sheet. Bake until golden brown, 15-20 minutes. Serve warm.

TOP TIP

Successful Scones

Scones are generally patted into a circle and cut into wedges. If the wedges are separated, the scones will have a crisper crust. If the wedges are cut and not separated, the scones will have a softer crust. Scones are done when they're golden brown on the top and bottom. The sides will always be a little light. Scones are best eaten on the day they are made.

GIVING THANKS

Nothing quite compares to a long dining room table of family and friends gathered around a golden-brown turkey. However, every good cook knows there's more to Thanksgiving than the famous bird. Delight your loved ones with a meal fit for a king with succulent side dishes, spiced desserts and other classics. The little ones will be thankful, too, for a lineup of Turkey Day treats especially for them.

A SENTIMENTAL THANKSGIVING 90

BLACK FRIDAY SLOW COOKER POTLUCK . . 102

GOBBLE, GOBBLE GOODIES 112

SUGAR & SPICE DESSERTS 122

A Sentimental Thanksgiving

If you're the lucky keeper of a recipe box or cookbook that once belonged to your mother, grandmother, aunt or another beloved relative, you probably stumbled upon a few that are smudged and annotated with her notes for getting it *just right*...the tried-and-true standbys she was proud to include in her holiday repertoire.

These are recipes to cherish, gems worth holding onto and passing along to future generations. Here you'll find treasured homemade, from-scratch heirloom recipes from cooks just like you and the heartwarming stories behind them.

From tender herb-rubbed turkey and all the classic trimmings to sweet potato pie, this will be a Thanksgiving to remember!

Almond-Herb Bread Dressing (p. 97) **Citrus Herb Turkey** (p. 97)
Sour Cream & Chives Mashed Potatoes (p. 97)

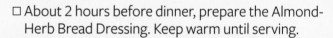

Countdown to Thanksgiving Dinner

It's the **most wonderful meal of the year.** Make it foolproof, too, with these **mouthwatering dishes** and this handy timeline for getting everything done. Here's your guide to the **ultimate Thanksgiving feast!**

Giving Thanks

A FEW WEEKS BEFORE

☐ Prepare two grocery lists—one for nonperishable items to buy now and one for perishable items to buy a few days before Thanksgiving.

☐ Create Thankful Tree centerpiece. (See page 101.)

TWO DAYS BEFORE

☐ Buy remaining grocery items.

☐ Bake the Brown Sugar Pecan Cake, but do not dust with confectioners' sugar or drizzle with butterscotch. Store in an airtight container.

☐ Wash china, stemware and table linens.

THE DAY BEFORE

☐ Prepare the dough for Cape Cod Bay Brown Bread, letting it rise according to recipe directions. Bake bread. Cover or store each loaf in an airtight container until ready to serve.

☐ Make the Smooth & Creamy Pumpkin Soup. Let cool and store in an airtight container in the refrigerator.

☐ Bake the Fluffy Sweet Potato Custard Pie; refrigerate until ready to serve.

☐ Prepare the Cheese Ball Roll-Ups, but do not slice. Refrigerate until ready to serve.

☐ Prepare the Holiday Cranberry Salad; refrigerate until ready to serve.

☐ Set the table.

THANKSGIVING DAY

☐ Early in the day, prepare the Sour Cream & Chives Mashed Potatoes. Let cool. Cover and store in the refrigerator.

☐ About 3-4 hours before dinner, prepare the Citrus Herb Turkey. Keep warm until serving.

☐ About 2 hours before dinner, prepare the Almond-Herb Bread Dressing. Keep warm until serving.

☐ About 1 hour before dinner, prepare Andrea's Stuffed Mushrooms and Thanksgiving Green Beans. Keep dishes warm until serving.

RIGHT BEFORE DINNER

☐ As guests arrive, prepare Aunt Dorothy's Russian Tea and slice the Cheese Ball Roll-Ups.

☐ Warm the Smooth & Creamy Pumpkin Soup in a stockpot or microwave just before serving.

☐ Warm the Sour Cream & Chives Mashed Potatoes in the oven just before serving.

☐ Dust Brown Sugar Pecan Cake with confectioners' sugar. Then drizzle with butterscotch, if desired, just before serving.

ANDREA'S STUFFED MUSHROOMS

My husband and I live in the Midwest, but he is originally from New York. This was his favorite Thanksgiving appetizer/side dish, so I asked his mother for the recipe. Now I make it every year in honor of his childhood home. My mother-in-law taught me to use a grapefruit spoon to easily stuff the mushrooms. I sprinkle on a bit of smoked paprika to add a little spice and festive color.
—Sara Drost, Ste. Genevieve, MO

Prep: 20 min. • **Bake:** 30 min.
Makes: 2 dozen

- 24 large fresh mushrooms
- 1 small onion, halved
- 5 tablespoons butter, divided
- ½ cup seasoned bread crumbs
- ½ cup shredded Parmesan cheese
- 1 large egg
- 2 tablespoons half-and-half cream
  Smoked paprika

1. Preheat oven to 350°. Remove stems from mushrooms; set caps aside. Place stems and onion in a food processor; pulse until finely chopped.
2. In a large skillet, heat 4 tablespoons butter over medium heat. Add onion mixture; cook and stir 2-3 minutes or until tender. Transfer to a small bowl; cool slightly. Stir in bread crumbs, cheese, egg and cream. Stuff into mushroom caps.
3. Place in an ungreased 13x9-in. baking dish. Dot with remaining butter. Bake 30-35 minutes or until mushrooms are tender. Sprinkle with paprika.

TOP TIP

Preparing Mushrooms for Stuffing

To prepare mushrooms for stuffing, hold the mushroom cap in one hand and grab the stem with the other hand. Twist to snap off the stem. Mince or finely chop stems or proceed as recipe directs. If there is any liquid, spoon chopped stems onto paper towel and squeeze or pat dry.

CAPE COD BAY BROWN BREAD

CAPE COD BAY BROWN BREAD

This reminds me of the brown bread my grandmother made whenever we traveled out east to visit. The aroma evokes fond memories of her New England home during the peak of fall. I use blackstrap molasses and agave nectar to make mine a little different without sacrificing any of the flavor. Cranberries are another special touch, but this would also taste delicious with raisins.
—Kellie Foglio, Salem, WI

Prep: 40 min. + rising
Bake: 30 min. + cooling
Makes: 2 loaves (12 slices each)

- 2 packages (¼ ounce each) active dry yeast
- 3 tablespoons molasses
- 2 teaspoons agave nectar or honey
- 2⅔ cups warm water (110° to 115°)
- ½ cup dried cranberries
- 2 tablespoons wheat bran
- 1 teaspoon salt
- 6 to 7 cups whole wheat flour

TOPPING
- 1 tablespoon 2% milk
- 1 tablespoon old-fashioned oats

1. In a small bowl, dissolve the yeast, molasses and agave nectar in ⅔ cup warm water. In a large bowl, combine the cranberries, wheat bran, salt, yeast mixture, 4 cups flour and remaining water; beat on medium speed 3 minutes until smooth. Stir in enough remaining flour to form a soft dough (dough will be sticky).
2. Turn dough onto a floured surface; knead until smooth and elastic, about 6-8 minutes. Place in a greased bowl, turning once to grease the top. Cover with plastic wrap and let rise in a warm place until doubled, about 1 hour.
3. Turn onto a lightly floured surface; divide in half. Shape into loaves. Place in two greased 8x4-in. loaf pans. Cover with kitchen towels; let rise in a warm place until almost doubled, about 1 hour. Preheat oven to 400°.
4. Brush tops with milk. Sprinkle with oats. Bake 30-40 minutes or until golden brown. Remove from pans to wire racks; cool completely.

HOLIDAY CRANBERRY SALAD

My mom made this every Thanksgiving and Christmas, and I have continued the tradition. We now are on our fourth generation of sharing and enjoying this salad, as my grandson makes a special request for it every year. I also serve this as a side dish when I make a chicken pot pie.
—Peggy Tagge, Stokesdale, NC

Prep: 10 min. + chilling
Makes: 12 servings (½ cup each)

- 1½ cups boiling water
- 1 package (3 ounces) lemon gelatin
- 1 package (3 ounces) cherry gelatin
- 1 can (14 ounces) whole-berry cranberry sauce
- 1 can (20 ounces) crushed pineapple, undrained
- 1 celery rib, finely chopped
- ½ cup chopped pecans

In a large bowl, add boiling water to gelatins; stir 2 minutes to completely dissolve. Stir in cranberry sauce. Refrigerate 30-40 minutes or until slightly thickened. Stir in pineapple, celery and pecans. Transfer to a 6-cup ring mold coated with cooking spray. Refrigerate for 4 hours or until set.

SMOOTH & CREAMY PUMPKIN SOUP

My mother-in-law can no longer cook, but she shared this recipe with me. Now I make it for her, and she enjoys eating it as much as I enjoy making it. The pumpkin flavor makes a great addition to any Thanksgiving feast.
—Helen Espinosa, Miami, FL

Start to Finish: 30 min.
Makes: 10 servings (2½ quarts)

- 1 large pie pumpkin (about 4 pounds)
- 4 cups water
- 1 large onion, chopped
- ¼ cup butter, cubed
- 2 tablespoons chicken bouillon granules
- 6 garlic cloves, peeled and halved
- 1 teaspoon salt
- ½ teaspoon ground nutmeg
- ½ teaspoon pepper
- 1 can (7.6 ounces) media crema table cream

1. Cut a 4-in. circle around pumpkin stem; remove top and discard. Peel pumpkin; cut in half. Remove strings and seeds; discard seeds or save for roasting. Cut pumpkin into 1-in cubes. Place in a 6-qt. stockpot; add water.

2. Stir in onion, butter, bouillon, garlic, salt, nutmeg and pepper. Bring to a boil. Reduce the heat to medium-low; cook mixture, uncovered, 10-12 minutes or until pumpkin is tender.

3. Add cream; heat through. Puree soup using an immersion blender. Or, cool soup slightly and puree in batches in a blender; return to pan and heat through.

CHEESE BALL ROLL-UPS

I make a variation of my mom's cheese ball recipe every Christmas and throughout the year, too. It's one of my daughter's favorite appetizers. I changed it from a traditional cheese ball into a roll-up to make it a fun finger food. All the cheeses create an intensely flavorful bite. If you choose to mold the mixture into a ball, garnish with additional chopped walnuts.
—Marsha Warner, Folsom, CA

Prep: 15 min. + chilling
Makes: about 3 dozen

- 1 package (8 ounces) cream cheese, softened
- 1 cup finely shredded cheddar cheese
- ½ cup crumbled blue cheese
- 1½ teaspoons grated onion
- 1 garlic clove, minced
- ½ teaspoon seasoned salt
- ½ teaspoon Worcestershire sauce
- ⅛ teaspoon cayenne pepper
- 4 flour tortillas (10 inches)
- 1 cup chopped walnuts

1. In a small bowl, mix the first eight ingredients until blended. Spread over tortillas; sprinkle with walnuts. Roll up tightly; wrap in plastic wrap. Refrigerate at least 30 minutes.

2. Just before serving, unwrap and cut each tortilla crosswise into 10 slices.

THANKSGIVING GREEN BEANS

Momma only made these green beans at Thanksgiving because at the time, the ingredients were out of her everyday budget. Her original recipe inside her recipe box had five stars drawn on it. I would have to agree—it's worth it to celebrate with all the fresh ingredients.
—Marcia Shires, San Antonio, TX

Prep: 45 min. • **Bake:** 10 min.
Makes: 16 servings (¾ cup each)

- 2 cups (16 ounces) sour cream
- 2 teaspoons sugar
- 1 teaspoon salt
- ½ teaspoon dill weed
- 1 pound bacon strips, cut into 1-inch pieces
- 2 pounds fresh green beans, cut into 1½-inch pieces (6 cups)
- 1 pound medium fresh mushrooms, quartered
- 6 green onions, chopped
- 1 cup slivered almonds, optional
- 4 garlic cloves, minced
- 2 cups onion and garlic salad croutons
- 1½ cups shredded Monterey Jack cheese

1. Preheat oven to 350°. In a small bowl, combine sour cream, sugar, salt and dill weed. In a 6-qt. stockpot, cook bacon over medium heat until crisp, stirring occasionally.

2. Meanwhile, in a large saucepan, bring 6 cups water to a boil. Add beans in batches; cook, uncovered, 2-3 minutes or just until crisp-tender. Drain.

3. Remove bacon with a slotted spoon; drain on paper towels. Discard drippings, reserving 6 tablespoons in pan. Add mushrooms, onions and, if desired, almonds to drippings; cook and stir over medium heat 4-6 minutes or until mushrooms are tender. Add garlic; cook and stir 1 minute longer. Remove from heat; stir in beans, bacon and croutons. Stir in sour cream mixture. Transfer to an ungreased 13x9-in. baking dish. Sprinkle with cheese. Bake 10-15 minutes or until cheese is melted.

THANKSGIVING
GREEN BEANS

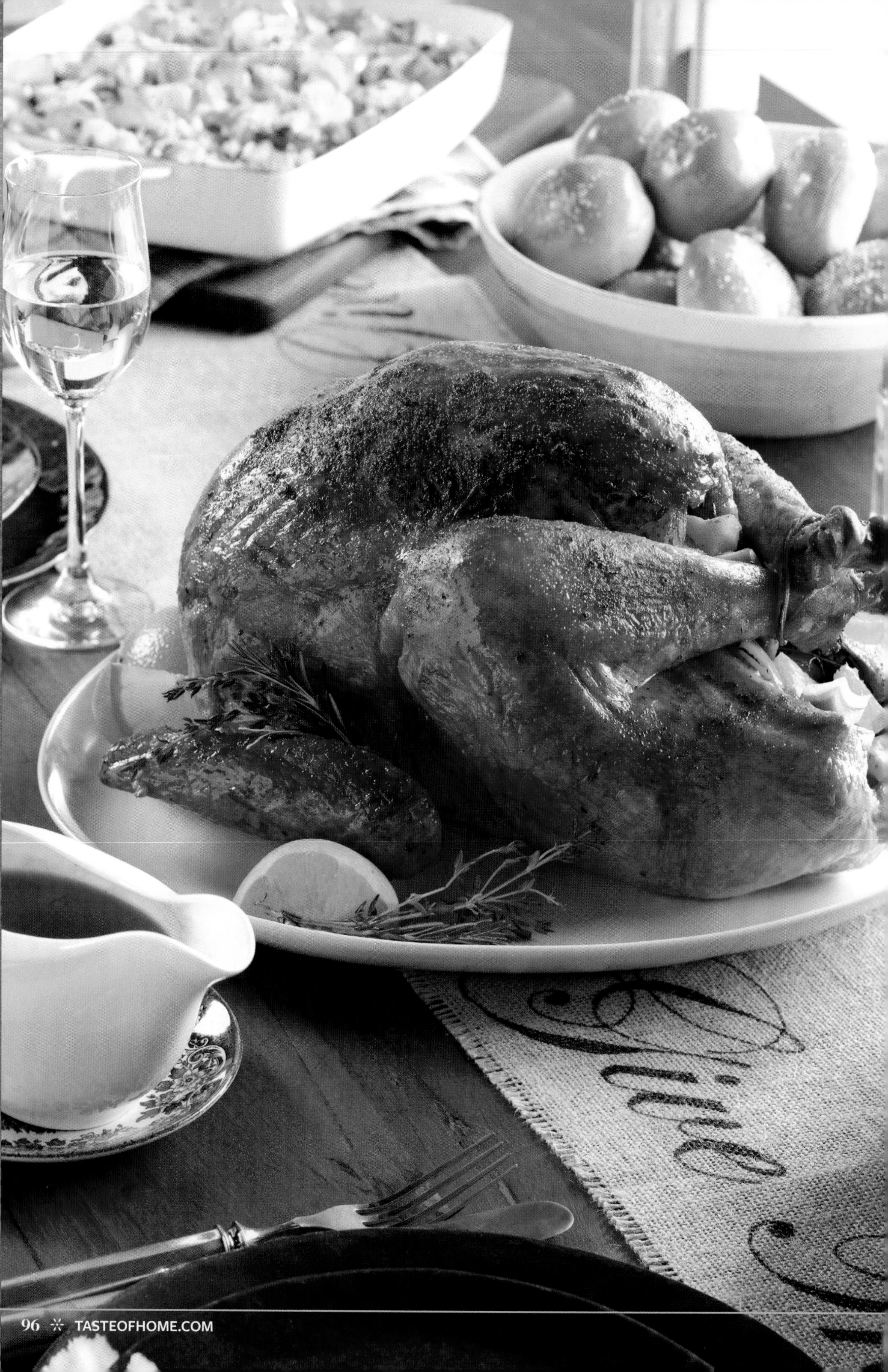

CITRUS HERB TURKEY

When it came to a roasting turkey, my grandmother had the magic touch: she would wrap her turkey in foil and cook it on low heat for 8 hours so it would bake up juicy and tender. This version doesn't take quite that long, but it's just as good.
—Portia Gorman, Los Angeles, CA

....

Prep: 40 min. • **Bake:** 2½ hours + standing
Makes: 12 servings

- 1 package (1 ounce) fresh rosemary, divided
- 1 package (1 ounce) fresh thyme, divided
- ¾ cup softened unsalted butter, divided
- 1 turkey (12 to 14 pounds)
- 2 teaspoons seasoned salt
- ½ teaspoon garlic powder
- ½ teaspoon pepper
- 1 medium apple, chopped
- 1 medium orange, chopped
- 1 small red onion, chopped
- 1 small sweet orange pepper, chopped

1. Preheat oven to 400°. Line a roasting pan with three pieces of heavy-duty foil (pieces should be long enough to cover turkey). Mince half the rosemary and thyme from each package (about ¼ cup total). In a small bowl, beat ½ cup butter and minced herbs until blended. With fingers, carefully loosen skin from turkey breast; rub butter mixture under the skin. Secure skin to underside of breast with toothpicks. Mix seasoned salt, garlic powder and pepper; sprinkle over turkey and inside turkey cavity.
2. Cube remaining butter. In a large bowl, combine butter, apple, orange, onion, orange pepper and remaining herb sprigs; spoon inside cavity. Tuck wings under turkey; tie drumsticks together. Place turkey in prepared pan, breast side up.
3. Bring edges of foil over turkey to cover. Roast, covered, 1 hour. Carefully open foil and fold it down. Reduce oven to 325°. Roast, uncovered, 1½ to 2 hours or until a thermometer inserted in thickest part of thigh reads 170°-175°. Cover loosely with foil if turkey browns too quickly.
4. Remove turkey from oven; tent with foil. Let stand 20 minutes before carving. Discard the fruit mixture from cavity. If desired, skim fat and thicken pan drippings for gravy. Serve with turkey.

ALMOND-HERB BREAD DRESSING

SOUR CREAM & CHIVES MASHED POTATOES

This recipe is a family favorite that always stirs up good memories. It's requested for Thanksgiving, Christmas, birthday parties, potlucks and other gatherings. It's simple to make and delicious to eat. If I make it early in the day I finish this dish for about 20 minutes in the oven, but you can use the stovetop to free up oven space for the turkey. See photo on page 91.
—Linda Williams, Florence, AL

....

Prep: 25 min. • **Cook:** 30 min.
Makes: 12 servings (¾ cup each)

- 5 pounds red potatoes (about 20 medium), peeled and quartered
- 1 carton (8 ounces) spreadable chive and onion cream cheese
- 1 cup (8 ounces) sour cream
- ½ cup butter, softened
- ¾ teaspoon salt
- ¼ teaspoon pepper
- 2 cups shredded cheddar cheese

1. Place potatoes in a 6-qt. stockpot; add water to cover. Bring to a boil. Reduce heat; cook, uncovered, 25-30 minutes or until tender. Drain.
2. In a large bowl, beat cream cheese and sour cream until blended. Add potatoes; beat until light and fluffy. Beat in butter, salt and pepper. Sprinkle with cheese. Let stand, covered, until cheese is melted.

ALMOND-HERB BREAD DRESSING

My grandmother made this dressing every Thanksgiving. She handed the recipe down to my mother, who passed it along to me, and I shared it with my daughter. It's a holiday staple we all cherish.
—Mindy Moore, Valencia, CA

....

Prep: 20 min. • **Bake:** 50 min.
Makes: 12 servings (¾ cup each)

- ¼ cup butter, cubed
- 2 celery ribs, finely chopped
- 2 medium onions, finely chopped
- ¾ cup chopped fresh parsley
- 1 loaf (1 pound) French bread, cut into ½-inch cubes
- 1 cup slivered almonds
- 2 large eggs, lightly beaten
- ¾ teaspoon salt
- ¼ teaspoon poultry seasoning
- ¼ teaspoon pepper
- 1¼ to 1¾ cups chicken or turkey broth

1. Preheat oven to 325°. In a 6-qt. stockpot, heat butter over medium heat. Add celery, onions and parsley; cook and stir 5-7 minutes or until vegetables are tender. Stir in bread, almonds, eggs, seasonings and enough broth to reach desired moistness.
2. Transfer to a greased 13x9-in baking dish. Bake, covered, 40 minutes. Bake, uncovered, 10-15 minutes longer or until lightly browned.

AUNT DOROTHY'S RUSSIAN TEA

When I was growing up I always looked forward to the Russian tea that my Aunt Dorothy made every Christmas Eve. As soon as the weather turned chilly, I would start longing for a hot, steamy cup. It wasn't until I was away at college that I finally thought to ask her for the recipe! I place the whole cloves into a tea ball strainer so they're easy to remove when the tea is ready. If you don't have a tea ball, use a cheesecloth as directed.
—Sharon Flenniken, Charlotte, NC

Start to Finish: 15 min.
Makes: 14 servings (1 cup each)

- 2 teaspoons whole cloves
- 1 cinnamon stick (2 inches)
- 12 cups water
- 6 tea bags
- 1½ cups sugar
- 1½ cups orange juice
- ¼ cup lemon juice

1. Place cloves and cinnamon stick on a double thickness of cheesecloth. Gather corners of cloth to enclose seasonings; tie securely with string. Place in a 6-qt. stockpot.
2. Add water; bring to a boil. Remove from heat. Add tea bags; steep, covered, 5 minutes according to taste. Meanwhile, in a small saucepan, combine sugar, orange juice and lemon juice; bring to a boil. Discard spice bag and tea bags. Stir juice mixture into tea. Serve immediately.

TOP TIP

Storing Tea

Store tea bags or loose tea at room temperature in an airtight container for up to 2 years. Be sure to keep tea away from moisture, direct sunlight and other spices or aromatic foods, as the tea can absorb their flavor or scent. It's also important to keep each kind of tea in a separate storage container to maintain their distinct and special flavors.

BROWN SUGAR PECAN CAKE

My great-aunt was famous in our family for her cooking. She lived in Kentucky and made a cake like this one many times during my childhood. I found a similar recipe years later, but changed it a bit to use what I had on hand. The added crunch of the pecans gives it a little southern flair that she would have loved.
—Lisa Varner, El Paso, TX

Prep: 20 min. • **Bake:** 70 min. + cooling
Makes: 16 servings

- 1½ cups butter, softened
- 2 cups packed brown sugar
- ½ cup sugar
- 6 large eggs
- 2 teaspoons vanilla extract
- 3 cups all-purpose flour
- ½ teaspoon baking powder
- 1 cup (8 ounces) sour cream
- 1½ cups chopped pecans
  Confectioners' sugar
  Vanilla ice cream and butterscotch ice cream topping, optional

1. Preheat oven to 350°. Grease and flour a 10-in. fluted tube pan.
2. In a large bowl, cream butter, brown sugar and sugar until light and fluffy. Add eggs, one at a time, beating well after each addition. Beat in vanilla. In another bowl, whisk flour and baking powder; add to creamed mixture alternately with sour cream, beating well after each addition. Fold in pecans.
3. Transfer batter to prepared pan. Bake 70-80 minutes or until a toothpick inserted in center comes out clean. Cool in pan 30 minutes before removing to a wire rack to cool completely. Dust cake with confectioners' sugar. If desired, serve with ice cream; drizzle with ice cream topping.

BROWN SUGAR PECAN CAKE

FLUFFY SWEET POTATO CUSTARD PIE

FLUFFY SWEET POTATO CUSTARD PIE

My grandmother made this dessert every Thanksgiving and Christmas. She passed the recipe to me and I started bringing the pies to parties at work. Feel free to add sweetened whipped cream and sprinkle on additional nutmeg for extra appeal. The secret to a perfect pie is to take no shortcuts. Soften, don't melt, the butter, and blend, blend, blend!
—Valerie Lockett, Tumwater, WA

Prep: 40 min. • **Bake:** 45 min. + cooling
Makes: 2 pies (8 servings each)

    Pastry for two single-crust pies
    (9 inches)
2 cups mashed cooked sweet potatoes
    (about 2 medium)
½ cup butter, softened
1 cup sugar
1 tablespoon all-purpose flour
2 teaspoons vanilla extract
½ teaspoon ground nutmeg
6 large eggs, separated
1 cup whole milk

1. Preheat oven to 350°. On a lightly floured surface, roll dough into two ⅛-in.-thick circles; transfer to two 9-in. pie plates. Trim pastry to ½ in. beyond rim of plates; flute edges.
2. In a large bowl, beat potatoes and butter until blended. Beat in sugar, flour, vanilla and nutmeg. Add egg yolks, one at a time, beating until blended. Add milk; beat well. With clean beaters, beat egg whites until stiff peaks form. Fold into sweet potato mixture.
3. Pour filling into pastry shells. Bake 45-55 minutes or until a knife inserted near the center comes out clean. Cover the edge of pie loosely with foil during the last 15 minutes if needed to prevent overbrowning. Remove foil. Cool on a wire rack; serve or refrigerate within 2 hours.

TOP TIP

Mashed Sweet Potatoes

To cook sweet potatoes for mashing, place whole scrubbed sweet potatoes in a large kettle; cover with water. Cover and boil gently for 30 to 45 minutes or until potatoes can easily be pierced with the tip of a sharp knife. Drain. When cool enough to handle, peel and mash.

THANKFUL TREE

This beautiful blessing tree does double duty as a decorative centerpiece and a fun way to talk to children about gratitude.

MATERIALS

Dried tree branches
Decorative branches from craft store
Balsa wood tags (available at craft stores)
Twine
Large vase or jar
Burlap square, about 2½ times the height of your vase
Photos of what you're thankful for
Scrapbook paper
Decoupage glue
Extra-fine glitter
Paintbrush

DIRECTIONS

1. On your computer, size photos to the approximate dimensions of the balsa wood tags and print out on ordinary copier paper.

2. Cut photos and scrapbook paper into the appropriate size for tags. Paint a layer of decoupage glue on one side of the tag. Put the photo in place and add another layer of glue over the photo. Let dry. Repeat on back with scrapbook paper. Let dry.

3. Use sharpened pencil to poke a hole through the paper on both sides. String with twine.

4. Pour glitter onto a sheet of paper. Brush a thin layer of glue around the edges of the tag and lightly press all sides into the glitter. Let dry.

5. Place vase in center of the burlap square. Pull up all sides; wrap at the top with twine.

6. Arrange branches in vase and trim as needed. Hang tags on branches.

7. After Thanksgiving, use the wood tags to decorate a Christmas tree or wreath.

THANKFUL TREE

Black Friday Slow Cooker Potluck

It's Black Friday, the day after Thanksgiving. Early birds are up and at 'em scouting out deals at their favorite stores. But serious shopping can work up a serious appetite. This year, plan a post-shopping potluck with a variety of slow-cooked sensations. Simply designate who is bringing what, then flip the switch on the slow cooker before you hit the stores. Later that afternoon, everyone meets up, brings their dish to pass and feasts on deliciously good eats!

Please all tastes with a quick prep dip, a delightful dessert, even a toasty fall beverage that will warm on a cool afternoon.

This lineup might inspire a new tradition. And it's not just for Black Friday. Plan a slow cooker spread to celebrate any shopping trip!

Black Bean Chicken Nachos (p. 110)

BBQ TURKEY MEATBALLS

What's a party without meatballs? We have these at all of our big gatherings, but they work just as well for an easy weeknight meal. If you prefer, you can make these with ground beef or even store-bought meatballs.
—Lisa Harms, Moline, MI

Prep: 45 min. • **Cook:** 3 hours
Makes: about 4 dozen

- 1 large egg, lightly beaten
- ⅔ cup soft bread crumbs
- ¼ cup finely chopped onion
- ½ teaspoon pepper
- 2 pounds ground turkey

SAUCE
- 1 bottle (20 ounces) ketchup
- ¼ cup packed brown sugar
- 2 tablespoons Worcestershire sauce
- 1 teaspoon garlic salt
- ½ to 1 teaspoon hot pepper sauce

1. Preheat oven to 375°. Combine egg, bread crumbs, onion and pepper. Add turkey; mix lightly but thoroughly. Shape into 1-in. balls. Place on a greased rack in a 15x10x1-in. pan. Bake meatballs until lightly browned, 15-20 minutes.
2. Transfer meatballs to a 3-qt. slow cooker. Mix sauce ingredients; pour over top. Cook, covered, on low until meatballs are cooked through, 3-4 hours.

TOP TIP

Slow Cooker Tips

Select the proper size slow cooker for the amount of food you are making. For example, to serve a small amount of dip, smaller slow cookers are ideal. To entertain or cook for a crowd, larger slow cookers work best. A slow cooker should be from half to two-thirds full. The lid on your slow cooker seals in steam to cook the food. So unless the recipe instructs you to stir or add ingredients, do not lift the lid while the slow cooker is cooking. Every time you sneak a peek, the food will take longer to cook. The majority of slow cookers have clear lids to satisfy curious cooks.

SLOW COOKER CRAB DIP

With just 10 minutes of prep time, this creamy and delicious crab dip couldn't be easier. The recipe comes from my hometown cookbook. My co-workers rave about it at every work potluck!
—Julie Novotney, Rockwell, IA

Prep: 10 min. • **Cook:** 2 hours
Makes: 2 cups

- 1 package (8 ounces) cream cheese, softened
- ½ cup grated Parmesan cheese
- ½ cup mayonnaise
- 4 green onions, finely chopped
- ½ teaspoon garlic powder
- 1 can (6 ounces) crabmeat, drained, flaked and cartilage removed
- ½ cup sliced almonds, toasted
   Assorted crackers

1. In a 1½-qt. slow cooker, combine first five ingredients. Stir in crab. Cook, covered, on low until heated through, 2-3 hours.
2. Just before serving, sprinkle with almonds. Serve with crackers.

GARDEN GREEN BEANS & POTATOES

Fresh green beans paired with red potatoes make for an easy and filling addition to any spread. To make it even better, add crumbled bacon!
—Kelly Zinn, Cicero, IN

Prep: 10 min. • **Cook:** 6 hours
Makes: 16 servings (¾ cup each)

- 2 pounds fresh green beans, trimmed
- 1½ pounds red potatoes, quartered
- 1 medium onion, chopped
- ½ cup beef broth
- 1½ teaspoons salt
- 1 teaspoon dried thyme
- ½ teaspoon pepper
- ¼ cup butter, softened
- 1 tablespoon lemon juice

In a 6-qt. slow cooker, combine the first seven ingredients. Cook, covered, on low until beans are tender, 6-8 hours. Stir in butter and lemon juice. Remove with a slotted spoon.

SLOW COOKER CRAB DIP

SIX-BEAN
CHILI

SIX-BEAN CHILI

When it's cold and frosty outside, this meatless chili is sure to warm you up. It's packed with fiber, protein and flavor. Serve it with sliced avocado. Or add shredded cheese, corn tortilla chips or a side of your favorite corn bread.
—Liz Bellville, Jacksonville, NC

Prep: 20 min. • **Cook:** 6 hours
Makes: 14 servings (about 3½ quarts)

- 1 large white onion, chopped
- 2 large carrots, coarsely chopped
- ½ cup frozen corn
- 3 large garlic cloves, minced
- 1 can (16 ounces) chili beans, undrained
- 1 can (16 ounces) kidney beans, rinsed and drained
- 1 can (15½ ounces) navy beans, rinsed and drained
- 1 can (15½ ounces) great northern beans, rinsed and drained
- 1 can (15 ounces) pinto beans, rinsed and drained
- 1 can (15 ounces) black beans, rinsed and drained
- 2 cans (14½ ounces each) fire-roasted diced tomatoes, undrained
- 1 can (28 ounces) crushed tomatoes
- 1 can (4 ounces) chopped fire-roasted green chilies
- 1 tablespoon chili powder
- 2 teaspoons ground cumin
- 2 teaspoons ground chipotle pepper
  Chopped avocado, optional

In a 6- or 7-qt. slow cooker, combine the first 16 ingredients. Cook, covered, on low until vegetables are tender, 6-8 hours. If desired, serve with avocado.

SPICED CRANBERRY-APPLE PUNCH

SPICED CRANBERRY-APPLE PUNCH

This festive and fruity punch is made with five kinds of juice plus cinnamon and allspice for a well-balanced flavor that's a delightful change of pace for a punch.
—Jennifer Stout, Blandon, PA

Prep: 10 min. • **Cook:** 4 hours
Makes: 16 servings (¾ cup each)

- 4 cups apple juice
- 4 cups orange juice
- 2 cups cranberry juice
- 1 can (11.3 ounces) pineapple nectar
- ½ cup sugar
- 2 teaspoons lemon juice
- 3 to 4 cinnamon sticks (3 inches)
- 8 whole allspice
- 8 to 10 orange slices
  Apple slices and fresh cranberries, optional

1. In a 5- or 6-qt. slow cooker, mix first six ingredients. Place cinnamon sticks and allspice on a double thickness of cheesecloth. Gather corners of cloth to enclose seasonings; tie securely with string. Place spice bag and orange slices in slow cooker. Cook, covered, on low for 4-5 hours to allow flavors to blend.
2. Discard spice bag and orange slices. If desired, top punch with apple and cranberries. Serve warm.

SWEET ONION CREAMED CORN

A friend from church gave me this easy and delicious recipe over 40 years ago, and I still make it regularly. She was from the South, and whenever I cook it, I think about her fondly.
—Nancy Heishman, Las Vegas, NV

....

Prep: 25 min. • **Cook:** 3 hours
Makes: 8 servings

- 5 bacon strips, chopped
- 1 large sweet onion, chopped
- 1 medium sweet red pepper, chopped
- 5 cups frozen corn (about 24 ounces), thawed
- 2 cups cubed fully cooked ham
- ½ cup half-and-half cream
- 1 tablespoon brown sugar
- 1 tablespoon dried parsley flakes
- 1 teaspoon smoked paprika
- ½ teaspoon salt
- ½ teaspoon pepper
- 1 package (8 ounces) cream cheese, cubed and softened

1. In a large skillet, cook bacon over medium heat until crisp, stirring occasionally. Remove with a slotted spoon; drain on paper towels.
2. Cook and stir onion and sweet red pepper in bacon drippings over medium-high heat until tender, 5-6 minutes.
3. In a greased 4-qt. slow cooker, combine corn, ham, cream, brown sugar, parsley, paprika, salt, pepper, bacon and onion mixture. Cook, covered, on low until heated through, 3-4 hours. Stir in cream cheese; cook, covered, 10 minutes longer. Stir before serving.

SWEET ONION CREAMED CORN

SLAW-TOPPED BEEF SLIDERS

When I was working full time, I would rely on these delicious, fast-to-fix beef sliders for simple meals. To ease on prep time and avoid extra clean-up, I used bagged coleslaw mix and bottled slaw dressing.
—Jane Whittaker, Pensacola, FL

Prep: 20 min. • **Cook:** 6 hours
Makes: 1 dozen

- 3 cups coleslaw mix
- ½ medium red onion (about ⅔ cup)
- ⅛ teaspoon celery seed
- ¼ teaspoon pepper
- ⅓ cup coleslaw salad dressing

SANDWICHES
- 1 boneless beef chuck roast (2 pounds)
- 1 teaspoon salt
- ½ teaspoon pepper
- 1 can (6 ounces) tomato paste
- ¼ cup water
- 1 teaspoon Worcestershire sauce
- 1 small onion, diced
- 1 cup barbecue sauce
- 12 slider buns or dinner rolls, split

1. Combine coleslaw, onion, celery seed and pepper. Add salad dressing; toss to coat. Refrigerate until serving.
2. Sprinkle roast with salt and pepper; transfer roast to a 5-qt. slow cooker. Mix tomato paste, water and Worcestershire sauce; pour over roast. Top with onion. Cook, covered, on low for 6-8 hours or until meat is tender.
3. Shred meat with two forks; return to slow cooker. Stir in barbecue sauce; heat through. Serve beef on buns; top with coleslaw. Replace tops.

PUMPKIN PIE PUDDING

My husband loves anything pumpkin, and this creamy, comforting dessert is one of his favorites. We make this super easy pudding year-round, but it's especially nice in fall.
—Andrea Schaak, Bloomington, MN

Prep: 10 min. • **Cook:** 6 hours
Makes: 6 servings

- 1 can (15 ounces) solid-pack pumpkin
- 1 can (12 ounces) evaporated milk
- ¾ cup sugar
- ½ cup biscuit/baking mix
- 2 large eggs, beaten
- 2 tablespoons butter, melted
- 2½ teaspoons pumpkin pie spice
- 2 teaspoons vanilla extract
  Sweetened whipped cream or vanilla ice cream, optional

1. Combine first eight ingredients. Transfer to a greased 3-qt. slow cooker.
2. Cook, covered, on low until a thermometer reads 160°, 6-7 hours. If desired, serve with whipped cream or vanilla ice cream.

BLACK BEAN CHICKEN NACHOS

WARM CINNAMON-APPLE TOPPING

You'll quickly warm up to the old-fashioned taste of this fruit topping! I like to spoon it over vanilla ice cream or slices of pound cake.
—Doris Heath, Franklin, NC

Prep: 10 min. • **Cook:** 3½ hours
Makes: about 6 cups

- 3 medium tart apples, peeled and sliced
- 3 medium pears, peeled and sliced
- 1 tablespoon lemon juice
- ½ cup packed brown sugar
- ½ cup maple syrup
- ¼ cup butter, melted
- 2 tablespoons cornstarch
- ½ cup chopped pecans
- ¼ cup raisins
- 2 cinnamon sticks (3 inches)
  Ice cream or pound cake

1. In a 3-qt. slow cooker, toss apples and pears with lemon juice. Mix brown sugar, maple syrup, butter and cornstarch; pour over fruit. Stir in the pecans, raisins and cinnamon sticks.
2. Cook, covered, on low until fruit is tender, 3-4 hours. Discard cinnamon sticks. Serve with ice cream or cake.

BLACK BEAN CHICKEN NACHOS

One of my very favorite local restaurants, Zeppelins, has the best chicken nachos. Their famous dish inspired me to create my own but with the convenience of using the slow cooker. I always use fresh cilantro because it's economical and it makes the dish pop with flavor.
—Natalie Hess, Cedar Rapids, IA

Prep: 10 min. • **Cook:** 4 hours
Makes: 8 servings

- 1½ pounds boneless skinless chicken breast
- 2 jars (16 ounces each) black bean and corn salsa
- 1 each medium green pepper and sweet red pepper, chopped
  Tortilla chips
- 2 cups shredded Mexican cheese blend
  Fresh cilantro leaves
  Optional toppings: minced fresh cilantro, pickled jalapeno slices and sour cream

1. Place chicken, salsa and peppers in a 3- or 4-qt. slow cooker. Cook, covered, on low until meat is tender, 4-5 hours.
2. Remove chicken; shred with two forks. Return to slow cooker. Using a slotted spoon, serve chicken over chips; sprinkle with cheese and cilantro. Add toppings of your choice.

TOP TIP

Chopped Nut Measurements

Chopping an ingredient before or after measuring it can make a difference in the outcome of a recipe. Here's a trick that might help you remember. If the word "chopped" comes before the ingredient when listed in a recipe, then chop the ingredient before measuring. If the word "chopped" comes after the ingredient, then chop after measuring.

WARM CINNAMON-APPLE TOPPING

Gobble, Gobble Goodies

Please the little ones with an array of super kid-friendly foods this Thanksgiving. They'll be delighted with the yummy options made just for them—and adults will like them too!

Enjoy irresistible recipes, including pizza casserole and cauliflower with a white cheddar sauce that makes even little ones love the veggie. Plus, who wouldn't want to end dinner with the Chocolate Caramel Turkey Legs on page 120?

Use a paper tablecloth and set out markers so kids can doodle away (or draw silly faces on gourds and pumpkins) as they eat. Everyone will want a seat at the kids' table this year!

Deluxe Pizza Casserole (p. 118) **Two-Bean Hummus** (p. 114)

APPLE
PECAN
SALAD

APPLE PECAN SALAD

I remember being excited right before Thanksgiving and Christmas, because that's when my family made this salad. There were five children and only the oldest helped peel the apples. It was fun when one of our boyfriends would come for the holiday for the first time. My dad would give him a huge bowl of grapes, hand him a sharp paring knife and tell him to start peeling. We all kept a straight face until he had the first grape peeled!
—Debra Slone, Crossville, TN

Prep: 20 min. + chilling
Makes: 20 servings (¾ cup each)

- ¾ cup Miracle Whip
- ½ cup 2% milk
- ⅓ cup sugar
- 3 pounds medium apples, cut into ½-inch pieces
- 1 pound seedless red grapes, halved
- 1 package (10 ounces) miniature marshmallows
- 3 cups chopped pecans

Whisk together Miracle Whip, milk and sugar until smooth. Place fruits in another bowl; add dressing and toss to coat. Gently stir in marshmallows and pecans. Refrigerate, covered, at least 2 hours before serving.

TWO-BEAN HUMMUS

My children love this easy hummus and even like to help me make it! Hummus is a great way to sneak in some beans and add important soluble fiber into their diets. I use this hummus in a bread bowl as the body of a turkey for my vegetable platter at Thanksgiving.
—Kelly Andreas, Eau Claire, WI

Start to Finish: 15 min.
Makes: 2 cups

- 1 can (15 ounces) garbanzo beans or chickpeas, rinsed and drained
- 1 can (15 ounces) white kidney or cannellini beans, rinsed and drained
- ¼ cup olive oil
- 2 tablespoons lemon juice
- 2 garlic cloves, minced
- ¼ teaspoon salt
  Assorted fresh vegetables

Process the first six ingredients in a food processor until smooth. Transfer to a serving bowl or divide into small individual serving cups; serve with vegetables.

TURKEY VEGETABLE PLATTER

Make the vegetable platter extra fun this Thanksgiving by arranging veggies into a simple turkey design. Kids (and adults!) will rush to the table to check out your adorable creation, and they won't wait to sample the crunchy, tasty treats. Bonus—it's healthy, too!

TURKEY HEAD AND BODY:

Cut the end off a small cucumber; place cut side down on a clean work surface. Insert two whole cloves into end of cucumber for eyes. Cut a small piece off the pointy end of peeled carrot; set remainder aside. Cut a small horizontal slit in carrot piece. Using a toothpick, attach carrot piece into cucumber to serve as the beak. Insert a small piece of sweet red pepper into the slit of the carrot to serve as the wattle. Place the hummus in a small serving bowl or bread bowl and place near the edge of a round platter. Place the finished turkey head onto the top of the hummus, cut side down. Trim two webbed feet from the remaining carrot and place outside the serving bowl, feet pointing down.

TURKEY FEATHERS:

Wash and trim a variety of assorted veggies: broccoli florets, small cherry tomatoes, cucumbers, sweet yellow pepper, radishes, sugar snap peas, carrot sticks and celery sticks. Using the photo above as a guide, arrange vegetables around the hummus bowl to resemble tail feathers on a turkey.

TWO-BEAN
HUMMUS

**CRESCENT
CHICKEN
BUNDLES**

CRESCENT CHICKEN BUNDLES

When I was expecting our third child, this was one of the meals I put in the freezer ahead of time. We now have four kids, and they all like these rich chicken pockets. For Thanksgiving, you might substitute ham or turkey for the chicken.
—Jo Groth, Plainfield, IA

Prep: 15 min. • **Bake:** 20 min.
Makes: 8 servings

- 6 ounces cream cheese, softened
- 4 tablespoons butter, melted, divided
- 2 tablespoons minced chives
- 2 tablespoons milk
- ½ teaspoon salt
- ¼ teaspoon pepper
- 4 cups cubed cooked chicken
- 2 tubes (8 ounces each) refrigerated crescent rolls
- 1 cup crushed seasoned stuffing

1. Preheat oven to 350°. Beat cream cheese, 2 tablespoons butter, chives, milk, salt and pepper until blended. Stir in chicken.
2. Unroll the crescent roll dough and separate into eight rectangles; press perforations together. Spoon about ½ cup chicken mixture in the center of each rectangle. Bring edges up to the center and pinch to seal. Brush with remaining butter. Sprinkle with crushed stuffing, lightly pressing down.
3. Transfer to ungreased baking sheets. Bake until golden brown, 20-25 minutes.

Freeze option: Freeze unbaked bundles on baking sheets until firm; transfer to a freezer container. May be frozen for up to 2 months. To use, thaw in refrigerator. Bake as directed, increasing the time as necessary to heat through.

GREEN PEA CASSEROLE

GREEN PEA CASSEROLE

This has been our family's favorite vegetable casserole for 20 years now! The kids always ask me to make it for Thanksgiving dinner.
—Barbara Preneta, Unionville, CT

Prep: 15 min. • **Bake:** 20 min.
Makes: 8 servings

- 5 cups frozen peas (about 20 ounces), thawed
- 1 celery rib, chopped
- ½ cup mayonnaise
- ⅓ cup chopped onion
- ¼ teaspoon salt
- ¼ teaspoon pepper
- 1 package (6 ounces) stuffing mix

Preheat oven to 350°. Mix the first six ingredients; transfer to a greased 11x7-in. baking dish. Prepare stuffing mix according to package directions. Spread over pea mixture. Bake, uncovered, until lightly browned, 20-25 minutes.

TOP TIP

Flavor Boost

To add a mild fruity flavor to this Green Pea Casserole, substitute apple juice for the water when preparing the package of stuffing mix that will go on top. If you're serving traditional dressing cooked inside a turkey as a side dish, replace the stuffing mix in this recipe with french-fried onions, crushed corn flakes, crumbled ranch-flavored crackers or slivered almonds.

CAULIFLOWER WITH WHITE CHEDDAR SAUCE

My mother served this cheesy cauliflower on Thanksgiving and Christmas for as long as I can remember. I've embellished the recipe over the years, but I've kept the family tradition around for 47+ years of marriage. When I visit my children and their families, this dish is a must for them as well! You can easily double the recipe for larger groups.
—Charlene Chambers, Ormond Beach, FL

Start to Finish: 25 min.
Makes: 8 servings

- 1 large head cauliflower, cut into florets (about 6 cups)
- 5 teaspoons cornstarch
- ½ teaspoon salt
- ⅛ teaspoon white pepper
- 1¼ cups 2% milk
- 2 tablespoons butter
- 1 cup shredded extra sharp white cheddar cheese
  Paprika, optional

1. In a large saucepan, place steamer basket over 1 in. of water. Place the cauliflower in basket. Bring water to a boil. Reduce heat to maintain a simmer; steam, covered, just until tender, 10-12 minutes.
2. Meanwhile, in a small saucepan, mix cornstarch, salt and white pepper. Stir in milk and butter until smooth. Bring to a boil, stirring constantly; cook and stir until thickened, 2-4 minutes.
3. Stir in the cheese until melted. Drain cauliflower. Transfer to a serving bowl; top with sauce. If desired, sprinkle with paprika.

DELUXE PIZZA CASSEROLE

This is the family's favorite dish for special occasions, and we always make it for my granddaughter's birthday. Mushrooms are a wonderful addition if you like them.
—Vickie Oldham, Dubuque, IA

Prep: 30 min. • **Bake:** 20 min.
Makes: 12 servings

- 3 cups uncooked spiral pasta
- 1 pound ground beef
- ½ pound bulk pork sausage
- 1 medium onion, chopped
- 1 medium green pepper, chopped
- 1 jar (24 ounces) meatless pasta sauce
- 1 can (15 ounces) pizza sauce
- 1 teaspoon brown sugar
- 2 cups shredded part-skim mozzarella cheese
- 1 package (3½ ounces) sliced pepperoni
- ¼ cup grated Parmesan cheese

1. Preheat oven to 350°. Cook pasta according to package directions for al dente; drain. Meanwhile, in a Dutch oven, cook and crumble beef and sausage with onion and pepper over medium-high heat until meat is no longer pink and vegetables are tender, 6-8 minutes; drain.
2. Stir in pasta sauce, pizza sauce and brown sugar. Bring to a boil. Reduce heat; simmer, uncovered, 10 minutes, stirring occasionally. Stir in pasta. Transfer to a greased 13x9-in. baking dish. Top with mozzarella cheese and pepperoni. Sprinkle with Parmesan cheese.
3. Bake, uncovered, until lightly browned and cheese is melted, 20-25 minutes. Cut into pieces.

DELUXE PIZZA CASSEROLE

CHOCOLATE CARAMEL TURKEY LEGS

Make your little turkeys feel like VIPs this holiday with pretzel "drumsticks" from my blog, amyscookingadventures.com.
— Amy Lents, Grand Forks, ND

Makes: 20 servings

40 caramels
20 honey wheat braided pretzel twists
3 oz. melted chocolate

Microwave the caramels on high until softened, 10-15 seconds. Mold two softened caramels around the lower half of each braided pretzel to resemble a turkey leg. Dip in melted chocolate; allow excess to drip off. Place on waxed paper; let stand until set. Store in an airtight container for 1-2 weeks.

PUMPKIN CUPCAKES WITH SPICED FROSTING

My aunt makes the most delicious pumpkin pies for Thanksgiving. But my kids prefer cupcakes for dessert, so I created these for all the youngsters at our holiday table!
—Aimee Shugarman, Liberty Township, OH

Prep: 15 min. • **Bake:** 25 min. + cooling
Makes: 1 dozen

  1 **cup canned pumpkin**
  2 **large eggs**
 ½ **cup sugar**
 ½ **cup packed brown sugar**
 ¼ **cup unsweetened applesauce**
 ¼ **cup canola oil**
  1 **cup all-purpose flour**
  1 **teaspoon baking powder**
 ½ **teaspoon baking soda**
 ¼ **teaspoon salt**
1½ **teaspoons ground cinnamon**
1½ **teaspoons pumpkin pie spice**
FROSTING
  1 **can (16 ounces) vanilla frosting**
  1 **cup whipped topping**
  1 **teaspoon ground cinnamon**
36 **pieces candy corn**

1. Preheat oven to 350°. Line 12 muffin cups with paper or foil liners. Beat first six ingredients until well blended. In another bowl, whisk flour, baking powder, baking soda, salt and spices; gradually beat into pumpkin mixture.
2. Fill prepared cups two-thirds full. Bake until a toothpick inserted in center comes out clean, 25-30 minutes. Cool in pans for 10 minutes before removing to wire racks to cool completely.
3. Mix the frosting, whipped topping and cinnamon. Pipe or spoon onto cupcakes; top with candy corn. Refrigerate leftovers.

LIME CHIFFON JELLO

As kids, we always looked forward to my aunt bringing this wonderful dish to Thanksgiving and Christmas dinner.
—Mary Richart, Roaring Branch, PA

Prep: 25 min. + chilling
Makes: 12 servings

  1 **package (3 ounces) lime gelatin**
 ¼ **cup sugar**
  1 **cup boiling water**
  1 **can (12 ounces) evaporated milk**
 ¾ **cup graham cracker crumbs**
  3 **tablespoons butter, melted**

1. Place gelatin and sugar in a bowl. Add boiling water to gelatin mixture; stir for 2 minutes to completely dissolve. Refrigerate until very thick, about 30 minutes.
2. Meanwhile, place milk and mixer beaters in a bowl. Freeze until ice crystals form around edge of bowl, about 30 minutes. Beat milk on high speed until light and fluffy. While beating, pour in thickened jello mixture; beat on high until soft peaks form.
3. Pour into an 11x7-in. dish. Mix cracker crumbs and butter; sprinkle over top. Refrigerate, covered, at least 4 hours before serving.

TOP TIP

Pumpkin from Scratch

"Pie pumpkins" are the most flavorful variety for use in baking. Pick when fully ripened—the color will be deep orange, and the stem will easily break loose when ready to harvest. Wash, peel and remove seeds. Cut pumpkin into chunks and steam until soft. Puree using a food mill or processor. Cool and pack into freezer bags or containers in the amounts needed for recipes. Use cup-for-cup in place of canned pumpkin.

**PUMPKIN CUPCAKES
WITH SPICED FROSTING**

Sugar &
Spice Desserts

These desserts are definitely everything nice! Fall is the perfect time to serve up something sweet and full of spices like nutmeg, cinnamon, ginger and cardamom. The flavors of the season make terrific treats, and the recipes here will give you some fresh ideas for combining them.

Whether you are prepping for a casual or a formal get-together, we've got you covered with a simple ginger apple-pear crisp, a tasty bananas foster, spiced brownie bites and more. You're sure to impress whoever you serve.

But don't wait for guests or Thanksgiving—you can enjoy these fine desserts any time of the year!

Pumpkin Cake with Whipped Cinnamon Frosting (p. 127)

GINGER APPLE-PEAR CRISP

Taste autumn aromas—apples, cinnamon and spices—in this delicious recipe. It's even better with a scoop of vanilla or pumpkin ice cream! Whipped cream is always an option.
—Holly Battiste, Barrington, NJ

Prep: 20 min. • **Bake:** 40 min.
Makes: 8 servings

- 4 medium tart apples, peeled and sliced
- 4 medium pears, peeled and sliced
- ¼ cup sugar
- 1 tablespoon lemon juice
- 1 tablespoon grated fresh gingerroot
- ½ teaspoon salt
- ½ teaspoon vanilla extract

TOPPING
- 1 cup old-fashioned oats
- ½ cup all-purpose flour
- ½ cup packed brown sugar
- 1 teaspoon ground cinnamon
- ¼ teaspoon ground nutmeg
- ⅛ teaspoon salt
- ⅓ cup cold butter, cubed

1. Preheat oven to 375°. In a large bowl, toss first seven ingredients. Transfer to a greased 2½-qt. baking dish.
2. In a bowl, mix first six topping ingredients; cut in butter until crumbly. Sprinkle over fruit.
3. Bake until golden brown and fruit is tender, 40-45 minutes. Serve warm.

MOLASSES SPICE CAKE

This recipe has been in my personal collection for 30 years. The spice flavors are nicely balanced, and the molasses and coffee make it dark and moist. You can use either instant coffee with 1 cup boiling water or brewed coffee in this sheet cake.
—Dawn Lowenstein, Huntingdon Valley, PA

Prep: 25 min. • **Bake:** 20 min. + cooling
Makes: 24 servings

- 1 cup butter, softened
- 1 cup sugar
- 2 large eggs
- ½ cup molasses
- 2 cups all-purpose flour
- 1 teaspoon salt
- 1 teaspoon baking soda
- 1 teaspoon ground ginger
- 1 teaspoon ground cinnamon
- 1 teaspoon ground cloves
- 1 cup brewed coffee, cooled

ICING
- ½ cup butter, softened
- 1 teaspoon vanilla extract
- 3 cups confectioners' sugar
- 3 to 4 tablespoons 2% milk

1. Preheat oven to 325°. Grease a 15x10x1-in. pan.
2. Cream butter and sugar until light and fluffy. Add eggs, one at a time, beating well after each addition. Beat in molasses. In another bowl, whisk together flour, salt, baking soda and spices; add to the creamed mixture alternately with coffee, beating well after each addition. Spread into the prepared pan.
3. Bake until toothpick inserted in center comes out clean, 20-25 minutes. Cool completely in pan on a wire rack.
4. For icing, beat butter and vanilla until creamy. Gradually beat in confectioners' sugar and enough milk to reach desired consistency. Spread over cake.

CHAI TEA CUPCAKES

My brother made me a batch of cupcakes using the flavors from my all-time favorite coffeehouse drink—chai tea latte. What brotherly love!
—Allison LaMarca, Cypress, TX

Prep: 25 min. + cooling
Bake: 15 min. + cooling
Makes: 1 dozen

- 1 cup 2% milk
- 3 chai tea bags
- ½ cup butter, softened
- 1 cup sugar
- 1 teaspoon vanilla extract
- 2 large eggs
- 2 cups all-purpose flour
- 2 teaspoons baking powder
- 3 teaspoons ground cinnamon
- 1½ teaspoons ground nutmeg
- 1½ teaspoons ground cloves
- 1 teaspoon ground ginger
  Pinch salt

FROSTING
- ½ cup butter, softened
- 1½ teaspoons vanilla extract
- 4½ cups confectioners' sugar
- 5 to 6 tablespoons 2% milk
  Additional nutmeg, optional

1. Preheat oven to 350°. Line 12 muffin cups with paper or foil liners.
2. In a small saucepan, bring milk to a simmer (do not boil); remove from heat. Add tea bags; steep, covered, 10 minutes. Discard tea bags; cool tea completely.
3. Cream butter and sugar until light and fluffy. Add vanilla and eggs, one at a time, beating well after each addition. In another bowl, whisk together flour, baking powder, spices and salt; add to creamed mixture alternately with steeped milk, beating well.
4. Fill prepared cups three-fourths full. Bake until a toothpick inserted in the center comes out clean, 15-18 minutes. Cool in pans for 10 minutes before removing to wire racks to cool completely.
5. For frosting, beat butter and vanilla until creamy. Gradually beat in confectioners' sugar and enough milk to reach desired consistency. Spread over cupcakes. If desired, sprinkle with nutmeg.

GINGER
APPLE-PEAR
CRISP

BANANAS
FOSTER
SUNDAES

BANANAS FOSTER SUNDAES

I have wonderful memories of eating bananas Foster in New Orleans, and as a dietitian, I wanted to find a healthier version. I combined the best of two recipes and added my own tweaks to create this Southern treat.
—Lisa Varner, El Paso, TX

Start to Finish: 15 min.
Makes: 6 servings

- 1 tablespoon butter
- 3 tablespoons brown sugar
- 1 tablespoon orange juice
- ¼ teaspoon ground cinnamon
- ¼ teaspoon ground nutmeg
- 3 large firm bananas, sliced
- 2 tablespoons chopped pecans, toasted
- ½ teaspoon rum extract
- 3 cups reduced-fat vanilla ice cream

1. In a large nonstick skillet, melt butter over medium-low heat. Stir in brown sugar, orange juice, cinnamon and nutmeg until blended. Add bananas and pecans; cook until bananas are glazed and slightly softened, 2-3 minutes, stirring gently.
2. Remove from the heat; stir in extract. Serve with ice cream.
Note: To toast nuts, cook in a skillet over low heat until lightly browned, stirring occasionally.

TOP TIP

Make Your Own Cinnamon Sugar

You can buy bottles of prepared cinnamon sugar in the spice aisle of your grocery store. But why not make your own? Mix ½ cup sugar and 1 tablespoon ground cinnamon. Store in an airtight container to use in recipes or sprinkle over buttered toast at breakfast.

PUMPKIN CAKE WITH WHIPPED CINNAMON FROSTING

PUMPKIN CAKE WITH WHIPPED CINNAMON FROSTING

My mom made this for me, and one bite can completely take me back to my childhood. You can easily convert it into a great carrot cake recipe: just use grated carrots in place of pumpkin and add raisins.
—Melissa Pelkey Hass, Waleska, GA

Prep: 35 min. • **Bake:** 25 min. + cooling
Makes: 12 servings

- 4 large eggs
- 2 cups sugar
- 1 cup canola oil
- 2 cups all-purpose flour
- 2 teaspoons ground cinnamon
- 1 teaspoon baking soda
- 1 teaspoon baking powder
- ½ teaspoon salt
- ½ teaspoon ground ginger
- ½ teaspoon ground allspice
- 1 can (15 ounces) pumpkin
- ½ cup chopped pecans

FROSTING
- 1 cup butter, softened
- 3 teaspoons ground cinnamon
- 2 teaspoons vanilla extract
- 7½ cups confectioners' sugar
- ⅔ to ¾ cup heavy whipping cream
  Cinnamon sugar, optional

1. Preheat oven to 350°. Line bottoms of two greased 9-in. round pans with parchment paper; grease paper.
2. Beat eggs, sugar and oil until well blended. In another bowl, whisk together flour, cinnamon, baking soda, baking powder, salt, ginger and allspice; gradually beat into egg mixture. Stir in pumpkin and pecans.
3. Transfer to prepared pans. Bake until a toothpick inserted in center comes out clean, 25-30 minutes.
4. Cool in pans for 10 minutes before removing to wire racks; remove paper. Cool completely.
5. For frosting, beat butter, cinnamon and vanilla until creamy. Gradually beat in confectioners' sugar and enough cream to reach desired consistency.
6. Using a long serrated knife, cut each cake horizontally in half. Spread ¾ cup frosting between layers; spread remaining frosting over top and sides of cake. If desired, sprinkle with cinnamon sugar.

SNICKERDOODLE CHEESECAKE

My maternal grandmother preferred sewing and quilting to cooking and baking, but there were some things that she cooked and baked really well. She was the only person I knew who made snickerdoodles. I always enjoyed these simple but yummy cookies. Since cheesecake is my favorite dessert, I couldn't resist coming up with a snickerdoodle cheesecake. I think of my grandmother each time I make it! Sometimes I'll drizzle the slices with maple syrup.

—Lisa Varner, El Paso, TX

Prep: 25 min. • **Bake:** 70 minutes + chilling
Makes: 16 servings

- 2 cups cinnamon graham cracker crumbs (about 14 whole crackers)
- ½ cup butter, melted
- 3 packages (8 ounces each) cream cheese, softened
- 1 cup sugar, divided
- 1 teaspoon ground cinnamon
- 1 teaspoon vanilla extract
- 4 large eggs, lightly beaten
- 1½ cups cinnamon baking chips
- 2 cups (16 ounces) sour cream

1. Preheat oven to 325°. Place a greased 9-in. springform pan on a double thickness of heavy-duty foil (about 18 in. square). Wrap foil securely around pan.
2. Mix cracker crumbs and melted butter. Press onto bottom and 1½ in. up sides of prepared pan.
3. Beat cream cheese and ¾ cup sugar until smooth. Beat in cinnamon and vanilla. Add eggs; beat on low speed just until blended. Fold in baking chips. Pour into crust. Place springform pan in a larger baking pan; add 1 in. of hot water to larger pan.
4. Bake until center is just set and top appears dull, 70-80 minutes. Remove springform pan from water bath. Cool cheesecake on a wire rack 10 minutes. Loosen sides from pan with a knife; remove the foil. Cool 1 hour longer. Refrigerate cake overnight, covering when completely cooled.
5. Remove rim from pan. Mix sour cream and remaining sugar; spread over cheesecake.

CARDAMOM COOKIES

Cardamom, almond extract and walnuts enhance the flavor of these buttery, melt-in-your-mouth cookies.

—Mary Steiner, West Bend, WI

Prep: 35 min. • **Bake:** 15 min./batch
Makes: about 6 dozen

- 2 cups butter, softened
- 2½ cups confectioners' sugar, divided
- 1 teaspoon ground cardamom
- ⅛ teaspoon salt
- 1½ teaspoons almond extract
- 3¾ cups all-purpose flour
- 1 cup finely chopped walnuts

1. Preheat oven to 350°. Cream butter, 1½ cups confectioners' sugar, cardamom and salt until light and fluffy. Beat in the extract. Gradually beat in flour. Stir in the walnuts.
2. Shape the dough into 1-in. balls; place 2 in. apart on ungreased baking sheets. Bake until edges are golden, 15-17 minutes.
3. While warm, roll cookies in remaining confectioners' sugar. Cool on wire racks.

SNICKERDOODLE CHEESECAKE

TOP TIP

Storing Cheesecake

Cover and refrigerate cheesecake for up to 3 days. To freeze, place entire cheesecake or individual slices on a baking sheet and freeze until firm. Wrap in heavy-duty plastic wrap and place in a freezer bag. Freeze cheesecake for up to 2 months. Thaw in the refrigerator.

SPICED
BROWNIE
BITES

SPICED BROWNIE BITES

My son and I came up with this recipe together to satisfy our cravings for chocolate and spice.
—Anna Nicoletta, East Stroudsburg, PA

....

Prep: 40 min. • **Bake:** 15 min. + cooling
Makes: about 3½ dozen

- 8 ounces bittersweet chocolate, coarsely chopped
- ½ cup butter, cubed
- 4 large eggs
- 1 cup sugar
- ¾ cup packed brown sugar
- 1¼ cups all-purpose flour
- ⅓ cup baking cocoa
- ¾ teaspoon cayenne pepper
- ¾ teaspoon Chinese five-spice powder
- ½ teaspoon salt

GLAZE

- 1 cup (6 ounces) semisweet chocolate chips
- 4 tablespoons butter, cubed
- 1 tablespoon light corn syrup
  Chopped crystallized ginger

1. Preheat oven to 350°. In a metal bowl or top of a double boiler over barely simmering water, melt chocolate and butter; stir until smooth. Cool slightly.
2. In a large bowl, beat eggs and sugars until blended; stir in chocolate mixture. In another bowl, mix flour, cocoa, spices and salt; gradually add to chocolate mixture, mixing well.
3. Fill greased mini-muffin cups almost full. Bake until centers are set, 12-15 minutes (do not overbake). Cool in pans 5 minutes before removing to wire racks to cool completely.
4. For glaze, in a small metal bowl or top of a double boiler over barely simmering water, melt chocolate chips and butter with corn syrup, stirring until smooth. Remove from heat; cool until slightly thickened, about 30 minutes.
5. Dip tops of brownies into glaze. Top with ginger.

CINNAMON ALMOND BRITTLE

It simply wouldn't be the start of the holidays at our house without this old-time favorite twist on peanut brittle. No one believes how easy it is to make... and it doesn't stick to your teeth!
—Lynette Kleinschmidt, Litchfield, MN

....

Prep: 15 min. • **Cook:** 20 min. + cooling
Makes: about 2 pounds

- 1 teaspoon plus 3 tablespoons butter, cubed
- 2 cups sugar
- ¾ cup light corn syrup
- ¼ cup water
- 3 cups slivered almonds, toasted
- 2 teaspoons ground cinnamon
- ½ teaspoon salt
- 1½ teaspoons baking soda
- 1 teaspoon vanilla extract

1. Preheat oven to 200°. Grease two baking sheets with 1 teaspoon butter; place in oven to warm.
2. In a large heavy saucepan, combine sugar, corn syrup and water. Bring to a boil, stirring constantly to dissolve sugar. Using a pastry brush dipped in water, wash down the sides of the pan to eliminate sugar crystals. Cook, without stirring, over medium heat until a candy thermometer reads 240° (soft-ball stage). Stir in almonds, cinnamon, salt and remaining butter; cook until thermometer reads 300° (hard-crack stage), stirring frequently and brushing sides of pan as needed.
3. Remove from heat; stir in baking soda and vanilla. Immediately pour onto prepared pans, spreading to ¼-in. thickness. Cool completely.
4. Break brittle into pieces. Store between layers of waxed paper in an airtight container.
Note: We recommend that you test your candy thermometer before each use by bringing water to a boil; the thermometer should read 212°. Adjust your recipe temperature up or down based on your test.

CARDAMOM CRUMB CAKE

This cake has a thick cardamom-scented crumb topping, and it brings the family to the table fast when the aroma drifts from the oven to the living room.
—Lily Julow, Lawrenceville, GA

....

Prep: 25 min. • **Bake:** 30 min. + cooling
Makes: 15 servings

- 1 cup butter, melted
- ½ cup sugar
- ½ cup packed brown sugar
- ½ teaspoon ground cardamom
- ¼ teaspoon salt
- 2½ cups all-purpose flour

CAKE

- 3 cups all-purpose flour
- 1¼ cups sugar
- 1½ teaspoons baking powder
- 1 teaspoon salt
- ½ teaspoon grated orange peel
- ¼ teaspoon ground cardamom
- 2 large eggs
- 1 cup 2% milk
- ¾ cup butter, melted

1. Preheat oven to 350°. Grease a 13x9-in. pan. Mix first five ingredients until blended; stir in flour until crumbly.
2. In a large bowl, whisk together first six cake ingredients. In another bowl, whisk together eggs, milk and melted butter; add to dry ingredients, stirring just until moistened.
3. Transfer to prepared pan. Top with crumb mixture. Bake until a toothpick inserted in the center comes out clean, 30-35 minutes. Cool in pan on a wire rack.

EASTER GATHERINGS

It's time to kiss the chilly winter air goodbye and welcome back our dear friend, the sun. Spring brings better moods and many opportunities to celebrate, from outdoor meals on the patio to church potlucks. And this section gives you even more reasons to rejoice: time-saving Easter recipes with no more than five ingredients that let you savor the fresh flavors of the season.

FOOD & FELLOWSHIP POTLUCK.......... 134

EASTER EGG LUNCHEON 144

5-INGREDIENT EASTER DINNER.......... 154

SPRING STAPLES 164

Food & Fellowship
Potluck

Fellowship, friends and of course fantastic food! That's what has drawn folks to church suppers for generations. Finding the perfect potluck recipe for Easter or anytime is no longer just luck with this lineup of unforgettable culinary creations at your fingertips.

Discover decadent make-and-take party favorites and traditional springtime classics. From fun finger foods and comforting main courses to sensational sides and dreamy desserts, this selection makes it easy to find the ideal contribution.

So don't be surprised when your pan comes home empty. With these impressive crowd-pleasers, guests will be piling their plates high and begging you for the recipe!

Chicken & Swiss Casserole (p. 141) **Fruit with Poppy Seed Dressing** (p. 138)
Chocolate-Coconut Layer Bars (p. 142) **Garlic-Dill Deviled Eggs** (p. 137)

"Easter isn't complete without deviled eggs. Fresh dill and garlic perk up the flavor of these irresistible appetizers."

—KAMI HORCH, CALAIS, ME

GARLIC-DILL DEVILED EGGS

Prep: 20 min. + chilling
Makes: 2 dozen

- 12 hard-cooked eggs
- ⅔ cup mayonnaise
- 4 teaspoons dill pickle relish
- 2 teaspoons snipped fresh dill
- 2 teaspoons Dijon mustard
- 1 teaspoon coarsely ground pepper
- ¼ teaspoon garlic powder
- ⅛ teaspoon paprika or cayenne pepper

1. Cut eggs lengthwise in half. Remove yolks, reserving whites. In a bowl, mash yolks. Stir in all remaining ingredients except paprika. Spoon or pipe filling into egg whites.
2. Refrigerate, covered, for at least 30 minutes before serving. Sprinkle deviled eggs with paprika.

APRICOT-CHIPOTLE CHEESE SPREAD

The creamy cheese, sweet preserves and spicy chipotle is just the right combo for this easy cracker spread. If you want to try some variations, use cherry or raspberry preserves in place of the apricot.
—Barb Templin, Norwood, MN

Prep: 10 min. + chilling
Makes: 2 cups

- 12 ounces cream cheese, softened
- 1 cup shredded cheddar cheese
- 2 garlic cloves, minced
- ½ teaspoon onion powder
- ½ cup apricot preserves
- 3 teaspoons minced fresh gingerroot
- 3 teaspoons minced chipotle peppers in adobo sauce
  Assorted crackers and vegetables

1. In a large bowl, beat cream cheese, cheddar cheese, garlic and onion powder until blended. Shape cheese mixture into a log. Wrap in plastic wrap; refrigerate at least 2 hours.
2. In a small bowl, mix preserves, ginger and chipotle peppers until blended. Spoon over cream cheese. Serve with crackers and vegetables.

How to Make Classic Deviled Eggs

Egg aficionados, rejoice! There are endless variations on this fun finger food. Begin by following these easy steps for basic deviled eggs, then season as desired.

1

2

HARD COOK the eggs. Arrange in a single layer and add water to cover by 1 inch. Bring to a rolling boil, uncovered. Remove from the heat. Cover and let stand 14-17 minutes.

DRAIN the hot water and cover the eggs in cold water. Gently crack the shells and return to the cold water. Let stand 1 hour. After one hour, the shells will peel off easily.

3

4

TRIM a small part of the egg white from both sides to prevent wobbly eggs. Halve eggs lengthwise and gently squeeze whites or use a small spoon to remove the yolk. Place the yolks in a bowl.

MASH the yolks with the back of a fork until crumbly. Stir in the rest of the filling ingredients.

5

6

SPOON or pipe filling into egg whites until slightly mounded.

GARNISH with paprika or your favorite herbs or spices.

FRUIT WITH POPPY SEED DRESSING

FRUIT WITH
POPPY SEED DRESSING

Easy to prepare, cool and colorful, this refreshing, good-for-you fruit salad is a springtime favorite.
—Peggy Mills, Texarkana, AR

Prep: 20 min. + standing
Makes: 12 servings (1 cup each)

- 3 tablespoons honey
- 1 tablespoon white vinegar
- 1 teaspoon ground mustard
- ¼ teaspoon salt
- ¼ teaspoon onion powder
- ⅓ cup canola oil
- 1 teaspoon poppy seeds
- 1 fresh pineapple, cut into 1½-inch cubes
- 3 medium kiwifruit, halved and sliced
- 2 cups fresh strawberries, halved

1. In a small bowl, whisk the first five ingredients. Gradually whisk in oil until blended. Stir in poppy seeds; let dressing stand 1 hour.
2. In a large bowl, combine fruits. Drizzle with dressing; toss gently to coat.

ONION & GARLIC
SODA BREAD

This is one of my favorite recipes for soda bread. It's versatile, as you can do endless sweet or savory variations. I serve it sliced alongside assorted spreads and cheeses.
—Theresa Vujosevic, Hamburg, NJ

Prep: 20 min. • **Bake:** 35 min. + cooling
Makes: 1 loaf (12 wedges)

- 1 tablespoon olive oil
- 1 medium onion, chopped
- 5 garlic cloves, minced
- 4 cups all-purpose flour
- 1 teaspoon salt
- 1 teaspoon baking soda
- ¼ cup cold butter, cubed
- 1 large egg
- 1½ cups buttermilk

1. Preheat oven to 425°. In a small skillet, heat oil over medium-high heat. Add onion; cook and stir 3-5 minutes or until light golden brown. Add garlic; cook and stir 30 seconds longer. Cool.
2. In a large bowl, whisk flour, salt and baking soda. Cut in butter until mixture resembles coarse crumbs. Stir in cooled onion mixture; make a well in center. In a small bowl, whisk egg and buttermilk; pour into well. Using a wooden spoon, mix dough until too stiff to stir. Turn onto a lightly floured surface; knead gently 10 times. Shape into a round loaf.
3. Transfer to a greased baking sheet. Using a sharp knife, cut a shallow "X" on top of loaf. Bake 35-40 minutes or until golden brown.
4. Remove from pan to a wire rack; serve bread warm.

ARTICHOKE SHRIMP
PASTA SALAD

I have enjoyed this recipe for as long as I can remember. My mom made it famous, and she passed it down to me on my wedding day. It's one of those potluck staples that folks can't get enough of.
—Mary McCarley, Charlotte, NC

Prep: 20 min. • **Cook:** 10 min. + chilling
Makes: 12 servings (1⅓ cups each)

- 1 package (16 ounces) bow tie pasta
- 2 pounds peeled and deveined cooked shrimp (31-40 per pound)
- 2 cans (7½ ounces each) marinated quartered artichoke hearts, drained
- 2 cans (2¼ ounces each) sliced ripe olives, drained
- 2 cups (8 ounces) crumbled feta cheese
- 8 green onions, sliced
- ½ cup chopped fresh parsley
- ¼ cup chopped fresh basil

DRESSING

- ½ cup white wine vinegar
- ½ cup olive oil
- ¼ cup lemon juice
- 2 tablespoons chopped fresh basil
- 2 teaspoons Dijon mustard
  Fresh ground pepper, optional

1. Cook pasta according to package directions for al dente. Drain pasta; rinse with cold water and drain well. In a large bowl, combine pasta, shrimp, artichokes, olives, feta cheese, green onions, parsley and basil.
2. In a small bowl, whisk the vinegar, oil, lemon juice, basil, mustard and, if desired, pepper. Pour dressing over pasta mixture; toss to coat. Refrigerate, covered, 2 hours before serving.

ARTICHOKE
SHRIMP
PASTA SALAD

TRIPLE CHEESE POTATO CAKE WITH HAM

MAKE-AHEAD VEGGIE SALAD

Assemble this colorful mix of vegetables and let it soak up the sweet and sour dressing overnight. The next day, you'll be ready to go with a refreshing salad that tastes extraordinary!
—Shirley Glaab, Hattiesburg, MS

Prep: 35 min. + marinating
Makes: 30 servings (½ cup each)

1 package (24 ounces) frozen shoepeg corn, thawed
1 package (16 ounces) frozen peas, thawed
1 package (16 ounces) frozen French-style green beans, thawed
1 large red onion, chopped
4 celery ribs, thinly sliced
2 medium carrots, thinly sliced
1 medium green pepper, chopped
1 medium sweet red pepper, chopped
1 jar (4½ ounces) sliced mushrooms, drained
1 jar (4 ounces) diced pimientos, drained
½ cup sugar
½ cup olive oil
½ cup red wine vinegar
¾ teaspoon salt
¼ teaspoon pepper

In a large bowl, combine the first 10 ingredients. Place remaining ingredients in a jar with a tight-fitting lid; shake well. Pour over the vegetable mixture; toss to coat. Refrigerate, covered, 8 hours or overnight, stirring occasionally.

TRIPLE CHEESE POTATO CAKE WITH HAM

This delicious and exquisite souffle-like side dish combines the classic flavors of ham, chives and three different cheeses. The crispy crust and fluffy interior make it over-the-top amazing.
—Rebekah Radewahn, Wauwatosa, WI

Prep: 35 min. • **Bake:** 35 min.
Makes: 12 servings

¼ cup plus 1 tablespoon dry bread crumbs, divided
3 pounds medium potatoes, peeled and cubed (about 8 cups)
½ cup heavy whipping cream
¼ cup butter, cubed
3 tablespoons minced fresh chives
1 teaspoon salt
¼ teaspoon pepper
3 large eggs
4 slices Swiss cheese
4 slices part-skim mozzarella cheese
4 ounces thinly sliced deli ham, cut into ½-inch pieces
⅓ cup grated Parmesan cheese
1 tablespoon butter, melted

1. Preheat oven to 350°. Grease a 9-in. springform pan; dust pan with ¼ cup bread crumbs.
2. Place potatoes in a Dutch oven; add water to cover. Bring to a boil. Reduce heat; cook, uncovered, 10-15 minutes or until tender. Drain; return to pan. Mash potatoes, gradually adding cream, cubed butter, chives, salt and pepper. Cool mixture slightly.
3. Add eggs, one at a time, stirring to blend after each addition. Spread half of potato mixture into prepared pan. Layer with cheese slices, ham and remaining potatoes. In a small bowl, mix Parmesan cheese and remaining bread crumbs; stir in butter. Sprinkle over potatoes.
4. Bake 35-40 minutes or until golden brown. Cool on a wire rack, 10 minutes. Loosen sides of cake from pan with a knife. Serve warm.

CHICKEN & SWISS CASSEROLE

It's nice to have an alternative to the traditional baked ham on Easter. This comforting casserole is always a crowd pleaser. Using rotisserie chicken from the deli keeps prep simple.
—Christina Petri, Alexandria, MN

Prep: 30 min. • **Bake:** 10 min.
Makes: 8 servings

5½ cups uncooked egg noodles (about ½ pound)
3 tablespoons olive oil
3 shallots, chopped
3 small garlic cloves, minced
⅓ cup all-purpose flour
2 cups chicken broth
¾ cup 2% milk
1½ teaspoons dried thyme
¾ teaspoon grated lemon peel
½ teaspoon salt
¼ teaspoon ground nutmeg
¼ teaspoon pepper
5 cups cubed rotisserie chicken
1½ cups frozen peas
2 cups shredded Swiss cheese
¾ cup dry bread crumbs
2 tablespoons butter, melted

1. Preheat oven to 350°. Cook noodles according to package directions; drain. In a large skillet, heat oil over medium heat. Add shallots and garlic; cook and stir 45 seconds. Stir in flour; cook and stir 1 minute. Add broth, milk, thyme, lemon peel, salt, nutmeg and pepper. Stir in the chicken and peas; heat through. Stir in noodles and cheese.
2. Transfer to a greased 13x9-in. baking dish. In a small bowl, mix bread crumbs and butter; sprinkle over top of casserole. Bake 8-10 minutes or until top is browned.

FROSTED CARROT CAKE COOKIES

CHOCOLATE-COCONUT LAYER BARS

I'm a huge fan of Nanaimo bars, the no-bake dessert named for the city in British Columbia. For fun, I reinvented this treat with coconut lovers in mind. See photo on page 135.
—Shannon Dobos, Calgary, AB

....

Prep: 20 min. + chilling
Makes: 3 dozen

- ¾ cup butter, cubed
- 3 cups Oreo cookie crumbs
- 2 cups sweetened shredded coconut
- ½ cup cream of coconut

FILLING
- ⅓ cup butter, softened
- 3 tablespoons cream of coconut
- ¼ teaspoon coconut extract
- 3 cups confectioners' sugar
- 1 to 2 tablespoons 2% milk

TOPPING
- 1½ cups semisweet chocolate chips
- 4 teaspoons canola oil
- 3 Mounds candy bars (1¾ ounces each), coarsely chopped, optional

1. Microwave butter on high until melted; stir until smooth. Stir in cookie crumbs, coconut and cream of coconut until blended (mixture will be wet). Spread onto bottom of an ungreased 13x9-in. baking pan. Refrigerate until set, about 30 minutes.
2. For the filling, beat butter, cream of coconut and extract until smooth. Gradually beat in confectioners' sugar and enough of the milk to reach a spreading consistency. Spread over crust.
3. For topping, microwave chocolate chips and oil until melted; stir until smooth. Cool slightly; spread over filling. If desired, sprinkle with chopped candy bars. Refrigerate.

FROSTED CARROT CAKE COOKIES

I took my favorite carrot cake recipe and slightly tweaked it to make cookies. Just like the cake, the yummy bites are filled with shredded carrot, pineapple and raisins—and topped with a homemade cream cheese frosting.
—Lawrence Earl, Sumner, MI

....

Prep: 30 min.
Bake: 10 min./batch + cooling
Makes: about 4½ dozen

- 1 cup butter, softened
- 1 cup sugar
- 1 cup packed brown sugar
- 2 large eggs
- 1 teaspoon vanilla extract
- 3 cups all-purpose flour
- 1 teaspoon baking soda
- ½ teaspoon salt
- 1 medium carrot, shredded
- ½ cup crushed pineapple, drained and patted dry
- ½ cup golden raisins

FROSTING
- 6 ounces cream cheese, softened
- 3¾ cups confectioners' sugar
- 1½ teaspoons vanilla extract
- 2 to 3 tablespoons 2% milk
  Toasted chopped walnuts, optional

1. Preheat oven to 350°. In a large bowl, cream butter, sugar and brown sugar until light and fluffy. Beat in eggs and vanilla. In another bowl, whisk flour, baking soda and salt; gradually beat into creamed mixture. Stir in carrot, pineapple and raisins.
2. Drop dough by tablespoonfuls 2 in. apart onto ungreased baking sheets. Bake cookies for 10-12 minutes or until light brown. Remove from pans to wire racks to cool completely.
3. In a small bowl, beat cream cheese until smooth. Gradually beat in the confectioners' sugar, vanilla and enough milk to reach a spreading consistency. Frost cookies. If desired, sprinkle with walnuts. Store in an airtight container in the refrigerator.

Freeze option: Drop dough by tablespoonfuls onto waxed paper-lined baking sheets; freeze until firm. Transfer to resealable plastic freezer bags; return to freezer. To use, bake the cookies as directed.

LEMON
LAYER CAKE

LEMON LAYER CAKE

This citrusy cake with a luscious cream cheese frosting will garner plenty of raves. The flavor, a duet of sweet and tangy notes, really sings.
—Summer Goddard, Springfield, VA

Prep: 35 min. • **Bake:** 25 min. + cooling
Makes: 12 servings

1 cup butter, softened
1½ cups sugar
2 large eggs
3 large egg yolks
1 tablespoon grated lemon peel
2 tablespoons lemon juice
¾ cup sour cream
¼ cup 2% milk
2½ cups all-purpose flour
1 teaspoon salt
1 teaspoon baking powder
½ teaspoon baking soda

SYRUP
½ cup sugar
½ cup lemon juice

FROSTING
2 packages (8 ounces each) cream
   cheese, softened
1 cup butter, softened
4 cups confectioners' sugar
1½ teaspoons lemon juice
⅛ teaspoon salt
   Lemon slices, optional

1. Preheat oven to 350°. Line bottoms of two greased 9-in. round baking pans with parchment paper; grease paper.
2. Cream butter and sugar until light and fluffy. Add eggs and egg yolks, one at a time, beating well after each addition. Beat in lemon peel and juice. In a small bowl, mix sour cream and milk. In another bowl, whisk together flour, salt, baking powder and baking soda; add to creamed mixture alternately with sour cream mixture.
3. Transfer to prepared pans. Bake until a toothpick inserted in center comes out clean, 24-28 minutes. Cool in pans 10 minutes before removing to wire racks; remove paper. Cool slightly.
4. For the syrup, in a small saucepan, combine sugar and lemon juice. Bring to a boil; cook until liquid is reduced by half. Cool completely.
5. For frosting, beat cream cheese and butter until smooth; beat in confectioners' sugar, lemon juice and salt until blended.
6. Using a long serrated knife, cut each cake horizontally in half. Brush layers with warm syrup; cool completely.
7. Place one cake layer on a serving plate; spread with 1 cup frosting. Repeat layers twice. Top with remaining cake layer. Frost top and sides with remaining frosting. If desired, top with lemon slices. Refrigerate any leftovers.

Easter Egg Luncheon

Hop to it this Easter with a lovely midday luncheon. As folks return from church services, egg hunts and other early-day festivities, their thoughts will turn to the delightful lineup of light and refreshing luncheon foods that await them.

This carefree, breezy menu is fast, fresh and easy. With everything from hearty sandwiches and dreamy desserts to the season's best salads and sides, each sunny favorite is guaranteed to wow your crowd. As a bonus, they're a snap to assemble, and some even can be made ahead to save you precious time on Easter Sunday.

This year, relax, have fun and keep it effortlessly simple with these ultra delicious recipes.

Fruity Chicken Salad Mini Sandwiches (p. 151) **Spinach-Orzo Salad with Chickpeas** (p. 147)

BAKED CRAB
WONTONS

BAKED CRAB WONTONS

These little crab bites put a smile on everyone's face. My family loves them for their size, texture and taste. I love them because they're quick and simple to make. They even won first prize in a cooking competition. Instead of baking them in the oven, you can deep fry them.
—Danielle Arcadi, Peoria, AZ

Start to Finish: 30 min.
Makes: 1½ dozen

- 18 wonton wrappers
  Cooking spray
- 4 ounces reduced-fat cream cheese
- ¼ cup reduced-fat mayonnaise
- ¼ teaspoon salt
- ¼ teaspoon pepper
- 1 can (6 ounces) crabmeat, drained, flaked and cartilage removed
- 2 green onions, thinly sliced
- ¼ cup shredded carrot
- ¼ cup finely chopped celery
  Sweet-and-sour sauce, optional

1. Preheat oven to 350°. Press wonton wrappers into greased mini muffin cups. Spritz wrappers with cooking spray. Bake until lightly browned, 5-7 minutes.
2. Beat cream cheese, mayonnaise, salt and pepper until smooth. Stir in remaining ingredients. Spoon into wonton cups. Bake until heated through, 9-11 minutes. If desired, serve wontons with sweet-and-sour sauce.

TOP TIP

Wonton Wrappers

One thing to keep in mind when using wonton wrappers is that they are delicate and dry out quickly. To avoid having them dry out and crack, place a clean damp towel over the opened package of wontons while using them. Also place an additional damp towel over the finished wontons until ready to cook and serve.

SPINACH-ORZO SALAD
WITH CHICKPEAS

SPINACH-ORZO SALAD WITH CHICKPEAS

The first version of this salad was an experiment in mixing together some random ingredients I had on hand. It was a success, and several people at the party asked for the recipe...which meant I had to re-create it! It's healthy, delicious and perfect for warm-weather days.
—Glen White, Kissimmee, FL

Start to Finish: 25 min.
Makes: 12 servings (¾ cup each)

- 1 can (14½ ounces) reduced-sodium chicken broth
- 1½ cups uncooked whole wheat orzo pasta
- 4 cups fresh baby spinach
- 2 cups grape tomatoes, halved
- 2 cans (15 ounces each) chickpeas or garbanzo beans, rinsed and drained
- ¾ cup chopped fresh parsley
- 2 green onions, chopped

DRESSING
- ¼ cup olive oil
- 3 tablespoons lemon juice
- ¾ teaspoon salt
- ¼ teaspoon garlic powder
- ¼ teaspoon hot pepper sauce
- ¼ teaspoon pepper

1. In a large saucepan, bring broth to a boil. Stir in the orzo; return to a boil. Reduce the heat; simmer, covered, until al dente, 8-10 minutes.
2. In a large bowl, toss spinach and warm orzo, allowing spinach to wilt slightly. Add the tomatoes, chickpeas, parsley and green onions.
3. Whisk together dressing ingredients. Toss with salad.

PINEAPPLE & COCONUT CARROT SALAD

I enjoyed a salad like this at a tropical-inspired restaurant. I tried to get the staff to give me the recipe but had no luck. So I went home and created my own! I will sometimes drain a can of mandarin orange slices and toss those in as well.
—Shirley Turpin, Williams, MN

Start to Finish: 20 min.
Makes: 12 servings (⅔ cup each)

- 1½ cups (12 ounces) sour cream
- ⅓ cup honey
- 2 teaspoons grated lime peel
- 3 tablespoons lime juice
- 2 teaspoons grated fresh gingerroot
- 1 teaspoon grated orange peel
- 1½ pounds carrots, shredded (about 5 cups)
- 1 can (20 ounces) unsweetened crushed pineapple, undrained
- 1½ cups flaked coconut
- 1½ cups golden raisins

In a large bowl, mix first six ingredients. Stir in the remaining ingredients. Refrigerate, covered, until serving.

PEPPER MANGO SALSA

Whenever I make this, the bowl is always left empty! The idea for a homemade mango salsa hit me after I saw a chef on television make something similar. It sounded so good, and it wasn't something I could find in a store at the time. The salsa is especially tasty served with artisan chips—the black bean and roasted garlic ones are my favorite. When strawberries are in season, I add them into the mix, too.
—Wendy Rusch, Cameron, WI

Prep: 15 min. + chilling
Makes: 6 cups

- 3 tablespoons lime juice
- 3 tablespoons honey
- 1 teaspoon olive oil
  Dash salt
  Dash coarsely ground pepper
- 3 medium mangoes, peeled and finely chopped
- 2 cups finely chopped fresh pineapple
- 1 large sweet red pepper, finely chopped

- 1 Anaheim or poblano pepper, seeded and finely chopped
- ½ cup finely chopped red onion
- ¼ cup chopped fresh cilantro
  Tortilla chips

1. Whisk together first five ingredients. In a large bowl, combine fruit, peppers, onion and cilantro; toss with lime juice mixture.

2. Refrigerate, covered, 1 hour to allow flavors to blend. Stir before serving. Serve with chips.

PARMESAN SNAP PEA PASTA

My family loves pasta! This simple dish is always a hit, especially during the spring when sugar snap peas are the sweetest. To keep us from getting in a rut, I change up the flavors.
—Crystal Jo Bruns, Iliff, CO

Start to Finish: 30 min.
Makes: 12 servings (¾ cup each)

- 1 pound fresh sugar snap peas (about 5 cups), trimmed
- 1 package (16 ounces) angel hair pasta
- 5 tablespoons olive oil, divided
- 1 medium red onion, finely chopped
- 3 garlic cloves, minced
- ½ teaspoon salt
- ¼ teaspoon crushed red pepper flakes
- ⅛ teaspoon coarsely ground pepper
- 1¼ cups grated Parmesan cheese, divided

1. In a 6-qt. stockpot, bring 16 cups water to a boil. Add peas; cook, uncovered, just until crisp-tender, 3-4 minutes. Using a strainer, remove peas from pot.

2. In same pot, add pasta to boiling water; cook according to package directions. Drain, reserving 1 cup cooking water; return to pot. Toss with 3 tablespoons oil.

3. In a large skillet, heat remaining oil over medium heat; saute the onion until tender, 2-3 minutes. Add garlic and seasonings; cook and stir 1 minute. Stir in the peas; heat through.

4. Toss with pasta, adding 1 cup cheese and reserved cooking water as desired. Sprinkle with remaining cheese.

HAM & SWISS BRAIDS

Satisfy hearty appetites with these golden loaves. Each slice is like a hot sandwich packed with ham, broccoli and Swiss cheese. Hot pepper sauce adds a nice kick, while refrigerated crescent rolls make it extra easy. The braids are perfect for a special occasion lunch or as an appetizer.
—Donna McCord, Fishers, IN

Prep: 30 min. • **Bake:** 25 min.
Makes: 2 loaves (6 servings each)

- ¾ cup mayonnaise
- 2 tablespoons Dijon mustard
- 2 tablespoons honey
- ⅛ teaspoon hot pepper sauce
- 2 cups chopped fully cooked ham (about 10 ounces)
- 1 cup (4 ounces) shredded Swiss cheese or crumbled goat cheese
- 1 cup chopped fresh broccoli florets
- 1 cup chopped fresh spinach
- 2 tubes (8 ounces each) refrigerated crescent rolls
- 1 large egg white, lightly beaten

1. Preheat oven to 375°. For filling, mix first four ingredients; stir in ham, cheese and vegetables.

2. Unroll one tube of crescent dough onto an ungreased baking sheet; seal perforations to form one long rectangle. Spoon half of the filling lengthwise down center third of rectangle. On each long side, cut 1-in. wide strips at an angle to within ½ in. of filling. Starting at one end, fold alternating strips at an angle across filling; seal ends. Brush with egg white. Repeat with remaining dough and filling.

3. Bake 20-25 minutes or until dark golden brown, rotating pans halfway through baking. Cool braids 5 minutes before slicing.

**FRUITY CHICKEN SALAD
MINI SANDWICHES**

FRUITY CHICKEN SALAD MINI SANDWICHES

Chicken salad ranks among the classics, and this version is great for parties of all kinds. Feel free to substitute green grapes for the red, or toss in extra strawberries when they're in season. The filling can also be served on a bed of salad greens.
—Marcy Kamery, Blasdell, NY

....

Start to Finish: 25 min.
Makes: 12 servings

- 6 cups chopped cooked chicken
- ¾ cup sliced fresh strawberries
- ½ cup halved seedless red grapes
- 2 celery ribs, finely chopped
- ⅓ cup chopped pecans, toasted
- ¾ cup sour cream
- ¾ cup mayonnaise
- ⅓ cup chopped fresh basil
- 2 teaspoons lemon juice
- ¾ teaspoon salt
- ¼ teaspoon garlic powder
- ¼ teaspoon pepper
- 24 potato dinner rolls or Hawaiian sweet rolls, split

1. Place first five ingredients in a large bowl. In a small bowl, mix the sour cream, mayonnaise, basil, lemon juice and the seasonings; stir into the chicken mixture. Refrigerate, covered, until serving.
2. To serve, fill each sandwich with ⅓ cup chicken mixture.

Note: To toast nuts, bake in a shallow pan in a 350° oven for 5-10 minutes, or cook nuts in a skillet over low heat until lightly browned, stirring occasionally.

BLACK RASPBERRY BARS

Black raspberries are a rare treat. Their flavor is sweeter than raspberries and more intense than blackberries. Black raspberries and black raspberry preserves can be hard to find if you don't live in a region where they're common. These bars also taste divine with apricot jam or fruit preserves of your choice.
—Penny Carey, Oxford, IN

....

Prep: 20 min. • **Bake:** 35 min. + cooling
Makes: 3 dozen

- ¾ cup butter, softened
- 1 cup sugar
- 1 large egg
- ½ teaspoon vanilla extract
- 2 cups all-purpose flour
- ¼ teaspoon baking powder
- 1½ cups flaked coconut
- ⅔ cup chopped walnuts
- 1 jar (10 ounces) seedless black raspberry preserves

1. Preheat oven to 350°. Cream butter and sugar until light and fluffy. Beat in the egg and vanilla. In another bowl, whisk together the flour and baking powder; gradually beat into creamed mixture. Stir in coconut and walnuts.
2. Reserve ¾ cup dough for topping. Press remaining dough onto the bottom of a greased 13x9-in. pan. Spread with preserves. Crumble reserved dough over top of bars.
3. Bake until golden brown, 35-40 minutes. Cool in pan on a wire rack. Cut into bars.

TOP TIP

Chicken Salad Bake

After a recent party, I had lots of leftover chicken salad. My family had our fill of sandwiches, so I decided to turn it into a lively leftover casserole. I mixed the chicken salad with cream of chicken soup, chopped sweet red pepper and coarsely crushed Triscuit crackers. I put the mixture in a 13x9-in. baking dish and baked it at 350° for about 25 minutes. Then I topped it with more crushed crackers and baked it for an additional 10 minutes. It was terrific. In fact, next time chicken salad is on the menu, I plan to make extra just so I can fix this tasty hot dish.
—Tricia J., Atlanta, GA

GLAZED CHOCOLATE ANGEL FOOD CAKE

GLAZED CHOCOLATE ANGEL FOOD CAKE

It's OK to lose track of how many slices of this delightful cake you eat. Light as air and loaded with big chocolate flavor, it's a guilt-free dessert that will become a standby at all your gatherings. Add fresh strawberries or raspberries and a dollop of sweetened whipped cream if desired.
—Mary Relyea, Canastota, NY

Prep: 20 min. • **Bake:** 40 min. + cooling
Makes: 12 servings

- 1½ cups egg whites (about 10 large)
- 1 cup cake flour
- 2 cups sugar, divided
- ½ cup baking cocoa
- 1 teaspoon cream of tartar
- 1 teaspoon vanilla extract
- ¼ teaspoon salt
- GLAZE
- ½ cup semisweet chocolate chips
- 3 tablespoons half-and-half cream

1. Place egg whites in a large bowl; let stand at room temperature 30 minutes.
2. Preheat oven to 350°. Sift flour, 1 cup sugar and cocoa together twice.
3. Add cream of tartar, vanilla and salt to egg whites; beat on medium speed until soft peaks form. Gradually add remaining sugar, 2 tablespoons at a time, beating on high after each addition until the sugar is dissolved. Continue beating until stiff glossy peaks form. Gradually fold in flour mixture, about ½ cup at a time.
4. Gently transfer to an ungreased 10-in. tube pan. Cut through batter with a knife to remove air pockets. Bake on lowest oven rack 40-50 minutes or until top springs back when lightly touched and cracks feel dry. Immediately invert pan; cool completely in pan, about 1 hour.
5. Run a knife around sides and center tube of pan. Remove cake to a serving plate. For glaze, in a microwave, melt chocolate chips with cream; stir until smooth. Drizzle over cake.

APRICOT COOLER

A mingling of apricot, pineapple and lemon flavors makes this soothing sipper so refreshing. I first tried it years ago at an outdoor wedding shower. It's the perfect complement not just for Easter but for any spring luncheon or buffet.
—Julie Peterson, Crofton, MD

Start to Finish: 10 min.
Makes: 12 servings (1 cup each)

- 1 can (12 ounces) frozen lemonade concentrate
- 1½ cups cold water
- 3 cups apricot nectar
- 3 cups unsweetened pineapple juice
- 2 cans (12 ounces each) lemon-lime soda, chilled
- Lemon slices
- Ice cubes

In a large pitcher, mix the lemonade concentrate and cold water. Stir in nectar, pineapple juice, soda and lemon slices. Serve over ice.

TWO-BERRY FLUFF SALAD

This fluffy salad is a welcome treat on warm Texas afternoons. Because there's a blueberry orchard near our home, we often pick fresh berries to use in this recipe and others. When blueberries and strawberries aren't in season, you can substitute frozen berries with equally good results.
—Karen Wenzel, Conroe, TX

Start to Finish: 15 min.
Makes: 12 servings (¾ cup each)

- 1 package (8 ounces) cream cheese, softened
- 1½ cups confectioners' sugar
- 2 cups heavy whipping cream
- 8 cups fresh strawberries (about 2 pounds), sliced
- 2 cups fresh blueberries
- Additional fresh strawberries and blueberries, optional

1. In a large bowl, beat cream cheese and confectioners' sugar until smooth. Slowly add cream, beating until thick and fluffy.
2. Fold in 8 cups strawberries and 2 cups blueberries. If desired, top salad with additional berries.

**TWO-BERRY
FLUFF SALAD**

5-Ingredient Easter Dinner

Easter dinner will practically fix itself with these fabulously simple recipes. Here you'll find dishes with no more than five ingredients (not counting water, salt, pepper and oil). Feast on starters, sides, delicious Bourbon-Spiced Glazed Ham (p. 160) for a main, and sweet dessert options such as Strawberry Shortcake Stacks (p. 163). Yum!

They may have fewer ingredients—and some take only minutes to prepare—but these dishes are full of flavor and aim to please. So if you're looking for something on the uncomplicated side, look here.

You'll be delighted by how easy it is to prepare your Easter meal, and your guests will be amazed at how terrific it tastes!

Buttery Carrots (p. 159) **Bourbon-Spiced Glazed Ham** (p. 160) **Easy Biscuit Muffins** (p. 160)

PESTO-GOAT CHEESE TOASTS

I came across this recipe years ago. Everyone who tries these little toasts absolutely loves them. The pesto is easy to find in the grocery store, and it blends beautifully with the tangy, creamy goat cheese.
—Jennifer Kunz, Troy, MI

Start to Finish: 20 min.
Makes: 16 servings

- 16 slices French bread (½ inch thick)
- 1 log (11 ounces) fresh goat cheese, cut into 16 slices
- 3 tablespoons prepared pesto

1. Preheat oven to 425°. Place bread slices on a baking sheet; top with cheese.
2. Bake until cheese begins to brown and bread is toasted, 10-12 minutes. Top with pesto. Serve warm.

LEMON-DILL CUCUMBER DIP

Fat-free Greek-style yogurt gives this quick and flavorful dip a rich, creamy texture. It's perfect served with fresh, crunchy veggies or toasted whole-wheat pita bread. The flavors are flexible, so customizing to taste is easy—add more cucumber for extra crunch or a little more garlic for extra bite.
—Jeremy McCarty, Asheville, NC

Prep: 10 min. + chilling
Makes: 12 servings (¼ cup each)

- 2½ cups fat-free plain Greek yogurt
- 1 small cucumber, peeled, seeded and finely chopped
- 2 tablespoons snipped fresh dill or 2 teaspoons dill weed
- 3 garlic cloves, minced
- 2 teaspoons grated lemon peel
- ¾ teaspoon salt
- ¼ teaspoon pepper
  Additional dill and lemon peel, optional

In a small bowl, mix the first seven ingredients; refrigerate, covered, until flavors are blended, about 1 hour. If desired, sprinkle with additional dill and lemon peel before serving.

How to Make Pesto

For a fresh twist, prepare your own homemade pesto. It calls for more than five ingredients, but you'll be pleasantly surprised how quick and easy it is to make using a food processor.

Start to Finish: 15 min. • **Makes:** 1¼ cups

- 2 cups loosely packed basil leaves
- 1 cup loosely packed Italian parsley
- ¼ cup slivered almonds, toasted
- 2 garlic cloves
- 4 teaspoons grated lemon peel
- ⅓ cup lemon juice
- 2 tablespoons honey
- ½ teaspoon salt
- ½ cup olive oil
- ½ cup grated Parmesan cheese

PLACE BASIL, parsley, slivered almonds and garlic in a small food processor; pulse until chopped.

ADD LEMON PEEL, lemon juice, honey and salt; process until blended. Continue processing while gradually adding oil in a steady stream.

ADD CHEESE; pulse until the mixture is blended.

STORE in an airtight container in the refrigerator for up to 1 week.

**PESTO-GOAT CHEESE
TOASTS**

FAVA BEAN &
PEA SALAD

FAVA BEAN & PEA SALAD

This is a springtime staple in my house; my mom has been making it forever. I know that when the favas are at the market I can always find this refreshing and tasty salad in her fridge! If fresh favas or peas are not available, frozen is fine—but if you use frozen favas, remember take off the tough outer skin.
—Francesca Ferenczi, New York, NY

Prep: 55 min. • **Cook:** 25 min.
Makes: 12 servings (¾ cup each)

- 3 cups shelled fresh fava beans (about 4 pounds unshelled) or 1 package (28 ounces) frozen fava beans, thawed
- 8 cups shelled fresh peas (about 8 pounds unshelled) or 8 cups frozen peas (about 32 ounces)
- 3 tablespoons olive oil, divided
- 4 ounces diced pancetta
- 8 shallots, thinly sliced
- ½ teaspoon salt
- ¼ teaspoon pepper

BUTTERY CARROTS

1. For fresh fava beans, add beans to a large pot of boiling water; return to a boil. Cook, uncovered, until tender, 4-5 minutes. Using a strainer, remove beans to a bowl of ice water to cool. Drain cooled beans; squeeze gently to remove skins. (If using frozen fava beans, prepare according to package directions.)
2. For fresh peas, add peas to boiling water; return to a boil. Cook, uncovered, just until tender, 2-4 minutes. Drain well; place in a large bowl. (If using frozen peas, cook according to package directions.)
3. In a large skillet, heat 1 tablespoon oil over medium heat. Add pancetta; cook and stir until crisp, about 5 minutes. Drain on paper towels, reserving drippings.
4. In the same pan, heat remaining oil and reserved drippings over medium heat. Add shallots; cook and stir until tender and lightly browned, 5-6 minutes. Stir in fava beans and heat through. Add to peas; stir in salt, pepper and pancetta. Serve warm.
Note: Three cups frozen shelled edamame may be substituted for fava beans; prepare according to package directions.

BUTTERY CARROTS

My mother made this recipe often when I was growing up. She got it from a friend who was a chef at a local restaurant my parents frequented. The onions really bring out the sweetness of the carrots. When I have carrots fresh from the garden, I don't even peel them, just scrub them well before cutting. For holiday buffets, I often double or triple this recipe.
—Mary Ellen Chambers, Lakewood, OH

Start to Finish: 20 min.
Makes: 12 servings (¾ cup each)

- 3 pounds medium carrots, halved crosswise and cut into strips
- 2 medium onions, halved and thinly sliced
- ½ cup butter, melted
- ½ cup chopped fresh parsley
- ½ teaspoon salt
  Coarsely ground pepper, optional

1. Place 2 in. of water in a 6-qt. stockpot. Add carrots and onions; bring to a boil. Reduce heat; simmer, covered, until carrots are crisp-tender, 10-12 minutes.
2. Drain the vegetables. Toss with remaining ingredients.

SAUTEED RADISHES

Who says radishes only belong in salads? Sauteed in wine and tarragon, these may just change the way you look at radishes forever. These can be served on their own, or added to your favorite au gratin recipe.
—*Taste of Home* Test Kitchen

Start to Finish: 25 min.
Makes: 12 servings (¾ cup each)

- ½ cup unsalted butter, cubed
- 6 pounds radishes, quartered (about 9 cups)
- ¼ cup white wine or water
- 2 teaspoons minced fresh tarragon or ½ teaspoon dried tarragon
- ½ teaspoon salt
- ¼ teaspoon pepper

In a 6-qt. stockpot, heat butter over medium heat. Add radishes; cook and stir for 2 minutes. Stir in wine; increase heat to medium-high. Cook, uncovered, until radishes are crisp-tender, 8-10 minutes. Stir in tarragon, salt and pepper.

BOURBON-SPICED GLAZED HAM

This bourbon-spiked ham makes a wonderful main course for a holiday feast. Any leftovers (if there are any leftovers) make great sandwiches.
—Karen Sublett-Young, Princeton, IN

Prep: 20 min. + marinating
Bake: 3 hours
Makes: 16 servings

- 7 to 9 pounds fully cooked bone-in ham
- 1 cup packed brown sugar
- 1 cup orange juice
- 1 cup bourbon
- 1½ teaspoons ground cloves

1. Place ham in a large resealable plastic bag. Whisk together remaining ingredients until blended; pour into bag. Seal bag and turn to coat. Refrigerate for 8 hours or overnight.
2. Preheat oven to 325°. Remove ham from marinade and place on a rack in a roasting pan; reserve remaining marinade, placing it in the refrigerator until ready to baste.
3. Using a sharp knife, score surface of ham with ¼-in. deep cuts in a diamond pattern. Bake, covered, 2 hours.
4. Baste with about half of the reserved marinade. Bake, uncovered, 1 to 1½ hours longer or until a thermometer reads 140°, basting two more times during the first half hour.

BROWNED BUTTER RED POTATOES

I've been making my own version of my Dad's potatoes for years, and it goes great with any meal. Browning the butter gives the potatoes a whole new taste.
—Anne Pavelak, Endicott, WA

Start to Finish: 30 min.
Makes: 12 servings (¾ cup each)

- 16 medium red potatoes (about 4 pounds), quartered
- 1 cup butter, cubed
- 6 to 8 garlic cloves, minced
- 2 teaspoons salt
- 1 teaspoon pepper

1. Place potatoes in a 6-qt. stockpot; add water to cover. Bring to a boil. Reduce heat; cook, uncovered, 15-20 minutes or until tender. Drain; return to pot.
2. Meanwhile, in a small heavy saucepan, melt butter over medium heat. Heat for 5-7 minutes or until light golden brown, stirring constantly. Stir in garlic; cook 30 seconds longer or until butter is golden brown. Add to potatoes; sprinkle with salt and pepper. Toss gently to combine.

EASY BISCUIT MUFFINS

Simple homemade biscuits, made with readily available ingredients—you'd never know there's mayonnaise in them! It's easy to adapt this recipe for jumbo-sized muffin tins; just give them a little more baking time.
—Taryn Ellis, Wyoming, MI

Prep: 10 min. • **Bake:** 25 min.
Makes: 1 dozen

- 3 cups all-purpose flour
- 4 teaspoons baking powder
- 1½ teaspoons sugar
- 1 teaspoon salt
- 1½ cups whole milk
- ½ cup mayonnaise

1. Preheat oven to 350°. Whisk together first four ingredients. In another bowl, whisk milk and mayonnaise until blended; add to dry ingredients, stirring just until moistened (batter will be thick).
2. Spoon ¼ cup mixture into each of 12 greased or paper-lined muffin cups. Bake until golden brown, 25-30 minutes. Cool for 5 minutes before removing from pan to a wire rack. Serve warm.

CLOCKWISE FROM TOP:
BUTTERY CARROTS (PAGE 159);
BOURBON-SPICED GLAZED HAM;
EASY BISCUIT MUFFINS

**STRAWBERRY
SHORTCAKE
STACKS**

STRAWBERRY SHORTCAKE STACKS

When my wonderful friend Kelly brought me a pint of strawberries, I didn't want to just eat them straight (tempting as it was). I decided to make strawberry shortcake with my own pretty, elegant spin. These light and airy puff pastry stacks let the fruit really shine.
—Jenny Dubinsky, Inwood, WV

Prep: 25 min. • **Bake:** 15 min. + cooling
Makes: 12 servings

- 1 sheet frozen puff pastry, thawed
- 4 cups fresh strawberries, sliced
- ¼ cup plus 3 tablespoons sugar, divided
- 1½ cups heavy whipping cream
- ½ teaspoon vanilla extract

1. Preheat oven to 400°. On a lightly floured surface, roll puff pastry to a 10-in. square; cut into 12 rectangles (approximately 3x2½-in.). Place on ungreased baking sheets. Bake until golden brown, 12-15 minutes. Remove to wire racks; cool completely.
2. In a large bowl, toss strawberries with ¼ cup sugar. Let stand for 30 minutes, stirring occasionally. In another bowl, beat cream until it begins to thicken. Add vanilla and remaining sugar; beat until stiff peaks form.
3. To serve, split pastries horizontally in half. Top each bottom half with 2 tablespoons whipped cream and 1 tablespoon strawberries; replace top half. Top with remaining whipped cream and strawberries.

TOP TIP

A Different Take on Strawberry Shortcake

Instead of sugar, I add frozen juice concentrate to the berries when I make strawberry shortcake. It adds an unexpected but fun flavor.
—Beth W., Tyler, TX

RHUBARB LEMONADE SLUSH

My family loves rhubarb, and this is such a fun way to enjoy it. It's nice to have in the freezer and bring out when guests drop by. Even people that aren't crazy about rhubarb enjoy it.
—Cathie Beard, Philomath, OR

Prep: 30 min. + freezing
Makes: 12 servings (1 cup each)

- 3 cups chopped fresh or frozen rhubarb
- 1 cup water
- ⅓ cup sugar
- 1 cup vodka
- ¾ cup thawed pink lemonade concentrate
- 1 bottle (2 liters) lemon-lime soda, chilled

1. In large saucepan combine rhubarb, water and sugar; bring to a boil. Reduce heat; simmer, covered, 5 minutes or until rhubarb is tender. Cool slightly.
2. Puree mixture in a blender; transfer to a 1-qt. freezer container. Stir in vodka and lemonade concentrate. Freeze, covered, until firm, at least 8 hours.
3. To serve, transfer mixture to a pitcher; stir in soda. Or, for each serving, place ⅓ cup rhubarb mixture in an 8-oz. glass; stir in ⅔ cup soda.

ROSEMARY-LEMON SHORTBREAD SANDWICH COOKIES

These beautiful shortbread sandwich cookies are always a welcome addition to our annual ladies holiday tea luncheon. The distinctive rosemary flavor, paired so well with the tangy lemon curd, has made them a favorite in our group for years!
—Jamie Jones, Madison, GA

Prep: 25 min. + chilling
Bake: 10 min./batch + cooling
Makes: about 2 dozen

- 1 cup butter, softened
- ¾ cup confectioners' sugar
- 2 cups all-purpose flour
- 4 teaspoons minced fresh rosemary
- ¼ teaspoon salt
- ½ cup lemon curd
  Additional confectioners' sugar

1. Cream butter and confectioners' sugar until light and fluffy. In another bowl, mix flour, rosemary and salt; gradually beat into creamed mixture. Divide dough in half. Shape each into a disk; wrap in plastic. Refrigerate until firm enough to roll, about 30 minutes.
2. Preheat oven to 350°. On a lightly floured surface, roll each portion of dough to ¼-in. thickness. Cut with a floured 2-in. round cookie cutter. Using a floured ⅞-in. round cookie cutter, cut out the centers of half of the cookies. Place solid and window cookies 1 in. apart on ungreased baking sheets.
3. Bake cookies until set, 9-11 minutes. Remove from pans to wire racks to cool completely.
4. To serve, spread lemon curd on bottoms of solid cookies; top with window cookies. Dust with additional confectioners' sugar.

GINGER BERRY COMPOTE

I make this dessert in the spring and summertime, and it's always a big hit. Serve it over angel food cake, ice cream or even over yogurt for breakfast. Delicious!
—Rebecca Cattell, Indianapolis, IN

Start to Finish: 20 min.
Makes: 20 servings (2 tablespoons each)

- 2 packages (12 ounces each) frozen unsweetened mixed berries
- ¼ cup sugar
- 1 teaspoon minced fresh gingerroot or ¼ teaspoon ground ginger
- 1 teaspoon grated orange peel

In a large saucepan, combine all the ingredients. Cook, uncovered, over medium heat until berries have softened and released their juices, 12-15 minutes, stirring occasionally. Serve warm or refrigerate and serve cold.

Spring Staples

When spring arrives, so do a host of delectable ingredients! Fresh is the name of the game, with early-harvest garden herbs and vegetables hitting the table along with seafood and spring lamb.

With the change in season, hearty, warming meals are put aside along with winter sweaters, but the weather's mild enough to still look forward to turning on the stove for the right dish. It's the perfect time for quick skillet meals, light pasta dishes, vegetable soups and wraps—plus tasty desserts!

This lineup of seasonal favorites brings traditional springtime ingredients to the front of the line for the springiest spread around!

Lemony Shrimp & Snow Pea Pasta (p. 169)

HERB-VINAIGRETTE POTATO SALAD

HERB-VINAIGRETTE POTATO SALAD

This is a great way to celebrate early produce from the garden. To add some more crunch, sprinkle with croutons.
—Debra Keil, Owasso, OK

Prep: 10 min. • **Cook:** 25 min.
Makes: 12 servings (¾ cup each)

- 3 **pounds small red potatoes, quartered**
- 1 **pound fresh asparagus, trimmed and cut into 2-inch pieces**
- 2 **cups sliced radishes**
- 6 **green onions, sliced**
- 2 **tablespoons chopped fresh chives**
- 2 **tablespoons chopped fresh parsley**

VINAIGRETTE
- ¾ **cup olive oil**
- ¼ **cup champagne vinegar or white vinegar**
- 1 **tablespoon Dijon mustard**
- ½ **teaspoon salt**
- ¼ **teaspoon coarsely ground pepper**

1. Place potatoes in a large saucepan; add water to cover. Bring to a boil. Reduce heat; cook, uncovered, for 10-15 minutes or until tender. Remove potatoes with a slotted spoon; cool. Return water to a boil. Add asparagus; cook, uncovered, for 2-3 minutes or just until crisp-tender. Remove asparagus and immediately drop into ice water. Drain and pat dry.

2. Transfer the potatoes and asparagus to a large bowl; add radishes, green onions and herbs. In a small bowl, whisk the vinaigrette ingredients until blended. Pour over potato mixture; toss gently to coat. Serve at room temperature or chilled. Stir before serving.

LEEK PROSCIUTTO PIZZA

This pizza is crazy good! It pops with flavor from caramelized leeks and garlic. The sweet onion is perfectly balanced by the salty prosciutto. I roast my own tomatoes when I have an abundance, but if you don't have fresh, canned tomatoes also work great. Don't be afraid of the four cloves of garlic—you'll love them.
—Trisha Kruse, Eagle, ID

Prep: 20 min. • **Bake:** 15 min.
Makes: 6 servings

- 1 **prebaked 12-inch pizza crust**
- 1 **tablespoon olive oil**
- 2 **medium leeks (white portion only), sliced**
- ½ **medium sweet onion, thinly sliced**
- 4 **garlic cloves, minced**
- 1 **cup fire-roasted diced tomatoes**
- 4 **ounces thinly sliced prosciutto**
- 2 **cups shredded part-skim mozzarella cheese**

1. Preheat oven to 425°. Place crust on an ungreased 12-in. pizza pan. In a large skillet, heat oil over medium-high heat. Add leeks and onion; cook and stir for 7-9 minutes or until lightly browned. Add garlic; cook and stir 1 minute longer.

2. Spread crust with tomatoes; top with the leek mixture, prosciutto and cheese. Bake for 12-15 minutes or until the edges are lightly browned.

CARROT-PARSNIP SOUP

Warm and comforting, this delicious soup makes a pretty presentation. Easy to prepare, it's a treat to serve for family dinners and special enough for guests.
—Lisa Speer, Palm Beach, FL

Prep: 15 min. • **Cook:** 20 min.
Makes: 4 servings

- 2 **tablespoons plus 1 cup peanut oil, divided**
- 1 **medium onion, chopped**
- ¾ **teaspoon ground cinnamon**
- ¼ **teaspoon salt**
- ¼ **teaspoon ground nutmeg**
- ⅛ **teaspoon coarsely ground pepper**
- 2 **garlic cloves, minced**
- 1 **pound medium carrots**
- 2 **medium parsnips, peeled and chopped**
- 4 **cups chicken stock**
- ½ **cup half-and-half cream**
  Minced chives, optional

1. In a large saucepan, heat 2 tablespoons oil over medium-high heat. Add onion, cinnamon, salt, nutmeg and pepper. Cook and stir for 6-8 minutes or until onion is tender. Add garlic; cook and stir 1 minute. Set 1 carrot aside; chop the remaining carrots. Add chopped carrots, parsnips and stock to onion mixture; bring to a boil. Reduce heat; simmer, covered, for 20-25 minutes or until the vegetables are tender.

2. Remove the soup from heat; cool slightly. Process in batches in a blender until smooth. Return soup to the pan; keep warm. Using a vegetable peeler, shave the remaining carrot lengthwise into very thin strips. In a small saucepan, heat remaining oil over medium-high heat. Fry the carrot strips for 2-3 minutes or until crispy, stirring occasionally. Drain on paper towels.

3. Gently reheat soup; stir in cream. Divide soup among four bowls. Top with the carrot strips and, if desired, chives.

CARROT-PARSNIP SOUP

PORK & VEGETABLE SPRING ROLLS

Rice paper wrappers are a quick, fun way to put salad ingredients into a hand-held snack or meal. Sometimes I switch things up and make this with shrimp or add cranberries. Go ahead, experiment!
—Marla Strader, Ozark, MO

Start to Finish: 30 min.
Makes: 4 servings

- 2 cups thinly sliced romaine
- 1½ cups cubed cooked pork
- 1 cup thinly sliced fresh spinach
- ¾ cup julienned carrot
- ⅓ cup thinly sliced celery
- ⅓ cup dried cherries, coarsely chopped
- 1 tablespoon sesame oil
- 12 round rice paper wrappers (8 inches)
- ¼ cup sliced almonds
- ¼ cup wasabi-coated green peas
  Sesame ginger salad dressing

1. In a large bowl, combine the first six ingredients. Drizzle with oil; toss to coat (image 1).
2. Fill a large shallow dish partway with water. Dip a rice paper wrapper into the water just until pliable, about 45 seconds (do not soften completely); allow the excess water to drip off (image 2).
3. Place wrapper on a flat surface. Layer salad mixture, almonds and peas across bottom third of wrapper (image 3). Fold in both sides of wrapper; fold the bottom edge over filling (image 4), then roll up tightly. Place on a serving plate, seam side down. Repeat with the remaining ingredients. Serve with dressing.

HOW-TO

How to Make Spring Rolls

Spring rolls look impressive, but they're easy to make. Two basic rules for spring-roll success—don't oversoak your wrapper and don't overstuff your roll!

PORK & VEGETABLE SPRING ROLLS

LEMONY SHRIMP & SNOW PEA PASTA

This pretty pasta is a family favorite—the kids love the light lemony flavor and I love that they devour the fresh veggies. You can use other types of pasta noodles for variety, like bow ties or corkscrews. See photo on page 165.
—Jennifer Fisher, Austin, TX

Start to Finish: 30 min.
Makes: 6 servings

- 1¾ cups uncooked gemelli or spiral pasta
- 2 tablespoons olive oil, divided
- 2 cups fresh snow peas
- 1 pound uncooked shrimp (26-30 per pound), peeled and deveined
- 3 garlic cloves, minced
- ¾ teaspoon salt, divided
- ¼ teaspoon plus ⅛ teaspoon pepper, divided
- 1 cup grape tomatoes, halved

DRESSING
- ¼ cup lemon juice
- 2 tablespoons chopped fresh parsley
- 2 tablespoons olive oil
- 2 garlic cloves, minced
- 2 teaspoons grated lemon peel
  Additional grated lemon peel and chopped fresh parsley, optional

1. Cook pasta according to the package directions. Meanwhile, in a large nonstick skillet, heat 1 tablespoon oil over medium heat. Add the peas; cook and stir for 2-3 minutes or until crisp-tender. Remove and keep warm.

2. In the same pan, heat the remaining oil over medium-high heat. Add shrimp; cook and stir for 2-3 minutes or until the shrimp turn pink. Add garlic, ½ teaspoon salt and ¼ teaspoon pepper; cook and stir 1 minute longer.

3. Drain the pasta, reserving ½ cup of the pasta water. Add pasta to the shrimp mixture; stir in peas and tomatoes. In a small bowl, whisk together lemon juice, parsley, oil, garlic, lemon peel and the remaining salt and pepper. Pour over the shrimp mixture; toss to coat, adding enough of the reserved pasta water to moisten the pasta. If desired, sprinkle with additional lemon peel and parsley.

MUSHROOM & SPINACH EGGS BENEDICT

Eggs Benedict is a great dish to experiment with, and this is my favorite version. The earthy flavors of mushrooms and spinach blend beautifully in this new twist on an old classic.
—Elizabeth Dumont, Madison, MS

Prep: 45 min. • **Cook:** 15 min.
Makes: 6 servings

- 12 slices pancetta
- 2 tablespoons butter
- 4 cups sliced assorted fresh mushrooms
- 2 shallots, chopped
- 2 garlic cloves, minced
- ¼ cup balsamic vinegar
- 16 cups fresh spinach
- ¼ teaspoon pepper
- ⅛ teaspoon salt
- 1 tablespoon white vinegar
- 12 large eggs

HOLLANDAISE SAUCE
- 3 large egg yolks
- ¼ cup water
- 2 tablespoons lemon juice
- 1 cup butter, melted
- ¼ teaspoon salt
- ⅛ teaspoon pepper
- 6 English muffins, split and toasted
  Minced chives

1. In a large skillet, cook pancetta over medium heat until crisp. Remove with a slotted spoon; drain on paper towels.
2. In the same skillet, melt butter. Add mushrooms and shallots. Cook and stir over medium heat until tender. Add garlic; cook 1 minute longer. Stir in balsamic vinegar. Bring to a boil; cook until liquid is almost evaporated. Add spinach, pepper and salt; cook until the spinach is wilted.
3. Place 2-3 in. of water in a large skillet with high sides; add white vinegar. Bring to a boil; reduce heat and simmer gently. Working in batches, break cold eggs, one at a time, into a custard cup or saucer; holding the cup close to the surface of the water, slip each egg into water.
4. Cook, uncovered, until the egg whites are completely set and the yolks are still soft, about 4 minutes.
5. For the sauce, in a double boiler or metal bowl over simmering water, constantly whisk egg yolks, water and lemon juice until mixture reaches 160°

or is thick enough to coat the back of a spoon. Reduce heat to low. Very slowly drizzle in warm melted butter, whisking constantly. Whisk in salt and pepper.
6. With a slotted spoon, lift eggs out of the water. On each muffin half, layer pancetta, the mushroom mixture and an egg; spoon sauce over top. Sprinkle with chives. Serve immediately.

SALMON PATTIES WITH GARLIC-DILL SAUCE

These cute little patties are a great way to get my whole family to enjoy salmon, even my toddler! And I love the fresh flavor the lemon and dill add.
—Brandi Murphy, McMinnville, TN

Prep: 45 min. + chiling
Cook: 10 min./batch
Makes: 6 servings (¾ cup sauce)

- ¾ cup mayonnaise
- 1 small garlic clove, minced
- 1½ teaspoons lemon juice
- 1½ teaspoons grated lemon peel
- ¼ teaspoon dill weed
  Pinch cayenne pepper
  Dash salt

SALMON
- 4 frozen salmon fillets (4 ounces each), thawed
- ½ teaspoon salt
- ¼ teaspoon pepper
- 3 large eggs
- 1½ cups panko (Japanese) bread crumbs
- 4 green onions, chopped
- 1 garlic clove, minced
- ½ teaspoon salt
- 2 tablespoons olive oil

1. Preheat oven to 350°. In a small bowl, mix the first seven ingredients. Refrigerate until serving.
2. Sprinkle salmon with salt and pepper. Bake 6-8 minutes or until the fish just begins to flake easily with a fork. Cool slightly; remove skin if necessary. In a small bowl, combine eggs, bread crumbs, green onions, garlic and salt. Flake the salmon; add to the bread crumb mixture, mixing thoroughly. Shape into twelve 2½-in. patties. Refrigerate, covered, 30 minutes.
3. In a large skillet, heat oil over medium-high heat. Add patties in batches; cook for 3-4 minutes on each side or until golden brown. Serve with dipping sauce.

HERBED LAMB CHOPS WITH CRISPY POTATOES

My mother's cooking is the inspiration behind this recipe. I adapted her scrumptious Easter leg of lamb so it can be served any day of the week.
—Bryn Namavari, Chicago, IL

Prep: 40 min. + standing • **Cook:** 20 min.
Makes: 4 servings

- 3 tablespoons olive oil
- 2 garlic cloves, halved
- ⅓ cup lightly packed fresh basil leaves
- ¼ cup fresh parsley leaves
- ¼ cup fresh oregano leaves
- ¼ cup coarsely chopped chives
- 2 tablespoons fresh rosemary leaves
- 1 teaspoon salt
- 1 teaspoon pepper
- 8 lamb loin chops (1 inch thick and 3 ounces each)

POTATOES
- 2 tablespoons olive oil
- 4 medium red potatoes, cut into ½-inch cubes
- 1 teaspoon lemon-pepper seasoning
- ¾ teaspoon salt
- ½ teaspoon paprika
- 4 cups fresh baby spinach
- 2 tablespoons pine nuts, toasted

1. Place the first nine ingredients in a food processor; pulse until blended. Spread over both sides of chops. Let stand for 30 minutes.
2. Meanwhile, in a large nonstick skillet, heat oil over medium-high heat. Add potatoes; cook for 15-20 minutes or until tender and golden brown, stirring occasionally. Sprinkle with lemon pepper, salt and paprika; remove from the pan. Keep warm.
3. Grill chops, covered, over medium heat for 3-4 minutes on each side or until the meat reaches desired doneness (for medium-rare, a thermometer should read 135°; medium, 140°; medium-well, 145°.)
4. Toss spinach with potatoes; sprinkle with pine nuts. Serve with lamb chops.
Note: To toast nuts, bake in a shallow pan in a 350° oven for 5-10 minutes or cook in a skillet over low heat until lightly browned, stirring occasionally.

TANGY LEMON TART

Our family adores lemon desserts. I like to make this lemony tart for brunch. For extra-special events, I bake it in my heart-shaped tart pan.
—Joyce Moynihan, Lakeville, MN

Prep: 15 min. + chilling
Bake: 45 min. + cooling
Makes: 14 servings

- ¾ cup butter, softened
- ½ cup confectioners' sugar
- 1½ cups all-purpose flour
- FILLING
- ¾ cup sugar
- 1 tablespoon grated lemon peel
- ¾ cup lemon juice
- 3 large eggs
- 3 large egg yolks
- 4 ounces cream cheese, softened
- 1 tablespoon cornstarch
   Sweetened whipped cream, optional

1. Preheat oven to 325°. In a large bowl, cream butter and confectioners' sugar until smooth. Gradually beat in flour. Press dough onto bottom and up sides of an ungreased 11-in. fluted tart pan with removable bottom. Refrigerate for 15 minutes.
2. Line unpricked pastry with a double thickness of foil. Fill with pie weights, dried beans or uncooked rice. Bake for 18-22 minutes or until edges are lightly browned. Remove the foil and weights; bake 5-7 minutes longer or until bottom is golden brown. Cool on a wire rack.

3. In a large bowl, beat the sugar, lemon peel, lemon juice, eggs, egg yolks, cream cheese and cornstarch until blended; pour into crust. Bake 18-22 minutes or until filling is set. Cool on a wire rack. If desired, serve with whipped cream. Refrigerate any leftovers.
Note: Let pie weights cool before storing. Beans and rice may be reused for pie weights, but not for cooking.

RHUBARB-BUTTERMILK COFFEE CAKE

Take advantage of rhubarb's short season and surprise your family with this moist and tender coffee cake. There's a nice balance of tangy and sweet in each bite.
—Cindy Ashley, Gregory, MI

Prep: 30 min. • **Bake:** 25 min.
Makes: 9 servings

- 2 cups diced fresh or frozen rhubarb
- ¼ cup plus ⅔ cup sugar, divided
- ½ cup butter, softened
- 2 large eggs
- 1½ teaspoons vanilla extract
- 1½ cups all-purpose flour
- 1 teaspoon baking powder
- ½ teaspoon salt
- ⅛ teaspoon baking soda
- ¾ cup buttermilk
- 2 tablespoons brown sugar
- ½ teaspoon ground cinnamon

1. Preheat oven to 350°. In a small bowl, combine rhubarb and ¼ cup sugar. In a large bowl, cream butter and the remaining sugar until light and fluffy. Add the eggs, one at a time, beating well after each addition. Stir in vanilla. In another bowl, whisk flour, baking powder, salt and baking soda; add to the creamed mixture alternately with the buttermilk, beating well after each addition. Fold in the rhubarb mixture.
2. Pour into a greased 9-in. square baking pan. In a small bowl, mix brown sugar and cinnamon; sprinkle over batter. Bake for 25-30 minutes or until a toothpick inserted near the center comes out clean. Serve warm or at room temperature.
Note: If using frozen rhubarb, measure the rhubarb while still frozen, then thaw completely. Drain in a colander, but do not press the liquid out.

STRAWBERRY LADYFINGER ICEBOX CAKE

This cake is inventive and yet familiar. Be sure to use a springform pan; otherwise you cannot invert the cake or remove it from the pan. If it breaks while you're transferring the cake to the serving plate, just push it back together and press gently.
—Stella Ohanian, Porter Ranch, CA

Prep: 35 min. + chilling
Makes: 12 servings

- 6 cups fresh strawberries, sliced
- 4 teaspoons balsamic vinegar
- 38 crisp ladyfinger cookies (about 23 ounces)
- 2 cartons (8 ounces each) mascarpone cheese, softened
- 2 cups heavy whipping cream
- ½ cup sugar
- 2 teaspoons vanilla extract
- 12 fresh strawberries

1. In a large bowl, mix strawberries and vinegar. Let stand 30 minutes. Line the bottom of a 9-in. ungreased springform pan with parchment paper. Trim ½ in. off one end of 22 ladyfingers. Arrange the ladyfingers, rounded sides up, along the sides of the prepared pan. Line the bottom of the pan with eight ladyfingers, trimming to fit if necessary.
2. In a large bowl, beat mascarpone cheese on low speed until fluffy. Add cream, sugar and vanilla; beat on medium until stiff peaks form. Spread 1½ cups of the cheese mixture evenly over cookies. With a slotted spoon, spoon half of the sliced strawberry mixture over top. Repeat layers. Layer with remaining ladyfingers, trimming to fit if necessary. Spread the remaining cheese over top.
3. Carefully cover with plastic wrap. Refrigerate for at least 8 hours or overnight. Remove the rim from the pan; arrange fresh strawberries over the top of the cake.

STRAWBERRY
LADYFINGER
ICEBOX CAKE

SPECIAL CELEBRATIONS

Looking for the perfect recipe to wow your sweetheart, or maybe something simply spooky for a Halloween movie night? Here you'll find seven sections dedicated to times worth celebrating that are often overshadowed—but still full of traditions, fun and flavor. We give you an array of standout recipes ranging from tempting cheese-laden indulgences to the best in hearty southern comfort food.

SEEING RED 176

MOTHER'S DAY BRUNCH. 186

REHEARSAL DINNER. 196

LOW COUNTRY BOIL 206

ROOFTOP FIREWORKS PARTY 216

CHEERS FOR CHEESE! 226

SCARY MOVIE NIGHT 236

Seeing Red

It's Valentine's Day and it's red all over—red food, that is! Bold and dramatic, red symbolizes love, passion and desire. So what better time to make a red dish for a special someone in your life?

Here you'll find a lovely array of rosy desserts along with a few other tantalizing dishes that boast crimson hues, such as classic tomato soup and a tempting red pepper sauce for pasta and chicken.

These bright and cheery delights can be part of a romantic meal for two, a heartfelt dinner for the entire family, or fun Valentine treats for the kids. Or invite your favorite gal pals to enjoy at a festive "Galentine's Day" celebration!

Blue Ribbon Red Velvet Cake (p. 184) **Butter Cookies** (p. 184)

QUICK TOMATO SOUP

There's nothing like a steamy bowl of classic tomato soup on a cold February day. The addition of sugar puts a sweet spin on this one. For extra fun, top with homemade heart-shaped croutons.
—Jane Ward, Churchville, MD

Start to Finish: 15 min.
Makes: 6 servings

- ¼ cup butter
- ¼ cup all-purpose flour
- 1 teaspoon curry powder
- ¼ teaspoon onion powder
- 1 can (46 ounces) tomato juice
- ¼ cup sugar
  Oyster crackers or croutons, optional

In a saucepan, melt butter. Stir in flour, curry powder and onion powder until smooth. Gradually add tomato juice and sugar. Cook, uncovered, until thickened and heated through, about 5 minutes. If desired, serve with crackers or croutons.

CHICKEN WITH RED PEPPER SAUCE & SPINACH

This tender moist chicken is dressed up with a savory sauce that combines roasted sweet red peppers, garlic and Italian seasonings. It's simple and pretty.
—Martha Pollock, Oregonia, OH

Start to Finish: 30 min.
Makes: 4 servings

- 1 large egg white
- ½ cup seasoned bread crumbs
- ¼ teaspoon salt
- 4 boneless skinless chicken breast halves (4 ounces each)
- 1 tablespoon olive oil
- 6 ounces fresh baby spinach (about 7½ cups)
- 1 jar (7 ounces) roasted sweet red peppers, drained
- 1 garlic clove, peeled
- ½ teaspoon Italian seasoning
- ½ cup crumbled feta cheese
  Fresh basil leaves, optional

1. In a shallow bowl, whisk egg white. In another shallow bowl, mix bread crumbs and salt. Dip chicken in egg white, then roll in crumb mixture.

2. In a large skillet, heat oil over medium heat. Add chicken breast halves; cook until a thermometer reads 165°, 4-5 minutes per side. Meanwhile, place spinach in a steamer basket; place in a large saucepan over 1 in. of water. Bring to a boil; cover and steam just until tender, 3-4 minutes.

3. Process peppers, garlic and Italian seasoning in a food processor until smooth. Transfer to a small microwave-safe bowl; cover and microwave until heated through.

4. Divide spinach among four plates. Serve with chicken; top chicken with about 2 tablespoons red pepper sauce, 2 tablespoons cheese and, if desired, basil.

BEET SALAD WITH ORANGE VINAIGRETTE

Beets and watercress topped with Gorgonzola and a sweet citrus dressing make a tantalizing new blend for a mixed salad. The combination of ingredients may seem unlikely, but I guarantee it will become a new favorite.
—Mary Moskovitz, Ventnor, NJ

Prep: 25 min. + chilling
Bake: 40 min. + cooling
Makes: 8 servings

- ½ cup orange juice
- 1 tablespoon olive oil
- 2 teaspoons white wine vinegar
- 1 teaspoon minced fresh rosemary or ¼ teaspoon dried rosemary, crushed
- 1 teaspoon chopped shallot
- ½ teaspoon grated orange peel
- ⅛ teaspoon salt
- ⅛ teaspoon pepper
- 4 fresh beets (about ½ pound)
- 1 bunch watercress
- ¼ cup walnut halves, toasted
- ¼ cup crumbled Gorgonzola cheese

1. For vinaigrette, place the first eight ingredients in a jar with a tight-fitting lid; shake well. Refrigerate 1 hour.

2. Preheat oven to 400°. Place beets in a 13x9-in. baking dish; add 1 in. of water. Bake, covered, until tender, 40-45 minutes. Cool; peel and cut into thin slices.

3. Just before serving, arrange watercress on a platter or individual plates; top with beets. Sprinkle with walnuts and cheese. Shake dressing again; drizzle over salad.

CREAMY STRAWBERRY CHEESECAKE

Perfect for entertaining, this dreamy dessert gets its delightful flavor from swirls of fresh strawberry sauce. The rich taste and velvety texture are wonderful to savor. And best of all, because you make it a day ahead of time, dessert will be ready anytime you are!
—Mia Trautwein, Goleta, CA

Prep: 40 min. • **Bake:** 30 min. + chilling
Makes: 8 servings

- 1½ cups sliced fresh strawberries
- ¼ cup sugar
- 1 tablespoon lemon juice
- 2 teaspoons cornstarch
- 1 tablespoon water

CRUST
- 1¼ cups graham cracker crumbs
- ¼ cup sugar
- ¼ cup butter, melted

FILLING
- 2 packages (8 ounces each) cream cheese, softened
- ½ cup sugar
- ½ cup sour cream
- ½ teaspoon vanilla extract
- 2 large eggs

1. Preheat oven to 350°. In a small saucepan, combine strawberries, sugar and lemon juice. Cook and stir over medium heat until the sugar is dissolved and mixture is bubbly, 2 minutes. Mix the cornstarch and water until smooth. Stir into pan. Bring to a boil; cook and stir until thickened, 2 minutes. Remove mixture from heat; cool.

2. Mix cracker crumbs and sugar; stir in butter. Press onto bottom and up sides of a 9-in. pie plate. Bake 10 minutes. Cool on a wire rack.

3. Beat cream cheese, sugar, sour cream and vanilla on medium speed until creamy. Add eggs; beat on low speed just until combined. Pour into prepared crust. Spoon cooled berry mixture over top; swirl into filling.

4. Bake until center is almost set, 30-35 minutes. Cool 1 hour on a wire rack. Refrigerate at least 4 hours or overnight.

QUICK
TOMATO
SOUP

SHRIMP POMODORO

SHRIMP POMODORO

My husband and I have hectic schedules, so I'm always looking for fast meals that have special-occasion appeal. Shrimp with garlic, tomatoes and pasta is a winner.
—Catherine Jensen, Blytheville, AR

Start to Finish: 20 min.
Makes: 4 servings

- 8 ounces uncooked thin spaghetti
- 1 tablespoon olive oil
- ¾ pound uncooked shrimp (26-30 per pound), peeled and deveined
- 2 cloves garlic, minced
- ¼ to ½ teaspoon crushed red pepper flakes
- 1 can (14½ ounces) petite diced tomatoes, undrained
- 10 fresh basil leaves, torn
- ½ teaspoon salt
- ⅛ teaspoon pepper
- ¼ cup grated Parmesan cheese

1. Cook the spaghetti according to the package directions.
2. In a large skillet, heat oil over medium-high heat. Add shrimp; cook until shrimp begin to turn pink, 1-2 minutes. Add garlic and pepper flakes; cook 1 minute longer.
3. Add tomatoes; bring to a boil. Reduce the heat; simmer, uncovered, until the shrimp turn pink, 2-3 minutes, stirring occasionally. Remove from heat; stir in basil, salt and pepper. Serve with spaghetti and cheese.

TOP TIP

Basil Timesaver

Instead of chopping fresh basil from my garden to add to my spaghetti sauce, I place several leaves in plastic bags and freeze them. I simply take out a handful of the frozen leaves and crumble them into the sauce.
—Betty D., Modesto, CA

CHOCOLATE-DIPPED ICE CREAM CONE CUPCAKES

CHOCOLATE-DIPPED ICE CREAM CONE CUPCAKES

I created this recipe based on our family's love of chocolate-dipped ice cream cones. Red heart-shaped sprinkles make them fun for Valentine's Day. Vary the color to match the occasion.
—Jennifer Gilbert, Brighton, MI

Prep: 40 min. • **Bake:** 15 min.
Makes: 2 dozen

- 1 package French vanilla or yellow cake mix (regular size)
- 24 ice cream cake cones (about 3 inches tall)

FROSTING
- 1 cup butter, softened
- ½ cup shortening
- 6 cups confectioners' sugar
- ¼ cup 2% milk
- 2 teaspoons vanilla extract

GLAZE
- 4 cups (24 ounces) semisweet chocolate chips
- ¼ cup shortening
- Colored sprinkles

1. Preheat oven to 350°. Grease 24 mini-muffin cups. Stand ice cream cones in additional mini-muffin cups.
2. Prepare cake mix batter according to package directions. Fill each greased muffin cup with 1 tablespoon batter. Divide remaining batter among ice cream cones (scant 2 tablespoons each).
3. Bake until a knife inserted in center comes out clean, 15-20 minutes. Cool in pans 5 minutes. Transfer both plain and cone cupcakes to wire racks; cool the cupcakes completely.
4. For the frosting, beat butter and shortening until blended. Gradually beat in confectioners' sugar, milk and vanilla on medium speed until soft peaks form.
5. To assemble, spread a small amount of frosting on bottom of each plain cupcake; attach to top of a cone cupcake. Spread remaining frosting over top cupcakes, rounding tops to resemble a scoop of ice cream. Freeze until the frosting is firm, 5-10 minutes.
6. For glaze, in a large metal bowl over simmering water, melt chocolate and shortening, stirring until smooth. Dip tops of cones in chocolate mixture. Decorate with sprinkles. Let stand until set.

CHOCOLATE TART WITH CRANBERRY RASPBERRY SAUCE

With its rich chocolate and fruity flavors, a little bit of this tart goes a long way. The berry-wine sauce lends an elegant touch.
—Diane Nemitz, Ludington, MI

Prep: 40 min. • **Bake:** 40 min. + cooling
Makes: 12 servings

- 1 cup all-purpose flour
- ½ cup old-fashioned oats
- ¼ cup sugar
- ½ cup cold butter, cubed
- 1½ cups unblanched almonds
- ½ cup packed brown sugar
- ½ cup dark corn syrup
- 2 large eggs
- 4 ounces bittersweet chocolate, melted
- 2 tablespoons butter, melted

SAUCE
- 2 cups fresh raspberries, divided
- 1 cup fresh or frozen cranberries, thawed
- ¾ cup sugar
- 2 tablespoons port wine or water

1. Preheat oven to 350°. Process flour, oats and sugar in a food processor until oats are ground. Add butter; pulse until crumbly. Press onto bottom and 1 in. up sides of an ungreased 10-in. springform pan. Bake until lightly browned, 14-16 minutes. Cool on a wire rack.

2. Process almonds in a food processor until coarsely chopped. Beat brown sugar, corn syrup, eggs, chocolate and melted butter; stir in almonds.

3. Pour into prepared crust. Bake until center is set and crust is golden brown, 25-30 minutes. Cool tart completely on a wire rack.

4. Meanwhile, in a small saucepan, combine 1 cup raspberries, cranberries, sugar and wine. Bring to a boil, stirring to dissolve sugar. Reduce heat to low; cook, uncovered, until cranberries pop, 4-5 minutes, stirring occasionally. Remove from heat; cool slightly.

5. Press berry mixture through a fine-mesh strainer into a bowl; discard seeds. Refrigerate sauce until serving.

6. Remove rim from pan. Serve tart with sauce and remaining raspberries.

CHOCOLATE TART WITH CRANBERRY RASPBERRY SAUCE

ROSY APPLE DUMPLINGS

Ground cinnamon and Red Hots give a cozy spiced flavor to the red sauce poured over these tender apple dumplings. Add a scoop of vanilla ice cream to cool the palate.
—Carol Hutchinson, Lansing, IL

Prep: 45 min. + chilling • **Bake:** 50 min.
Makes: 6 servings

- 2 cups all-purpose flour
- ¼ teaspoon salt
- 1 cup cold butter, cubed
- ½ cup cold water
- 6 medium tart apples, cored and peeled
- ¾ cup sugar
- ½ teaspoon ground cinnamon

SAUCE
- ¾ cup sugar
- ½ cup water
- ¼ cup Red Hots
- ¼ cup butter, cubed
- ¼ teaspoon ground cinnamon

1. Mix flour and salt; cut in butter until crumbly. Gradually add water to crumb mixture, tossing with a fork until dough forms a ball. Divide into six portions. Cover and refrigerate for at least 1 hour or until easy to handle.
2. Preheat oven to 350°. On a well floured surface, roll each portion into a 7-in. square. Place an apple on each pastry square. Mix the sugar and cinnamon; place 2 tablespoons sugar mixture into the core of each apple.
3. Gently bring up corners of pastry to center; pinch edges to seal. Place into a greased 13x9-in. baking dish. Bake the dumplings 15 minutes.
4. Meanwhile, in a small saucepan, combine sauce ingredients. Bring to a boil; cook and stir until smooth and blended. Pour over apples. Bake until apples are tender and pastry is golden brown, 35-40 minutes longer, basting occasionally with sauce. Serve warm.

CHERRY DESSERT LASAGNA

I think it's fun to incorporate pasta in a dessert. Not everyone in my family agrees, but try it— this is a fun and tasty way to end a meal.
—Linda Cifuentes, Mahomet, IL

Prep: 20 min. • **Bake:** 45 min.+ standing
Makes: 9 servings

- 1 container (15 ounces) whole-milk ricotta cheese
- ½ cup sugar
- 1 large egg
- ½ teaspoon ground cinnamon
- ¼ teaspoon almond extract
- 1 can (21 ounces) cherry pie filling
- 4 no-cook lasagna noodles

TOPPING
- ⅓ cup packed brown sugar
- ¼ cup all-purpose flour
- ¼ cup quick-cooking oats
- ½ teaspoon ground cinnamon
- 3 tablespoons cold butter, cubed
- ½ cup chopped almonds

1. Preheat oven to 350°. Mix first five ingredients. Spread half of the pie filling into a greased 8-in. square baking dish. Place two noodles on top, cutting to fit into baking dish. Layer with half of the ricotta cheese mixture and the remaining noodles. Top with remaining cheese mixture and pie filling.
2. For topping, mix brown sugar, flour, oats and cinnamon; cut in butter until crumbly. Stir in almonds. Sprinkle over top. Bake, uncovered, until bubbly, 45-50 minutes. Let dessert stand 30-45 minutes before serving.

BUTTER COOKIES

These classic cookies will melt in your mouth. They're favorites of my nephews, who love the tender texture and creamy frosting. Kids can help decorate, too.
—Ruth Griggs, South Hill, VA

....

Prep: 25 min. • **Bake:** 10 min./batch
Makes: about 6½ dozen

- 1 cup butter, softened
- ¾ cup sugar
- 1 large egg
- ½ teaspoon vanilla extract
- 2½ cups all-purpose flour
- 1 teaspoon baking powder
- ¼ teaspoon salt

FROSTING

- ½ cup butter, softened
- 4 cups confectioners' sugar
- 1 teaspoon vanilla extract
- 3 to 4 tablespoons 2% milk
  Red food coloring, optional

1. Preheat oven to 375°. Cream butter and sugar until light and fluffy. Beat in egg and vanilla. In another bowl, whisk flour, baking powder and salt; gradually beat into creamed mixture.
2. Using a cookie press fitted with a heart disk, press the dough 1 in. apart onto ungreased baking sheets. Bake until set but not brown, 6-8 minutes. Cool cookies on wire racks.
3. Beat the butter, confectioners' sugar, vanilla and enough milk to reach desired spreading consistency. If desired, tint frosting with food coloring. Decorate the cookies as desired.

TOP TIP

Using a Cookie Press

If you are using a cookie press for the first time, it may take a little practice to make perfectly shaped cookies. When too little dough is pressed out, the cookie will be too small and break easily. When too much dough is pressed out, the design will lose its form. When just the right amount of dough is pressed out, the baked cookie will have a uniform design and crisp indentations.

BLUE RIBBON RED VELVET CAKE

This two-layer beauty features a striking red interior. It calls for more baking cocoa than most red velvet cakes, making it extra chocolaty. Feel free to change the color of the food coloring to suit the occasion. I'm proud to say this recipe won a blue ribbon in the holiday cake division at the 2006 Alaska State Fair. I think it will be a winner in your house, too!
—Cindi DeClue, Anchorage, AK

....

Prep: 35 min. • **Bake:** 25 min. + cooling
Makes: 12 servings

- 1½ cups canola oil
- 1 cup buttermilk
- 2 large eggs
- 2 tablespoons red food coloring
- 1 teaspoon white vinegar
- 2½ cups all-purpose flour
- 1½ cups sugar
- 3 tablespoons baking cocoa
- 1 teaspoon baking soda

FROSTING

- 1 package (8 ounces) cream cheese, softened
- ½ cup butter, softened
- 2 teaspoons vanilla extract
- 3¾ cups confectioners' sugar

1. Preheat oven to 350°. Line bottoms of two greased 9-in. round pans with parchment paper; grease paper. Beat the first five ingredients until well blended. In another bowl, whisk together flour, sugar, baking cocoa and baking soda; gradually beat into oil mixture.
2. Transfer batter to prepared pans. Bake until a toothpick inserted in center comes out clean, 25-30 minutes. Cool in pans 10 minutes before removing to wire racks; remove paper. Cool completely.
3. Beat cream cheese, butter and vanilla until blended. Gradually beat in the confectioners' sugar until smooth. Using a long serrated knife, trim tops of cakes; set tops aside. Place one cake layer on a serving plate. Spread with ¾ cup frosting. Top with remaining cake layer, bottom side up. Frost top and sides of cake with the remaining frosting.
4. Break cake tops into pieces. Pulse in a food processor until fine crumbs form. Decorate cake with crumbs as desired.

BLUE RIBBON RED VELVET CAKE

BUTTER
COOKIES

Mother's Day Brunch

In May we set aside a special day to honor a most important woman: Mother. To celebrate this amazing lady, treat her to an assortment of homemade sweet and savory brunch dishes.

Whether you're serving her a leisurely breakfast in bread or hosting the entire family, you'll be sure to delight her—and everyone else—with a sunny cheese-filled frittata. Then bring on the spring flavors with some light and elegant side dishes like herb-happy pea salad, crab cake lettuce wraps, and strawberry bruschetta.

Deep-dish key lime pie and vanilla cupcakes topped with sweet-tart rhubarb compote make a fitting finale. Cheers (and love) to Mom!

Lime-Raspberry Pie with Coconut Cream (p. 194)

DOUBLE CHEESE ARTICHOKE FRITTATA

The combination of fresh flavors make this pretty egg bake a great entree for a special occasion brunch or light luncheon. Just add homemade sausage patties and strawberry-topped bruschetta to make it a complete meal.
—Joyce Moynihan, Lakeville, MN

Prep: 15 min. • **Bake:** 35 min.
Makes: 8 servings

- 1 package (8 ounces) frozen artichoke hearts
- 1 tablespoon butter
- 1 tablespoon olive oil
- 1 medium onion, chopped
- 1 garlic clove, minced
- ¼ teaspoon dried oregano
- ¾ cup shredded Parmesan cheese, divided
- 6 large eggs
- ½ cup 2% milk
- ¼ teaspoon salt
- ⅛ teaspoon white pepper
- ⅛ teaspoon ground nutmeg
- 1 cup shredded Monterey Jack cheese
     Minced chives, optional

1. Cook artichokes according to package directions; drain. Cool slightly; coarsely chop. Preheat oven to 350°.
2. In a large skillet, heat butter and oil over medium-high heat. Add the onion; cook and stir until tender. Add garlic; cook for 1 minute longer. Stir in oregano and artichokes; remove from heat.
3. Sprinkle ¼ cup Parmesan cheese in a greased 11x7-in. baking dish. Top with artichoke mixture.
4. In a large bowl, whisk eggs, milk, salt, pepper and nutmeg. Stir in Monterey Jack cheese and ¼ cup Parmesan cheese. Pour over artichoke mixture.
5. Bake, uncovered, 30 minutes. Sprinkle with remaining Parmesan cheese. Bake 6-8 minutes longer or until a knife inserted in the center comes out clean. If desired, sprinkle with minced chives.

VANILLA CUPCAKES WITH RHUBARB COMPOTE

Not too long ago I took up baking as a hobby and have loved it ever since. The inspiration for these sweet treats came from my love of Twinkies. I added the rhubarb compote to make them a bit more upscale for entertaining.
—Julia VanderMolen, Grand Rapids, MI

Prep: 50 min. + cooling
Bake: 20 min. + cooling
Makes: 1½ dozen

- ½ cup unsalted butter, softened
- 1½ cups sugar
- 3 large eggs
- 3 teaspoons vanilla extract
- 1½ cups all-purpose flour
- ½ teaspoon baking soda
- ¼ teaspoon salt
- ⅓ cup sour cream

TOPPING
- 1 carton (8 ounces) mascarpone cheese
- ¾ cup fat-free vanilla Greek yogurt
- 1 tablespoon honey

RHUBARB COMPOTE
- 2 cups chopped fresh rhubarb
- 2 tablespoons sugar
- 1 tablespoon water
- ¼ teaspoon ground ginger
- ½ cup quartered fresh strawberries

1. Preheat oven to 350°. Line 18 muffin cups with paper liners.
2. In a large bowl, cream butter and sugar until light and fluffy. Add eggs, one at a time, beating well after each addition. Beat in vanilla. In another bowl, whisk the flour, baking soda and salt; add to the creamed mixture alternately with the sour cream, beating well after each addition.
3. Fill the prepared cups two-thirds full. Bake 18-20 minutes or until a toothpick inserted in center comes out clean. Cool in pans 10 minutes before removing to wire racks to cool completely.
4. For topping, in a small bowl, mix mascarpone cheese, yogurt and honey. Refrigerate until serving.
5. For compote, in a small saucepan, bring rhubarb, sugar, water and ginger to a boil. Reduce heat; simmer, uncovered, until the rhubarb begins to soften, about 6-8 minutes.
6. Stir in strawberries; simmer gently until slightly thickened and strawberries are just softened, about 5 minutes. Cool completely.
7. Serve cupcakes with topping and strawberry rhubarb compote.

HOMEMADE SAGE SAUSAGE PATTIES

Oregano, garlic and sage add zippy flavor to these quick-to-fix ground pork patties. I've had this Pennsylvania Dutch recipe for years, and it always brings compliments.
—Diane Hixon, Niceville, FL

Prep: 10 min. + chilling • **Cook:** 15 min.
Makes: 8 servings

- 1 pound ground pork
- ¾ cup shredded cheddar cheese
- ¼ cup buttermilk
- 1 tablespoon finely chopped onion
- 2 teaspoons rubbed sage
- ¾ teaspoon salt
- ¾ teaspoon pepper
- ⅛ teaspoon garlic powder
- ⅛ teaspoon dried oregano

1. In a bowl, combine all ingredients, mixing lightly, but thoroughly. Shape into eight ½-in.-thick patties. Refrigerate 1 hour.
2. In a large nonstick skillet, cook patties over medium heat 6-8 minutes on each side or until a thermometer reads 160°.

CLOCKWISE FROM RIGHT: STRAWBERRY & CREAM BRUSCHETTA (PAGE 193); DOUBLE CHEESE ARTICHOKE FRITTATA; HOMEMADE SAGE SAUSAGE PATTIES

TOP TIP

Rubbed Sage

In recipes calling for "rubbed" sage, take the whole dried leaf and crush or rub it to make a finely textured but light and fluffy powder. Ground sage sold in the spice section is more concentrated; use half as much if the recipe calls for rubbed sage.

CHAMPAGNE SIPPER

HERBY PEA SALAD

We love spring vegetables. One Mother's Day I came up with this flavorful green salad that everyone enjoyed. You could increase the dressing and mix in some cooked small pasta, like acini de pepe, for a pasta salad.
—Ann Sheehy, Lawrence, MA

Start to Finish: 30 min.
Makes: 8 servings

- 1 tablespoon olive oil
- 2 medium leeks (white portion only), thinly sliced
- 3 small zucchini, halved and sliced
- ½ pound fresh asparagus, trimmed and cut into 2-inch pieces
- 3 cups frozen petite peas (about 16 ounces), thawed
- 2 tablespoons each minced fresh chives and parsley
- 1 to 2 tablespoons minced fresh tarragon

DRESSING
- 3 tablespoons olive oil
- 2 tablespoons rice or white wine vinegar
- ¾ teaspoon salt
- ½ teaspoon Dijon mustard
- ¼ teaspoon pepper

1. In a large skillet, heat oil over medium heat. Add leeks; cook and stir 4-6 minutes or until tender. In a Dutch oven, place steamer basket over 1 in. of water. In batches, place zucchini and asparagus in basket. Bring water to a boil. Reduce heat to maintain a low boil; steam, covered, 4-5 minutes or until crisp-tender. Remove and immediately drop into ice water. Drain and pat dry.
2. In a large bowl, combine peas, leeks, zucchini mixture and herbs. In a small bowl, whisk dressing ingredients. Pour over salad; toss to coat. Serve salad immediately.

CHAMPAGNE SIPPER

This is a terrific cocktail for a holiday celebration. And because you make it by the pitcher, you can mingle with your guests instead of tending bar.
—Moffat Frazier, New York, NY

Start to Finish: 10 min.
Makes: 12 servings

- 1½ cups sugar
- 1 cup lemon juice
- 3 cups cold water
- 1½ cups sweet white wine, chilled
- 1 bottle (750 milliliters) champagne, chilled
  Sliced fresh strawberries, optional

In a 3-qt. pitcher, dissolve sugar in lemon juice. Add cold water and white wine. Stir in champagne. If desired, serve cocktail with strawberries.

CRAB CAKE LETTUCE WRAPS

I love dishes that you can put together and eat with your hands. These little crab wraps are healthy, fast and flavorful.
—Joyce Huang, New York, NY

Start to Finish: 10 min.
Makes: 1 dozen

- 2 cans (6 ounces each) lump crabmeat, drained
- ¼ cup finely chopped celery
- ¼ cup seasoned stuffing cubes, coarsely crushed
- ¼ cup plain Greek yogurt
- ⅛ teaspoon salt
- ⅛ teaspoon pepper
- 12 Bibb or Boston lettuce leaves
  Finely chopped tomatoes, optional

In a large bowl, mix crab, celery, stuffing cubes, yogurt, salt and pepper. To serve, spoon 2 tablespoons crab mixture into each lettuce leaf. If desired, sprinkle with tomatoes. Fold lettuce over filling.

CRAB CAKE
LETTUCE
WRAPS

STRAWBERRY
& CREAM
BRUSCHETTA

STRAWBERRY & CREAM BRUSCHETTA

This is a dessert take on bruschetta. Sweet, cinnamony toast slices are topped with a cream cheese mixture, strawberries and almonds. They taste like miniature cheesecakes and are so yummy!
—Christi Meixner, Aurora, IL

Start to Finish: 25 min.
Makes: 2 dozen

- 1 French bread baguette (8 ounces), cut into 24 slices
- ¼ cup butter, melted
- 3 tablespoons sugar
- ½ teaspoon ground cinnamon
- 1 package (8 ounces) cream cheese, softened
- ¼ cup confectioners' sugar
- 2 teaspoons lemon juice
- 1 teaspoon grated lemon peel
- 2½ cups fresh strawberries, chopped
- ⅓ cup slivered almonds, toasted

1. Preheat oven to 375°. Place bread on an ungreased baking sheet; brush with butter. Combine sugar and cinnamon; sprinkle over bread. Bake 4-5 minutes on each side or until lightly crisp.
2. In a small bowl, beat cream cheese, confectioners' sugar, lemon juice and peel until blended; spread over toast. Top with strawberries; sprinkle with almonds.

TOP TIP
Strawberries 101
When buying or picking strawberries, look for those that are shiny, firm, plump and fragrant. A strawberry should be almost completely red, although some whiteness near the leafy cap is acceptable. Avoid berries with mold or bruised spots. Refrigerate unwashed strawberries with the caps on until ready to use. Just before using, wash and hull.

ONION-GARLIC HASH BROWNS

ONION-GARLIC HASH BROWNS

Quick to assemble, these slow-cooked hash browns are one of my go-to sides. Stir in hot sauce if you like a bit of heat. I top my finished dish with a sprinkling of shredded cheddar cheese.
—Cindi Boger, Ardmore, AL

Prep: 20 min. • **Cook:** 3 hours
Makes: 12 servings (½ cup each)

- ¼ cup butter, cubed
- 1 tablespoon olive oil
- 1 large red onion, chopped
- 1 small sweet red pepper, chopped
- 1 small green pepper, chopped
- 4 garlic cloves, minced
- 1 package (30 ounces) frozen shredded hash brown potatoes
- ½ teaspoon salt
- ½ teaspoon pepper
- 3 drops hot pepper sauce, optional
- 2 teaspoons minced fresh parsley

1. In a large skillet, heat butter and oil over medium heat. Add onion and peppers. Cook and stir until crisp-tender. Add garlic; cook 1 minute longer. Stir in hash browns, salt, pepper and, if desired, pepper sauce.
2. Transfer to a 5-qt. slow cooker coated with cooking spray. Cook, covered, 3-4 hours or until heated through. Sprinkle with parsley just before serving.

LEMON RICOTTA FRITTERS

These delicious fritters are golden brown outside, soft and cake-like inside, and have a lovely citrus flavor. They're great served with jam or honey.
—Tina Mirilovich, Johnstown, PA

Start to Finish: 30 min.
Makes: about 2 dozen

- 1 cup all-purpose flour
- 2 teaspoons baking powder
- 1½ teaspoons grated lemon peel
  - Pinch salt
- 3 large eggs
- 1 cup whole-milk ricotta cheese
- 3 tablespoons sugar
- ½ teaspoon lemon extract
  - Oil for deep-fat frying
  - Confectioners' sugar
  - Honey or strawberry jam

1. In a large bowl, whisk flour, baking powder, lemon peel and salt. In another bowl, whisk eggs, cheese, sugar and extract. Add to dry ingredients, stirring just until moistened.
2. In an electric skillet or deep fryer, heat oil to 375°. Drop batter by tablespoonfuls, several at a time, into hot oil. Fry 2-3 minutes or until golden brown. Drain on paper towels. Dust with confectioners' sugar. Serve warm with honey or jam.

**LIME-RASPBERRY PIE
WITH COCONUT CREAM**

LIME-RASPBERRY PIE WITH COCONUT CREAM

In my many family trips to Florida, I've had key lime pie from several restaurants, and each one is different. I wanted to create my own spin on the pie to make it my signature dessert. Whipped egg whites in the filling make it light and mousse-like, sweet raspberries balance the tart filling, and coconut and cashews add additional tropical character. Garnish with fresh raspberries and toasted shredded coconut if desired.

—Elise Easterling, Chapel Hill, NC

....

Prep: 50 min. • **Bake:** 25 min. + chilling
Makes: 12 servings

  3 large egg whites
 18 whole graham crackers, crushed
      (about 2½ cups)
 ½ cup packed brown sugar
 ½ cup unsalted cashews, finely
      chopped
 ¾ cup butter, melted
  2 cans (14 ounces each) sweetened
      condensed milk
 ¾ cup Key lime juice
  6 large egg yolks
 ¼ cup sugar

TOPPINGS
  1 can (13.66 ounces) coconut milk
  1 cup heavy whipping cream
 ½ cup confectioners' sugar
 ½ cup seedless raspberry jam
      Fresh raspberries and toasted flaked
        coconut, optional

1. Place egg whites in a small bowl; let stand at room temperature 30 minutes. Preheat oven to 350°.
2. In a large bowl, mix crushed crackers, brown sugar and cashews; stir in melted butter. Press onto bottom and 2 in. up sides of a greased 9-in. springform pan.
3. In a large bowl, mix condensed milk, lime juice and egg yolks until blended. With clean beaters, beat egg whites on medium speed until soft peaks form. Gradually add sugar, 1 tablespoon at a time, beating on high after each addition until sugar is dissolved. Continue beating until stiff peaks form. Fold into the milk mixture; pour into crust.
4. Bake 25-30 minutes or until filling is set. Cool 4 hours on a wire rack. Refrigerate 6 hours or overnight, covering when cold.
5. Spoon cream layer from top of coconut milk into a large bowl (discard remaining liquid). Add whipping cream and confectioners' sugar to bowl; beat until stiff peaks form.
6. Spread jam over pie. If desired, top with raspberries and coconut. Serve with whipped coconut cream.
Note: Light coconut milk is not recommended for this recipe.
Note: To toast coconut, bake in a shallow pan in a 350° oven for 5-10 minutes or cook in a skillet over low heat until golden brown, stirring occasionally.

MOTHER'S DAY GIFT BASKET

Celebrated on the second Sunday in May, Mother's Day is the time to honor and thank the moms in our lives—the special lady we call Mom, brand-new mommies, and even beloved aunts, grandmothers, great-grandmothers and godmothers. These outstanding women shower us with so much love throughout our lives. While we may not be able to repay them for all the homemade meals, words of wisdom, and thousands of hugs and kisses, we can treat them to a homemade gift from the heart.

To treat a special mom in your life to a well-deserved day of pampering, try this thoughtful gift idea. Fill a decorative basket (available at craft and hobby stores) with items she can use for a relaxing spa day at home. A few fun, simple and inexpensive gifts like these make the day last longer.

GIFT BASKET ITEMS
Bath soaks
Scented candle
Tea tins filled with Mom's favorite tea
Clear tea cup with infuser
Sleep mask
Journal
Stationery
Pens
Decorative "Best Mom Ever" plate

Rehearsal Dinner

It's the day before the big day! The rehearsal dinner is the last time to bring your dearest friends and family together for a smaller, more intimate gathering.

Casual elegance is key to the occasion, with dishes that are delicious and beautiful yet also low-stress. Set a stunning table with tempting Shrimp & Garlic Bruschetta, Lime Chicken with Blackberry Salsa, and Key Lime Trifle—and toast your loved ones with Peach Champagne!

Add a one-of-a-kind decor for lasting memories. Then relax and linger in the pleasure of such good food and company.

Special Occasion Cutout Cookies (p. 204) **Peach Champagne** (p. 198)
Lime Chicken with Blackberry Salsa (p. 201)

**PEACH
CHAMPAGNE**

SHRIMP & GARLIC BRUSCHETTA

My daughter brought this dish to a potluck dinner party at a professor's house. The students and professors voted and said hers was the best savory dish of the evening. Talk about a top grade!
—Pamela Schofield, Melrose, MA

Prep: 30 min. • **Bake:** 30 min.
Makes: 3 dozen

- 4 plum tomatoes, seeded and chopped
- 6 tablespoons olive oil, divided
- 6 garlic cloves, minced
- ¼ teaspoon salt
- ¼ teaspoon pepper
- 2 pounds uncooked small shrimp, peeled and deveined
- 1 cup crumbled feta cheese
- 1 tablespoon lemon juice
- 2 teaspoons minced fresh basil
- 2 teaspoons minced fresh parsley
- 36 slices French bread baguette (¼ inch thick)
- 1 garlic clove, halved

1. Preheat oven to 425°. In a 13x9-in. baking dish, combine the tomatoes, 4 tablespoons oil, the minced garlic, salt and pepper. Bake, uncovered, for 15 minutes. Stir in shrimp, cheese, lemon juice, basil and parsley. Bake, uncovered, 10-12 minutes longer or until the shrimp turn pink.

2. Meanwhile, brush baguette slices with the remaining oil. Place the bread on ungreased baking sheets. Bake for 1-2 minutes on each side or until lightly browned. Rub toast with the cut surface of garlic; discard garlic. Using a slotted spoon, top toast with the shrimp mixture.

PEACH CHAMPAGNE

I searched high and low for the perfect punch recipe and finally decided to create my own. This refreshing sipper is a big hit at parties, especially weddings. In summer I freeze fresh peaches and strawberries; if you don't have fresh fruit, store-bought frozen fruit works just as well.
—Linda Hall, Evington, VA

Start to Finish: 10 min.
Makes: 20 servings (¾ cup each)

- 1 package (16 ounces) frozen unsweetened sliced peaches
- 1 package (14 ounces) frozen unsweetened sliced strawberries
- 2 cans (5½ ounces each) peach nectar, chilled
- 1 cup peach schnapps liqueur
- 2 liters lemon-lime soda, chilled
- 2 bottles (750 milliliters each) champagne or other sparkling wine, chilled

In a punch bowl, combine peaches, strawberries, nectar and liqueur. Stir in soda and champagne just before serving.

TOMATO-GOAT CHEESE SPREAD

A good friend shared this recipe with me. It's super easy and so delicious... guests will love it! It's best served with crackers that aren't strongly seasoned.
—Linda Alexander, Madison, WI

Start to Finish: 10 minutes
Makes: 12 servings

- 1 jar (8½ ounces) julienned oil-packed sun-dried tomatoes
- 2 garlic cloves, minced
- 1 log (11 ounces) fresh goat cheese
  Minced fresh parsley, optional
  Assorted crackers

1. Drain the tomatoes, reserving 3 tablespoons of oil.

2. In a small skillet, heat the reserved oil, tomatoes and garlic over medium-high heat. Cook and stir for 5 minutes or until the garlic is golden and the tomatoes are heated through. To serve, place the cheese on a serving plate. Pour the tomato mixture over cheese. If desired, sprinkle with parsley. Serve with crackers.

TOP TIP

Minced Garlic

Jarred minced garlic that is store-bought, fresh garlic that's been finely chopped by hand and fresh garlic that's been put through a press can all be used interchangeably in recipes. Choose whichever is easiest and most convenient for you. Typically, ½ teaspoon minced garlic from a jar equals one fresh garlic clove, minced. The jarred garlic tends to be slightly milder than fresh.

TOMATO-GOAT CHEESE SPREAD

LIME CHICKEN WITH
BLACKBERRY SALSA

LIME CHICKEN WITH BLACKBERRY SALSA

I invented this recipe in a hurry one night and was over-the-top thrilled with how it came out! I've since served it to company; it always gets rave reviews. I love that it's so easy, and so healthy for my family, too. You can use grilled chicken instead of baked, if you like, and the spice level is up to you. If you like more kick in your food, use the whole 2 tablespoons of red pepper flakes. Otherwise, start with 1 tablespoon and adjust to taste.
—Joni Hilton, Rocklin, CA

Prep: 10 min. + marinating • **Grill:** 10 min.
Makes: 12 servings (6 cups salsa)

- 6 medium limes
- ½ cup olive oil
- 1 to 2 tablespoons crushed red pepper flakes
- 1 teaspoon salt
- 12 boneless skinless chicken breast halves (6 ounces each)

SALSA
- 3 cups fresh blackberries
- 3 medium tomatoes, finely chopped
- 6 green onions, finely chopped
- 1 cup fresh cilantro leaves
- ½ teaspoon salt

1. Finely grate peel from limes. Cut limes crosswise in half; squeeze juice from the limes. Place peel, lime juice, oil, pepper flakes and salt in a large resealable plastic bag. Add chicken; seal bag and turn to coat. Refrigerate for 4 hours or overnight.
2. In a bowl, combine the blackberries, tomatoes, green onions, cilantro and salt.
3. Drain chicken, discarding marinade. Grill, covered, over medium heat or broil 4 in. from heat for 4-5 minutes on each side or until a thermometer reads 165°. Serve with salsa.

CHICKPEA SALAD

CHICKPEA SALAD

This recipe is a crowd pleaser! My husband and I bring it to parties, barbecues and other gatherings. It's a light but flavorful side dish that brings a little bit of Greek flavor to any meal.
—Kristi Smith, Greenwood, IN

Prep: 10 min. + chilling
Makes: 12 servings (¾ cup each)

- 3 cans (15 ounces each) chickpeas or garbanzo beans, rinsed and drained
- 4 large cucumbers, seeded and cut into ½-inch pieces
- 2 packages (3½ ounces each) crumbled reduced-fat feta cheese (about 1⅓ cups)
- 1 cup finely chopped red onion
- ½ cup reduced-fat ranch salad dressing
- 2 tablespoons snipped fresh dill
- ¾ teaspoon salt
- ¼ teaspoon pepper

Combine the chickpeas, cucumbers, cheese and onion. In a second bowl, mix the ranch dressing, dill, salt and pepper. Pour over the salad; toss to coat. Refrigerate, covered, for 1 hour before serving.

TROPICAL TABBOULEH

This is an easy and refreshing dish for a hot summer day. It is perfect for picnics and potlucks.
—Sonya Labbe, West Hollywood, CA

Prep: 20 minutes + chilling
Makes: 12 servings (¾ cup each)

- 1½ cups bulgur, rinsed
- 2 cups chopped peeled mango (about 1 medium)
- 2 cups chopped peeled papaya (about 1 small)
- ½ cup thinly sliced red onion
- 1⅓ cups orange juice
- ¼ cup lime juice
- ¼ cup canola oil
- 1 teaspoon salt
- 2 medium tomatoes, seeded and chopped
- ½ cup chopped fresh cilantro

1. Combine bulgur, mango, papaya and onion. In another bowl, whisk the orange juice, lime juice, oil and salt. Pour over the bulgur mixture; toss to coat. Refrigerate, covered, 8 hours or overnight.
2. Just before serving, gently stir in the tomatoes and cilantro.

PROSCIUTTO HONEYDEW WITH BALSAMIC REDUCTION

I often saw these bites on restaurant menus and thought how simple they would be to prepare at home. The fresh mint from our garden adds a bright kick to these already delectable temptations. You could use different herbs with the prosciutto; herbes de Provence provides another level of taste.

—Jenn Tidwell, Fair Oaks, CA

Prep: 30 min. • **Cook:** 10 min.
Makes: about 7 dozen

- 1 large honeydew, peeled, seeded and cut into 1-inch cubes
- ¼ cup lime juice
- 2 tablespoons minced fresh mint
- ¼ teaspoon coarsely ground pepper
- 42 thin slices prosciutto, halved crosswise
- 6 tablespoons balsamic vinegar
- 3 tablespoons soy sauce
- 2 teaspoons sugar or honey
- 2 garlic cloves, minced

1. Combine melon, lime juice, mint and pepper; toss gently to coat. Wrap each melon cube with half a slice of prosciutto and secure with a toothpick. Arrange on a serving platter; cover and refrigerate.
2. Meanwhile, in a small saucepan, mix vinegar, soy sauce, sugar and garlic. Bring to a boil. Reduce heat; simmer 7-9 minutes or until slightly thickened. Cool to room temperature. Drizzle over melon.

MARINATED STEAK WITH GRILLED ONIONS

This marinade is magic—it will make even economy cuts of beef tender and delicious.

—Gail Garcelon, Beaverton, OR

Prep: 10 min. + marinating • **Grill:** 10 min.
Makes: 12 servings (1 cup cooked onions)

- 1¼ cups balsamic vinaigrette
- 4 teaspoons ground mustard
- 2¼ teaspoons Worcestershire sauce
- 2 garlic cloves, minced
- 3 beef top sirloin steaks (¾ inch thick and 1 pound each)
- 5 medium onions, sliced

1. Whisk together the vinaigrette, mustard, Worcestershire sauce and garlic. Pour ¼ cup of the mixture into a large resealable plastic bag. Add the beef; seal the bag and turn to coat. Refrigerate for 6 hours or overnight. Cover and refrigerate the remaining marinade.
2. Drain the beef, discarding marinade in the bag. Grill the steaks and onions, covered, over medium heat or broil 4 in. from heat until the meat reaches the desired doneness (for medium-rare, a thermometer should read 135°; medium, 140°; medium-well, 145°) and the onions are tender, 4-7 minutes per side. Drizzle the reserved marinade over the onions. Cut steak into thin slices; serve with onions.

GARDEN GREEN BEAN SALAD

When my sons were growing up, they preferred their green beans cold. So I started adding green beans to salads. This recipe is great to make in advance because the longer it marinates, the better it tastes.

—JoAnn Handley, Mount Dora, FL

Prep: 20 min.+ chilling
Makes: 16 servings

- 3 pounds fresh green beans, trimmed
- ¾ cup finely chopped sweet onion
- ½ cup balsamic vinaigrette
- ¼ cup olive oil
- 3 tablespoons lemon juice
- 3 tablespoons snipped fresh dill
- 3 tablespoons minced fresh basil
- 3 teaspoons minced fresh oregano
- 1 teaspoon seasoned salt
- 1 cup dry roasted peanuts

1. In a 6-qt. stockpot, bring 8 cups water to a boil. Add the beans in batches; cook, uncovered, for 3-5 minutes or just until crisp-tender. Remove the beans and immediately drop into ice water. Drain and pat dry. Place the beans and onion in a bowl. In a second bowl, whisk the vinaigrette, oil, lemon juice, herbs and seasoned salt. Pour over salad; toss to coat. Refrigerate, covered, for at least 1 hour.
2. Just before serving, sprinkle with peanuts.

KEY LIME TRIFLE

When I saw a recipe for a banana cream pie trifle I was inspired to invent a version that spun off my favorite pie, key lime. My family loved it! Some friends got to try it, and they enjoyed it immensely as well.
—Rebecah Lytle, Ocala, FL

KEY LIME TRIFLE

Prep: 30 min. • **Bake:** 10 min. + chilling
Makes: 16 servings (1 cup each)

- 2 cups graham cracker crumbs
- 1 cup chopped pecans
- ½ cup packed brown sugar
- 1 cup butter, melted

FILLING
- 2 packages (8 ounces each) cream cheese, softened
- 2 cans (14 ounces each) sweetened condensed milk
- 1½ cups Key lime juice

WHIPPED CREAM
- 3 cups heavy whipping cream
- ⅓ cup confectioners' sugar
- 3 teaspoons vanilla extract

TOPPING
- ½ cup chopped pecans, toasted
- ¼ cup flaked coconut, toasted

1. Preheat oven to 400°. Mix cracker crumbs, pecans and brown sugar; stir in butter. Press mixture onto the bottom of a 15x10-in. pan. Bake for 10-12 minutes. Stir to break up the crumbs; cool on a wire rack.
2. For filling, in another bowl, beat cream cheese and condensed milk until blended. Stir in lime juice. In a third bowl, beat the cream until it begins to thicken. Add the confectioners' sugar and vanilla; beat until stiff peaks form.
3. In a 4-qt. glass bowl, layer half of each of the following: crumb mixture, filling and whipped cream. Repeat layers. Sprinkle with pecans and coconut. Refrigerate, covered, at least 2 hours or overnight.

SPECIAL OCCASION CUTOUT COOKIES

Set aside ½ cup glaze for piping initials. Spread the remaining glaze over cookies. Let stand at room temperature until glaze is set, about 1 hour.

6. Cut a small hole in the tip of a pastry bag or in one corner of a food-safe plastic bag; insert a #2 round pastry tip. Tint the reserved glaze as desired; add to the pastry bag. Pipe initials on cookies. Let stand until glaze is set.

CHOCOLATE SALTED CARAMEL BARS

I love to experiment with different recipes and combine classic and new flavors. I've been making this shortbread for over 20 years and finally have found the perfect pairing! I love the new craze, salted caramel, and of course I love dark chocolate, so I layered these two flavors with my favorite shortbread crust. It's melt-in-your-mouth good, and it is quickly becoming a favorite with my family, friends and customers! For even more gooey goodness, drizzle bottled caramel sauce over top.

—Lisa Glenn, Sarasota, FL

Prep: 20 min. • **Bake:** 50 min. + cooling
Makes: 2½ dozen

- 2 **cups butter, softened**
- 1½ **cups confectioners' sugar**
- 1 **cup sugar**
- 6 **teaspoons vanilla extract**
- 4 **cups all-purpose flour**
- 1 **package (14 ounces) caramels**
- ⅓ **cup heavy whipping cream**
- 1 **teaspoon kosher salt**
- 2 **cups (12 ounces) dark chocolate chips**

1. Preheat oven to 325°. Beat butter, sugars and vanilla until light and fluffy. Gradually beat in flour, mixing well. Press 3 cups of dough onto the bottom of a greased 13x9-in. pan. Bake until set, 20-22 minutes.
2. Cool for 10 minutes on a wire rack. Meanwhile, in a small saucepan, melt the caramels with cream over low heat until smooth. Pour over crust. Sprinkle with salt, then chocolate chips. Drop remaining dough over top by teaspoonfuls. Bake until light golden brown, 30-35 minutes longer. Cool on a wire rack.

SPECIAL OCCASION CUTOUT COOKIES

This is a old family cookie recipe; after many years, I have yet to find another one as good. I've served these at family gatherings and of course it's my Christmas cut-out cookie recipe. I gave these as gifts to overnight guests when my daughter got married, and also as Valentine's Day presents. At family gatherings, everyone asks for them!

—Teresa Broullire, Niagara, WI

Prep: 1 hour + chilling
Bake: 10 min./batch + standing
Makes: about 3½ dozen

- 1 **cup butter, softened**
- 1½ **cups confectioners' sugar**
- 1 **large egg**
- 1 **teaspoon vanilla extract**
- ½ **teaspoon almond extract**
- 2½ **cups all-purpose flour**
- ½ **teaspoon baking soda**
- ½ **teaspoon cream of tartar**

GLAZE
- 4 **cups confectioners' sugar**
- ½ **cup light corn syrup**
- ¼ **cup lemon juice**
  Food coloring

1. Cream butter and confectioners' sugar until light and fluffy. Beat in the egg and extracts. In another bowl, whisk flour, baking soda and cream of tartar; gradually beat into the creamed mixture.
2. Divide the dough in half. Shape each half into a disk; wrap in plastic. Refrigerate for 1 hour or until firm enough to roll.
3. Preheat oven to 375°. On a lightly floured surface, roll each disk of dough to ¼-in. thickness. Cut with a floured 2-in. puzzle piece-shaped cookie cutter. Place 1 in. apart on ungreased baking sheets, interlocking cookies together in pairs.
4. Bake until edges are light brown, 7-9 minutes. Remove from pans to wire racks to cool completely.
5. For glaze, mix confectioners' sugar, corn syrup and lemon juice until smooth.

MONOGRAMMED BURLAP RUNNER

Transform a piece of plain burlap fabric into a decorative monogrammed table runner using standard sewing and art supplies. You can adorn it with one or two letters as you wish to represent the couple's first or last names. Rustic yet refined, this personalized runner is sure to become a family heirloom they will cherish for years to come.

MATERIALS

- **Burlap, cut to length of table plus 30 in. (15-in. drop at each end)**
- **Fabric paint**
- **Purchased clear stencils of choice (or make your own—see Note)**
- **Painter's tape**
- **Stiff stencil brush**
- **Small scissors or seam ripper**

NOTE

To make your own stencil, use a blank clear stencil (available at craft stores and online) and follow the directions below. Before stenciling the runner, stencil on a fabric scrap to determine how much paint and pressure to apply. If using the same stencil in reverse for symmetrical designs, wash and dry it completely before reusing it on the runner.

DIRECTIONS

MAKING A STENCIL (OPTIONAL)

1. Choose a monogram or other simple shape from a book or other source. Print or photocopy the design to transfer it to a sheet of paper, enlarging or reducing the design to the desired size as needed.
2. Use painter's tape to secure the paper design to a cutting mat. Tape a clear blank stencil on top. Use a craft knife to cut out the stencil design, applying even pressure for a clean stencil edge. Use a clear ruler or straightedge guide as needed.

TABLE RUNNER

1. Determine the desired width of the runner; choose a thread at the edge of that desired width. Using a seam ripper or small scissors, pull the thread out of the weave. Cut along the path of the missing thread to trim the fabric to its desired width.
2. Make a ½-in. fringe along all edges of the runner by gently removing a few edge threads.
3. Lay the runner flat on a work table. Use tape to secure runner above and below stenciling area.
4. Position the stencil in the center of the runner, about 12 in. from one short end. Tape the stencil in place.
5. Daub paint onto the burlap using a stiff stencil brush, working the paint into the fabric. When the paint is dry, carefully remove the stencil.
6. Continue stenciling each short end of runner in the same way, using one stencil at a time and securing each with tape. Allow the paint to dry before removing stencil and proceeding to the next design.

Low Country Boil

It's time to gather 'round the table, y'all! Get ready to serve up a hearty helping of southern charm with a seafood boil that's out-of-this-world good.

Similar to crawfish boils in Louisiana, South Carolina's famous Low Country boils are more of an event than a dish. Frogmore Stew (page 212) is the star attraction, complemented by southern staples such as classic skillet corn bread, black-eyed peas, bourbon-spiked pecan tart and a refreshing shandy twist on sweet tea.

No matter what side of the Mason-Dixon line you happen to call home, you and your crew will enjoy the down-home comfort of the South in each delicious forkful.

Frogmore Stew (p. 212) **Oven-Fried Corn Bread** (p. 210)

SWEET TEA
BOYSENBERRY
SHANDY

3 tablespoons red wine vinegar
2 tablespoons olive oil
2 tablespoons whole grain mustard
1 teaspoon sugar

Toss celery and apples with lemon juice. In another bowl, whisk together mayonnaise, apple cider, vinegar, oil, mustard and sugar. Pour over celery mixture; toss to coat. Refrigerate, covered, 1 hour. Stir before serving.

BBQ CHICKEN GRITS BITES

I love grits and barbecued chicken, so I decided to combine them into a fun and tasty appetizer. You can also use shredded pork instead of chicken.
—Jamie Jones, Madison, GA

Prep: 30 min. • **Bake:** 15 min.
Makes: 2½ dozen

2 cups 2% milk
¾ cup quick-cooking grits
¼ teaspoon salt
⅛ teaspoon pepper
4 ounces crumbled goat cheese, divided
¼ cup apricot preserves
¼ cup barbecue sauce
1½ cups chopped rotisserie chicken
3 green onions, thinly sliced

1. Preheat oven to 350°. Grease 30 mini muffin cups.
2. In a large saucepan, bring milk to a boil. Slowly stir in grits, salt and pepper. Reduce heat to medium-low; cook, covered, until thickened, about 5 minutes, stirring occasionally. Stir in 2 ounces cheese. Spoon 1 tablespoon mixture into each prepared muffin cup.
3. In a bowl, mix preserves and barbecue sauce; toss with chicken. Spoon about 1 teaspoon chicken mixture into each cup; press lightly into grits.
4. Bake until heated through, 15-20 minutes. Top with remaining cheese; sprinkle with green onions. Cool 5 minutes before removing from pans. Serve warm.

SWEET TEA BOYSENBERRY SHANDY

I love an ice-cold beer on a hot summer day. I also love sweet iced tea, so one day I got the great idea to mix the two. Wow! It was absolutely delish. I experimented with different flavorings, and this combination was my favorite.
—Kelly Williams, Forked River, NJ

Prep: 10 min. • **Cook:** 5 min. + chilling
Makes: 12 servings (¾ cup each)

1½ cups water
4 tea bags
¾ cup sugar
¾ cup boysenberry syrup
4 cups cold water
3 bottles (12 ounces each) white ale beer, chilled
1 medium orange, sliced, optional

1. In a large saucepan, bring water to a boil; remove from heat. Add tea bags; steep, covered, 3-5 minutes, according to taste. Discard tea bags. Stir in sugar and syrup until dissolved. Stir in cold water. Transfer tea mixture to a 3-qt. pitcher; refrigerate until cold.
2. Stir beer into tea mixture; serve immediately. If desired, top individual servings with orange slices.

APPLE-CELERY SALAD

I created this recipe one night when I had a craving for a twist on a traditional slaw. It was a hit, and now it's a staple at all our family get-togethers. Add a cup of raisins for variety.
—Hutch Hutchins, Hartsville, SC

Prep: 15 min. + chilling
Makes: 10 servings

12 celery ribs, cut into ¼-inch slices
3 medium apples, cut into chunks
1 tablespoon lemon juice
⅓ cup mayonnaise
¼ cup sparkling apple cider or unsweetened apple juice

BBQ CHICKEN
GRITS BITES

OVEN-FRIED CORN BREAD

Nothing says good southern cooking like a crisp corn bread baked in a cast-iron skillet. This is an old family recipe that has been passed down to each generation.
—Emory Doty, Jasper, GA

Prep: 20 min. • **Bake:** 15 min.
Makes: 8 servings

- 4 **tablespoons canola oil, divided**
- 1½ **cups finely ground white cornmeal**
- ¼ **cup sugar**
- 2 **teaspoons baking powder**
- 1 **teaspoon baking soda**
- 1 **teaspoon salt**
- 2 **large eggs**
- 2 **cups buttermilk**

1. Place 2 tablespoons oil in a 10-in. cast-iron skillet; place in oven. Preheat oven to 450°. Whisk together cornmeal, sugar, baking powder, baking soda and salt. In another bowl, whisk together eggs, buttermilk and remaining oil. Add to the cornmeal mixture; stir just until the batter is moistened.

2. Carefully remove hot skillet from oven. Add batter; bake until golden brown and a toothpick inserted in center comes out clean, 15-20 minutes. Cut into wedges; serve warm.

TOP TIP

Secrets for Successful Corn Bread

Here are some hints for making the best corn bread:

- Before using cornmeal, make sure it's fresh. It should have a slightly sweet smell. Rancid cornmeal will smell stale and musty.
- To avoid overmixing, stir the batter by hand just until moistened. Lumps in the batter are normal and desired.
- Don't let the mixed batter stand before baking. Have the oven preheated and the skillet or pan ready to go.
- Corn bread tastes best fresh from the oven. If that's not possible, serve it the same day it's made.
- If you like a corn bread with more crust, use a dark pan or skillet instead of one with a light finish.

OVEN-FRIED CORN BREAD

ROASTED PEPPER PIMIENTO-STYLE CHEESE

Pimiento cheese is sometimes known as "the caviar of the South." This spread is so good, it's been requested as gifts. It will keep for several days in the refrigerator (it gets even better overnight). Be sure to use real mayonnaise, not salad dressing, or the cheese will be too sweet. Serve with veggies and crackers or spread on top of grilled burgers.
—Jerri Gradert, Lincoln, NE

Prep: 55 min. + chilling
Makes: 4 cups

- 2 medium sweet red peppers
- 1 Anaheim pepper
- 1 jalapeno pepper
- 1 pound (16 ounces) cheddar cheese, finely shredded
- 4 ounces cream cheese, softened
- ½ cup mayonnaise
- 1 teaspoon sugar
- ½ teaspoon white pepper
- ½ teaspoon hot pepper sauce
- ⅛ teaspoon cayenne pepper, optional
  Assorted fresh vegetables and crackers

1. Broil peppers 4 in. from heat on a foil-lined baking sheet until skins blister, about 4-5 minutes. With tongs, rotate peppers a quarter turn. Broil and rotate until all sides are blistered and blackened. Immediately place peppers in a bowl; let stand, covered, 20 minutes.
2. Peel off and discard charred skin. Remove stems and seeds. Finely chop peppers. Beat the cheeses, mayonnaise, sugar, white pepper, pepper sauce and, if desired, cayenne until blended. Stir in peppers. Transfer to a serving bowl. Refrigerate, covered, at least 2 hours. Serve with vegetables and crackers.
Note: Wear disposable gloves when cutting hot peppers; the oils can burn skin. Avoid touching your face.

HAM BISCUITS WITH WHITE CHEDDAR

Salty ham and fluffy biscuits combine with tender apples, spicy mustard and tangy cheddar for a sweet and savory sandwich. To speed things up, use prepared biscuits instead of making them from scratch.
—Amanda Reed, Nashville, TN

Prep: 25 min. • **Bake:** 10 min.
Makes: 1½ dozen

- 2 cups all-purpose flour
- 3 teaspoons baking powder
- 1 teaspoon salt
- ½ cup butter, cubed
- ¾ cup 2% milk
- 3 medium apples, peeled and chopped
- 1 teaspoon lemon juice
- 3 tablespoons Dijon mustard
- 5 slices fully cooked ham, quartered
- 9 slices white cheddar cheese, halved

1. Preheat oven to 450°. Whisk together flour, baking powder and salt. Cut in the butter until mixture resembles coarse crumbs. Add milk; stir just until mixture forms a ball.
2. Turn onto a lightly floured surface; knead 5-6 times. Roll dough to ½-in. thickness; cut with a floured 2-in. biscuit cutter. Place 1 in. apart on an ungreased baking sheet. Bake until golden brown, about 9-11 minutes.
3. Meanwhile, in a large saucepan, heat apples and lemon juice over medium-high heat until just tender, about 6-8 minutes. Split biscuits; spread with mustard. Layer with ham, cheese and apple mixture; replace tops.

BLACK-EYED PEA
TOMATO SALAD

FROGMORE STEW

This picnic-style medley of shrimp, smoked kielbasa, corn and spuds is a specialty of South Carolina cuisine. It's commonly dubbed Frogmore Stew or Beaufort Stew in recognition of both of the Low Country communities that lay claim to its origin. No matter what you call it, this one-pot wonder won't disappoint!
—*Taste of Home* Test Kitchen

Prep: 10 min. • **Cook:** 35 min.
Makes: 8 servings

- 16 cups water
- 1 large sweet onion, quartered
- 3 tablespoons seafood seasoning
- 2 medium lemons, halved, optional
- 1 pound small red potatoes
- 1 pound smoked kielbasa or fully cooked hot links, cut into 1-inch pieces
- 4 medium ears sweet corn, cut into thirds
- 2 pounds uncooked medium shrimp, peeled and deveined
  Seafood cocktail sauce
  Melted butter
  Additional seafood seasoning

1. In a stockpot, combine water, onion, seafood seasoning and, if desired, lemons; bring to a boil. Add the potatoes; cook, uncovered, 10 minutes. Add kielbasa and corn; return to a boil. Reduce heat; simmer, uncovered, 10-12 minutes or until potatoes are tender. Add shrimp; cook 2-3 minutes longer or until shrimp turn pink.
2. Drain; transfer to a bowl or a large platter. Serve with cocktail sauce, butter and additional seasoning.

Low Country Boils

There's one rule of thumb for a Low Country Boil: the bigger the crowd, the bigger the pot! The famous stew is popular fare for picnics, family reunions, trips to the beach, even camping. It's best served from a large platter on a newspaper-covered table and eaten with the fingers.

BLACK-EYED PEA TOMATO SALAD

Spending time in the kitchen with my late aunt was so much fun because she was an amazing cook and a great teacher. This black-eyed pea salad was one of her specialties. It's easy to make and is a nice alternative to pasta or potato salad. Add cooked cubed chicken breast to make it a meal on its own.
—Patricia Ness, La Mesa, CA

Prep: 20 min. + chilling
Makes: 12 servings (¾ cup each)

- 4 cans (15½ ounces each) black-eyed peas, rinsed and drained
- 3 large tomatoes, chopped
- 1 large sweet red pepper, chopped
- 1 cup diced red onion
- 4 bacon strips, cooked and crumbled
- 1 jalapeno pepper, seeded and diced
- ½ cup canola oil
- ¼ cup sugar
- ¼ cup rice vinegar
- 2 tablespoons minced fresh parsley
- 1½ teaspoons salt
- ½ teaspoon pepper
- ⅛ teaspoon garlic powder

1. Combine the first six ingredients. In another bowl, whisk together remaining ingredients. Add to bean mixture; toss to coat. Refrigerate, covered, at least 6 hours or overnight.
2. Stir just before serving.
Note: Wear disposable gloves when cutting hot peppers; the oils can burn skin. Avoid touching your face.

FROGMORE
STEW

**FAVORITE
CHOCOLATE-
BOURBON
PECAN TART**

BANANA CRUMB PUDDING

Friends and family ask me to make my thick and creamy banana pudding for all occasions. They can't get enough of the wonderful flavor of the fruit and the vanilla wafer crumbs. You can also top the classic Southern treat with meringue instead of whipped cream.
—Yvonnia Butner, Pinnacle, NC

Prep: 15 min. • **Cook:** 20 min. + chilling
Makes: 10 servings

 1   cup sugar
 ½   cup cornstarch
 6   cups 2% milk
 5   large egg yolks
 ¼   cup butter, cubed
 1   teaspoon vanilla extract
 1   package (12 ounces) vanilla wafers, coarsely crushed
 4   medium bananas, sliced

TOPPING
 1   cup heavy whipping cream
 3   tablespoons sugar

1. In a large heavy saucepan, mix sugar and cornstarch. Whisk in milk. Cook and stir over medium heat until thickened and bubbly. Reduce heat to low; cook and stir 2 minutes longer. Remove from heat.
2. In a bowl, whisk a small amount of hot mixture into egg yolks; return all to pan, whisking constantly. Bring to a gentle boil; cook and stir 2 minutes. Remove from heat. Stir in butter and vanilla. Cool 15 minutes, stirring occasionally.
3. In a 3-qt. baking dish, layer a third of the pudding, half each of the crushed wafers and bananas. Repeat layers. Top with remaining pudding. Press plastic onto surface of pudding. Refrigerate, covered, 1 hour.
4. In a bowl, beat cream until it begins to thicken. Add sugar; beat until stiff peaks form. Just before serving, spread whipped cream over pudding.

FAVORITE CHOCOLATE-BOURBON PECAN TART

I grew up in Louisiana where, as in most of the South, pecan pie is a staple. This tart variation is extra good because it includes chocolate. I decided to up the decadence even more by adding bourbon and drizzling some caramel on top.
—Amber Needham, San Antonio, TX

Prep: 15 min. • **Bake:** 30 min. + cooling
Makes: 12 servings

     Pastry for single-crust pie (9 inches)
 ½   cup semisweet chocolate chips
 2   large eggs
 ¾   cup dark corn syrup
 ½   cup sugar
 ¼   cup butter, melted
 2   tablespoons bourbon
 ¼   teaspoon salt
 1   cup pecan halves, toasted
 ¼   cup hot caramel ice cream topping

1. Preheat oven to 375°. On a lightly floured surface, roll pastry dough to a 12-in. circle. Press pastry onto bottom and up sides of an ungreased 11-in. tart pan with removable bottom. Sprinkle with chocolate chips.
2. Beat eggs, corn syrup, sugar, butter, bourbon and salt. Stir in pecans. Pour over chocolate chips. Bake until the center of tart is just set and crust is golden brown, 30-35 minutes.
3. Cool on a wire rack. Cut into slices. Serve with caramel topping.

Note: To toast nuts, bake in a shallow pan in a 350° oven for 5-10 minutes or cook in a skillet over low heat until lightly browned, stirring occasionally.
Pastry for single-crust pie (9 inches): Combine 1¼ cups all-purpose flour and ¼ teaspoon salt; cut in ½ cup cold butter until crumbly. Gradually add 3-5 tablespoons ice water, tossing with a fork until dough holds together when pressed. Wrap in plastic and refrigerate 1 hour.

SPARKLING PEACH PUNCH

I sampled this refreshing punch at my company's open house. Normally I don't like punch because it's too sweet—but this was so good, I couldn't get enough! The caterer kindly shared the recipe with me. With only three ingredients, it's also easy to make.
—Ruth Baker, Akron, OH

Prep: 5 min. + freezing
Makes: 12 servings (¾ cup each)

 2   medium peaches
 2   liters carbonated water, chilled
 1   can (11½ ounces) frozen white grape peach juice concentrate, thawed

Peel and cut peaches into ¼-in. slices. Place on a waxed paper-lined 15x10-in. pan; freeze. Just before serving, mix carbonated water and concentrate in a punch bowl. Add peach slices.

LEMON TOWELETTES *(Shown at top left)*

Some foods, like the Frogmore Stew on page 212, are best eaten with hands instead of forks. With these adorable towelettes, guests can easily clean up messy fingers. Squeeze juice from the lemon slices over your hands to erase any lingering odors from seafood or spicy seasonings, then dry. Your hands will be sweet smelling and fresh.

To make the towelettes, fold an assortment of 20x20-in. cloth napkins into squares. Place a lemon slice on top of each towelette. Wrap the towelettes with a piece of jute twine and tie into a knot to secure. Place towelettes in a basket or decorative serving dish for guests to grab as they fill their plates.

Rooftop Fireworks Party

Are you ready for a bang-up Fourth of July? No need to apply the sunscreen or worry about melting away in the heat—this year's party is an evening affair, complete with fireworks and a rooftop view.

Your ultimate patriotic shindig starts with an array of tempting appetizers, including dips, salsa and bruschetta. The grill is fired up and ready for chicken wings, turkey sliders and even pizza! Enjoy a few sweet treats, then quench your thirst with the best summertime cocktails (turn to page 223 to see how easy it is to set up a bar).

Grab your city-dwelling crew and head upstairs for cool breezes, an unparalleled panoramic view and the best food and libations. This Fourth of July, your hip summer bash is the place to be!

Watermelon Margaritas (p. 224) **Fresh Herb Vegetable Dip** (p. 218)
Easy Strawberry Salsa (p. 218) **Grilled Tomato-Peach Pizza** (p. 221)
Turkey Sliders with Sesame Slaw (p. 221) **South-of-the-Border Bruschetta** (p. 222)

EASY
STRAWBERRY
SALSA

GRILLED CHERRY-GLAZED CHICKEN WINGS

Prep: 20 min. • **Grill:** 15 min.
Makes: 1 dozen

- 12 chicken wings (about 3 pounds)
- 3 tablespoons canola oil, divided
- 1 garlic clove, minced
- 1 cup ketchup
- ½ cup cider vinegar
- ½ cup cherry preserves
- 2 tablespoons Louisiana-style hot sauce
- 1 tablespoon Worcestershire sauce
- 3 teaspoons coarse salt, divided
- 1 teaspoon coarsely ground pepper, divided

1. Using a sharp knife, cut through the two wing joints; discard wing tips. In a small saucepan, heat 1 tablespoon oil over medium heat. Add garlic; cook and stir 1 minute. Stir in ketchup, vinegar, preserves, hot sauce, Worcestershire sauce, 1 teaspoon salt and ½ teaspoon pepper. Cook and stir mixture until heated through. Brush wings with remaining oil; sprinkle with remaining salt and pepper.
2. Grill, covered, over medium heat 15-18 minutes or until juices run clear, turning occasionally and brushing with glaze during the last 5 minutes of grilling. Serve with remaining glaze.

ANTIPASTO SKEWERS

Take the usual meat and cheese tray to a new level by threading classic antipasto ingredients onto skewers and drizzling them with a tangy vinaigrette.
—Amanda Dekrey, Fargo, ND

Start to Finish: 15 min.
Makes: 1 dozen

- 24 grape tomatoes (about 1 pint)
- 1 carton (8 ounces) cherry-size fresh mozzarella cheese
- 12 thin slices hard salami (about ¼ pound)
- 12 pimiento-stuffed Queen olives
  Italian vinaigrette, optional

On 12 wooden 6-in. skewers, alternately thread tomatoes, mozzarella, folded salami slices and olives. Refrigerate until serving. If desired, drizzle skewers with vinaigrette to serve.

FRESH HERB VEGETABLE DIP

I entertain a lot and am always looking for an easy crowd-pleaser. If it's one where I use fresh ingredients from my herb and vegetable garden, it's even better! I serve this dip in individual servings for large parties so each person has their own cup. See photo on page 217.
—Isabel Minunni, Poughkeepsie, NY

Start to Finish: 15 min.
Makes: 3 cups

- ¼ cup olive oil
- 3 tablespoons lemon juice
- 1½ cups (12 ounces) fat-free sour cream
- 2 medium ripe avocados, peeled and cubed
- 2 tablespoons chopped chives
- 2 tablespoons chopped fresh parsley
- 2 tablespoons chopped fresh basil
- 1 tablespoon chopped fresh tarragon
- 1 tablespoon chopped fresh thyme
- 1 garlic clove, halved
- ½ teaspoon salt
- ¼ teaspoon pepper
  Assorted fresh vegetables

Place the first 12 ingredients in a food processor; process until smooth. Refrigerate until serving. Serve with fresh vegetables.

EASY STRAWBERRY SALSA

My salsa is sweet, colorful and has just a little bit of a bite from jalapeno peppers. I use fresh strawberries and my own home-grown vegetables, but you can also use produce available year round. It's delicious with tortilla chips or even as a garnish to grilled chicken or pork.
—Dianna Wara, Washington, IL

Prep: 20 min. + chilling
Makes: 16 servings (¼ cup each)

- 3 cups chopped seeded tomatoes (about 4 large)
- 1⅓ cups chopped fresh strawberries
- ½ cup finely chopped onion (about 1 small)
- ½ cup minced fresh cilantro
- 1 to 2 jalapeno peppers, seeded and finely chopped
- ⅓ cup chopped sweet yellow or orange pepper
- ¼ cup lime juice
- ¼ cup honey
- 4 garlic cloves, minced
- 1 teaspoon chili powder
  Baked tortilla chip scoops

In a large bowl, combine the first 10 ingredients. Refrigerate, covered, at least 2 hours. Serve with chips.
Note: Wear disposable gloves when cutting hot peppers; the oils can burn skin. Avoid touching your face.

GRILLED CHERRY-GLAZED
CHICKEN WINGS

"When I take these grilled wings to events, there are never any leftovers! Friends and family love them."

—ASHLEY GABLE, ATLANTA, GA

GRILLED
TOMATO-PEACH
PIZZA

GRILLED TOMATO-PEACH PIZZA

This delicious pizza is unique, healthy and easy to make. The fresh flavors make it a perfect appetizer for a summer party.
—Scarlett Elrod, Newnan, GA

Prep: 20 min. + standing • **Grill:** 5 min.
Makes: 16 pieces

- 4 medium tomatoes, thinly sliced
- ¼ teaspoon salt
- 2 medium peaches, halved
  Cooking spray
- 1 tablespoon cornmeal
- 1 tube (13½ ounces) refrigerated pizza crust
- 4 ounces fresh mozzarella cheese, sliced
- 6 fresh basil leaves, thinly sliced
- ⅛ teaspoon coarsely ground pepper

1. Sprinkle tomatoes with salt; let stand 15 minutes. Drain tomatoes on paper towels and pat dry.
2. Coat grill rack lightly with cooking oil. Grill peaches, covered, over medium heat or broil 4 in. from heat 2-3 minutes on each side or until peaches have grill marks and are tender, turning once. Remove peaches; cool slightly. Cut into slices.
3. Coat a 15x10x1-in. baking pan with cooking spray; sprinkle with cornmeal. Unroll crust into pan, pressing into a 12x10-in. rectangle. Spritz with cooking spray. Invert dough onto grill. Grill, covered, over medium heat 2-3 minutes or until bottom is lightly browned. Remove from grill, inverting onto baking pan.
4. Layer grilled side of pizza with tomatoes, peaches and cheese. Return pizza to grill. Cook, covered, 3-4 minutes or until crust is lightly browned and the cheese is melted, rotating halfway through cooking to ensure an evenly browned crust. Sprinkle with basil and pepper.

TURKEY SLIDERS
WITH SESAME SLAW

TURKEY SLIDERS WITH SESAME SLAW

I'm a fan of sliders, especially if they are Asian-inspired. Sweet Hawaiian rolls make them especially tasty.
—Gloria Bradley, Naperville, IL

Prep: 20 min. • **Grill:** 10 min.
Makes: 12 servings

- ⅔ cup mayonnaise
- 2 tablespoons hoisin sauce
- 2 teaspoons Sriracha Asian hot chili sauce
- 1½ pounds ground turkey
- ½ cup panko (Japanese) bread crumbs
- 2 green onions, finely chopped
- 2 tablespoons reduced-sodium soy sauce, divided
- 2 teaspoons minced fresh gingerroot
- 2 tablespoons rice vinegar
- 2 teaspoons sugar
- 2 teaspoons sesame oil
- 6 small carrots, grated (about 1½ cups)
- ⅓ cup thinly sliced red onion
- 3 tablespoons chopped fresh cilantro
- 1 teaspoon sesame seeds, toasted
- 12 slider buns or dinner rolls, split and toasted

1. In a small bowl, mix mayonnaise, hoisin sauce and chili sauce. Refrigerate until serving.
2. In a large bowl, combine turkey, panko, green onions, 1 tablespoon soy sauce and minced fresh ginger, mixing lightly but thoroughly. Shape mixture into twelve ½-in.-thick patties.
3. In a small bowl, whisk vinegar, sugar, oil and remaining soy sauce. Add carrots, onion, cilantro and sesame seeds; toss to combine.
4. Coat grill rack lightly with cooking oil. Grill sliders, covered, over medium heat or broil 4 in. from heat for 3 minutes on each side or until a thermometer reads 165°. Spread cut sides of buns with mayonnaise mixture. Layer with burger and slaw. Replace tops.

TOP TIP

Ground Turkey

Not all ground turkey is the same. If you want to save calories, look for labels that say lean ground turkey or ground turkey breast (instead of ground turkey, which may contain light and dark meat).

SOUTH-OF-THE-BORDER BRUSCHETTA

RAZZY JAZZY BERRY TARTS

I serve these fresh fruit tarts every July at my family's Independence Day celebration. Sometimes I substitute blackberries and blackberry jam, and I often add slivered almonds to the fillings.
—Nicole Chatron, Tulsa, OK

Prep: 1 hour • **Bake:** 25 min.
Makes: 3 dozen

- 1 cup butter, softened
- 6 ounces cream cheese, softened
- 2 cups all-purpose flour
- ½ teaspoon salt
- 1½ cups fresh blueberries
- ⅔ cup blueberry preserves
- 1½ cups fresh raspberries
- ⅔ cup seedless raspberry jam

1. Preheat oven to 325°. In a large bowl, beat butter and cream cheese until smooth. In another bowl, whisk flour and salt; gradually add to creamed mixture. Drop by scant tablespoonfuls into 36 greased miniature muffin cups. With floured hands, press dough onto bottoms and up sides of cups; flute edges if desired.
2. Bake 20-25 minutes or until golden brown. Cool for 5 minutes before removing from pans to wire racks to cool completely.
3. On a lightly floured surface, roll the remaining dough to ⅛-in. thickness. Cut dough with a floured 1½-in. star-shaped cookie cutter; cut ¼-in. stripes with a small knife. Place stars and stripes on ungreased baking sheets. Bake 4-6 minutes or until lightly browned.
4. In a small bowl, combine blueberries and blueberry preserves; spoon into half of the tarts. In another bowl, combine raspberries and raspberry jam; spoon into remaining tarts. Top with cut-outs.

SOUTH-OF-THE-BORDER BRUSCHETTA

I like to get creative in the kitchen, and this is one of the first dishes I threw together without using a recipe. It boasts a zesty Mexican flavor everyone is sure to love.
—Rebecca Spoolstra, Pilot Point, TX

Prep: 20 min. + chilling • **Broil:** 5 min.
Makes: 12 servings

- 2 medium ripe avocados, peeled and finely chopped
- 3 tablespoons minced fresh cilantro
- 1 to 2 red chili peppers, finely chopped
- ¼ teaspoon salt
- 2 small limes
- 12 slices French bread baguette (½ inch thick)
  Crumbled cotija cheese, optional

1. In a small bowl, mix avocados, cilantro, chili peppers and salt. Finely grate lime peels. Cut limes crosswise in half; squeeze juice from limes. Stir lime peel and juice into avocado mixture. Refrigerate for 30 minutes.
2. Preheat broiler. Place bread slices on an ungreased baking sheet. Broil 3-4 in. from heat 1-2 minutes on each side or until golden brown. Top with avocado mixture. If desired, sprinkle with cheese.

FETA-CUCUMBER CHEESE BALLS

I found an old recipe for cucumber balls that I converted to a whole cheese ball. The light and refreshing flavor has made it one of my favorites. I've made variations on it for three different holidays—the 4th of July version with tomato and basil was gone by the end of the day!
—Shelly Bevington, Hermiston, OR

Prep: 20 min. + chilling
Makes: 2 dozen

- 1 package (8 ounces) reduced-fat cream cheese
- 1 package (4 ounces) crumbled tomato and basil feta cheese
- ⅛ teaspoon salt
- ½ cup peeled, seeded and finely chopped cucumber
- 1 cup finely chopped walnuts
- 24 fresh basil leaves
- 24 toothpicks

1. In a small bowl, mix cream cheese, feta cheese and salt until blended. Stir in cucumber. Refrigerate, covered, 30 minutes.
2. Shape tablespoonfuls of cheese mixture into balls. Roll in walnuts. Thread a folded basil leaf and cheese ball on each toothpick. Refrigerate until serving.

THE ESSENTIAL SUMMER BAR

If your idea of a great Fourth of July is sipping a cocktail with friends as you watch the fireworks, you'll need to make sure the bar's ready when you are. Don't worry if you're missing a few items—basics go a long way.

THE BASICS
Classic summer spirits: Rum • Bourbon or whiskey • Gin • Vodka •Tequila

BUILD ON THE BASE
Keeping a few secondary options around will help you customize your cocktails. Bitters and flavored liqueurs are usually used in small quantities, so a single bottle will log a lot of miles. Bitters—classic Angostura • Orange liqueur—Cointreau or Grand Marnier • Elderflower liqueur—St-Germain • Ginger liqueur—Domaine de Canton

FROM THE FARMERS MARKET
Fresh produce, especially celery and tomato • Citrus • Seasonal stone fruits and berries • Herbs

MIXERS
Mixers are the nonalcoholic liquid ingredients added to cocktails. Club soda •Tonic water • Colas and ginger ale • Juice • Simple syrups

THE TOOL KIT
An initial investment in a few key items will pay you back for years to come. Cocktail shaker and strainer • Muddler (or the handle of a wooden spoon) • Ice cube trays • Paring knife • Bottle/wine opener • Peeler • Hand-held citrus press • Straws

SIPPING PRETTY

Add these colorful ice cubes to drinks to make them extra special. Just fill an ice tray with water and pop in fresh herbs, citrus or berries, then let it all freeze.

BERRIES
Strawberries • Blueberries • Raspberries

HERBS
Basil • Mint

CITRUS
Lemon • Lime • Orange

WATERMELON MARGARITAS

Summer's best flavors get frosty in the party-sized cocktail we serve at all of our backyard shindigs. We mix sun-ripened watermelon and our favorite tequila with just the right amount of ice for a thick and boozy sipper that pairs perfectly with grilled fare.
—Alicia Cummings, Marshalltown, IA

Start to Finish: 20 min.
Makes: 12 servings (¾ cup each)

- 2 medium limes
- ⅓ cup sugar
- 8 cups cubed seedless watermelon (1 inch)
- 2 cups ice cubes
- 2 cups tequila
- 1 cup Triple Sec
- ¼ cup lime juice
  Sugar, optional

1. Cut one lime into 12 wedges; reserve for garnishes. Cut remaining lime into wedges. Using these wedges, moisten the rims of 12 margarita or cocktail glasses. Sprinkle sugar on a plate; hold each glass upside down and dip rim into sugar. Discard remaining sugar.
2. Place half of the watermelon in a blender; cover and process until pureed (this should yield 3 cups). Add half of each of the following: ice cubes, tequila, Triple Sec and lime juice. If desired, add sugar. Cover and process until blended.
3. Serve in prepared glasses. Repeat with remaining ingredients. Garnish with reserved lime wedges.

LEMON BASIL MOJITO MOCKTAILS

In this twist on the classic summer beverage, lemon and basil take the place of mint. For a grown-up version, just add your favorite rum or vodka.
—Cheryl Perry, Hertford, NC

Prep: 15 min. + chilling
Makes: 12 servings

- 1½ cups sugar
- 4 cups water
- 6 cups fresh basil leaves, divided
  Crushed ice, divided
- 2 bottles (1 liter each) club soda

GARNISH
  Fresh lemon wedges

1. In a small saucepan, bring sugar and water to a boil. Cook and stir until sugar is dissolved. Place half of the basil in a small bowl. With a mortar or wooden spoon, crush basil until aromas are released. Stir into sugar mixture. Remove from heat; cool completely. Strain basil; refrigerate until cold.
2. Place 2 cups crushed ice and remaining basil in a 4-qt. pitcher. Using a muddler or a wooden spoon, press basil leaves against ice until aromas are released. Stir in basil syrup and soda. Serve over crushed ice in tall glasses; squeeze lemon wedges into drink.

MINTY PINEAPPLE RUM

This delicious drink is a great way to use fresh mint and celebrate summer. If your pineapple isn't overly ripe, add a bit more sugar. Save any leftover pineapple and mint syrup in an airtight glass container, or freeze the mixture in ice cube trays to use later.
—Colleen Delawder, Herndon, VA

Start to Finish: 10 min.
Makes: 14 servings (¾ cup each)

- 6 tablespoons fresh lime juice (about 3 limes)
- 4 cups cubed fresh pineapple (1 inch)
- 40 fresh mint leaves
- ⅔ cup superfine sugar
- ⅛ teaspoon kosher salt
- 1½ cups light rum
  Ice cubes
- 7 cups club soda, chilled

GARNISH
  Fresh pineapple slices and additional fresh mint leaves

Place the first five ingredients in a blender; cover and process until pureed. Transfer to a 1½-qt. pitcher; stir in rum. Pour ⅓ cup into each glass. Add ice; pour ½ cup soda over ice. Garnish with a pineapple slice and additional mint leaves.

WATERMELON MARGARITAS;
LEMON BASIL MOJITO MOCKTAILS

Cheers for Cheese!

There's always room on the invite list for cheese! What better way to add comforting flair, eye-fetching appeal and easy assembly to your menu? From savory appetizers to decadent desserts, a lineup of cheesy favorites offers guests a sure to please buffet of flavor.

Start with Party Cheese Bread or Mushroom-Stuffed Baked Brie, and then move onto a casual entree such as Amazing Mac & Cheese Pizza. For a sweet ending to any gathering, try New York Cheesecake with Shortbread Crust.

Whether you feel like Beer-Cheese Velvet Soup or Fruit-Topped Cheese Blitzes, raise your glass in a cheer for cheese! It's the perfect addition to any party—any time of year.

Party Cheese Bread (p. 234)

AMAZING MAC & CHEESE PIZZA

I love pizza, and I love macaroni and cheese. After lots of experimenting, I figured out a wonderful way to combine the two. The pizza is a big hit with my colleagues, friends and family!
—Martha Muellenberg, Vermillion, SD

Prep: 20 min. • **Cook:** 40 min.
Makes: 6 slices

- 1 cup uncooked elbow macaroni
- 1 loaf (1 pound) frozen pizza dough, thawed
- 2 teaspoons olive oil
- ½ teaspoon dried rosemary, crushed
- 8 slices process American cheese
- 1 package (8 ounces) shredded Velveeta cheese
- 2 cups shredded part-skim mozzarella cheese
- ¾ cup shredded cheddar cheese
- 8 bacon strips, cooked and crumbled
- ¼ teaspoon dried oregano

1. Preheat oven to 400°. Cook macaroni according to package directions; drain.
2. Press dough into a greased 14-in. pizza pan. Brush with oil; sprinkle with the rosemary. Top with American cheese.
3. Toss together shredded cheeses; sprinkle half of the mixture over pizza. Toss remaining cheese mixture with bacon, oregano and macaroni; distribute over top. Bake until crust is golden brown and cheese is melted, 35-40 minutes.

TOP TIP
Flavor Boost

For an extra tease to the taste buds, knead a dash or two of dried herbs into the pizza dough before pressing it into the pan. (Don't over work the dough or it might become tough.) Try basil, oregano, rosemary or Italian seasonings for a surefire sensation.

NEW YORK CHEESECAKE WITH SHORTBREAD CRUST

Light, creamy and smooth, this traditional New York cheesecake will melt in your mouth. I rely on a tender change-of-pace shortbread crust instead of a graham cracker crust. Try topping it with berries. This recipe takes time, but it's not difficult, and the result is well worth the effort.
—Karen Nielson, St. George, UT

Prep: 50 min. • **Bake:** 1¼ hours + chilling
Makes: 16 servings

- 1 cup all-purpose flour
- ¼ cup sugar
- 1 teaspoon grated lemon peel
- ½ cup cold butter, cubed
- 2 large egg yolks
- 1 teaspoon vanilla extract

FILLING
- 5 packages (8 ounces each) cream cheese, softened
- 1¾ cups sugar
- ½ cup heavy whipping cream
- 3 tablespoons all-purpose flour
- 2 teaspoons vanilla extract
- 2 teaspoons lemon juice
- 1½ teaspoons grated lemon peel
- 5 large eggs, lightly beaten
- 2 large egg yolks

1. Preheat oven to 325°. Place a greased 9-in. springform pan on a double thickness of heavy-duty foil (about 18 in. square). Wrap foil securely around pan. Place on a baking sheet.
2. In a small bowl, mix flour, sugar and lemon peel; cut in butter until crumbly. Add egg yolks and vanilla, tossing with a fork until mixture pulls together.
3. Press onto bottom and 1½ in. up the sides of prepared pan. Bake until lightly browned, roughly 12-16 minutes. Cool on a wire rack.
4. Beat cream cheese and sugar until smooth. Beat in cream, flour, vanilla, lemon juice and peel. Add eggs and egg yolks; beat on low speed just until blended. Pour into crust. Place springform pan in a larger baking pan; add 1 in. of hot water to larger pan.
5. Bake until center is just set and top appears dull, 1¼ to 1½ hours. Remove springform pan from water bath. Cool cheesecake on a wire rack 10 minutes. Loosen sides from pan with a knife; remove the foil. Cool 1 hour longer. Refrigerate overnight, covering when completely cooled. Remove rim of pan.

BEER-CHEESE VELVET SOUP

This soup was a hit with a group of German exchange teachers who visited our high school. I usually serve it with soft pretzels or crusty bread, and it's also a treat with slices of cooked bratwurst or kielbasa stirred into it.
—Paula Zsiray, Logan, UT

Start to Finish: 25 min.
Makes: 8 servings

- ¾ cup butter, cubed
- ¾ cup all-purpose flour
- 1 bottle (12 ounces) light beer
- 4 cups chicken or vegetable stock, divided
- 2 teaspoons Worcestershire sauce
- 1 teaspoon ground mustard
- ½ teaspoon salt
- ¼ teaspoon pepper
- ¼ teaspoon cayenne pepper
- 4 cups shredded cheddar cheese

1. In a large saucepan, melt butter over medium heat. Stir in flour until blended; gradually whisk in beer until smooth. Whisk in stock, Worcestershire sauce, mustard, salt, pepper and cayenne.
2. Bring to a boil, stirring constantly; cook and stir until thickened, 1-2 minutes. Reduce heat. Gradually stir in shredded cheese until melted.

AMAZING MAC & CHEESE PIZZA

STUFFED JALAPENO
GRILLED CHEESE

STUFFED JALAPENO GRILLED CHEESE

Not your ordinary grilled cheese, these sandwiches are all grown up! Made with a comforting combination of jalapenos, roasted garlic, cream cheese, bacon and provolone, they please just about all adults—and even adventurous kids!
—Melissa Haines, Valparaiso, IN

Prep: 40 min. + standing • **Cook:** 10 min.
Makes: 6 servings

- 1 whole garlic bulb
- 2 teaspoons olive oil
- ⅛ teaspoon salt
- 6 jalapeno peppers
- 1 package (8 ounces) cream cheese, softened
- 2 tablespoons shredded Parmesan cheese
- 2 tablespoons Worcestershire sauce
- 2 tablespoons butter, softened
- 12 slices multigrain bread
- 6 slices smoked provolone cheese
- 12 cooked bacon strips

1. Preheat oven to 425°. Remove papery outer skin from garlic bulb, but do not peel or separate the cloves. Cut off top of garlic bulb, exposing individual cloves. Drizzle cut cloves with oil. Sprinkle with salt. Wrap in foil. Bake until the cloves are soft, 25-35 minutes. Unwrap the garlic and cool to room temperature.

2. Meanwhile, cut peppers lengthwise in half; remove stems and seeds. Place peppers on a foil-lined baking sheet, skin side up. Broil 4 in. from heat until skins blister, about 5 minutes. Immediately place peppers in a small bowl; let stand, covered, 10 minutes. Peel off and discard charred skin. Cut pepper strips in half.

3. Preheat griddle over medium heat. In a small bowl, squeeze the garlic from skins; mash with a fork. Beat in cream cheese, Parmesan cheese and Worcestershire sauce until blended.

4. Spread butter over one side of each bread slice. Spread cheese mixture over unbuttered side of six bread slices. Layer each with jalapeno pepper pieces, 1 slice provolone cheese and 2 bacon strips. Top with remaining bread slices, buttered side up. Grill the sandwiches until golden brown and cheese is melted, 4-6 minutes on each side.

MUSHROOM-STUFFED BAKED BRIE

MUSHROOM-STUFFED BAKED BRIE

My husband loves sauteed mushrooms and I love brie, so I decided to experiment and see if I could create an appetizer that we both love. After so many attempts, I came up with this recipe that our friends love, too. I like to serve it with baguette slices on the side, to help scoop up the gooey cheesy goodness.
—Arlene Jacobson, Grand Terrace, CA

Prep: 30 min. • **Bake:** 30 min.
Makes: 8 servings

- 2 tablespoons butter
- 1 tablespoon olive oil
- ½ pound sliced fresh mushrooms
- 1 small onion, finely chopped
- 3 garlic cloves, minced
- 1 teaspoon dried thyme
- 1 teaspoon dried rosemary, crushed
- ⅛ teaspoon seasoned salt
- ⅛ teaspoon pepper
- 1 sheet frozen puff pastry, thawed
- 1 round (8 ounces) Brie cheese, halved horizontally
- 1 large egg, lightly beaten

1. Preheat oven to 400°. In a large skillet, heat butter and oil over medium-high heat. Add mushroom and onion; saute 6-8 minutes or until golden brown. Add garlic and seasonings; cook 1 minute longer. Remove from heat; transfer to a bowl and refrigerate until cooled.

2. On a lightly floured surface, unfold puff pastry. Place 1 Brie half on pastry, cut side up. Top with mushroom mixture and remaining Brie half, cut side down. Pull corners of pastry up over cheese, pinching together to seal on top. Place on an ungreased baking sheet, seam side down. Brush top and sides of pastry with egg. Bake until puffed and browned, about 30-35 minutes.

TOP TIP

Make it Memorable

Use a second sheet of thawed puff pastry to dress up the baked brie. With a small cookie cutter, cut shapes from the second sheet. Gently press the decorative cutouts on top of the wrapped brie before brushing the entire appetizer with the beaten egg. Bake as directed.

STUFFED SHELLS WITH ARRABBIATA SAUCE

This Italian classic takes on a distinctive Latin American flourish with the addition of chorizo. The sausage adds an extra kick to a dish that's already a favorite.
—Crystal McDuffy, Fairfax, VA

Prep: 30 min. • **Bake:** 20 min.
Makes: 12 servings

- 1 package (12 ounces) jumbo pasta shells
- 1 pound ground beef or turkey
- ½ pound fresh chorizo or bulk spicy pork sausage
- ½ large onion, chopped (about 1 cup)
- 3 garlic cloves, minced
- 1 package (10 ounces) frozen chopped spinach, thawed and squeezed dry
- ¾ teaspoon salt, divided
- ½ teaspoon pepper, divided
- 1 carton (15 ounces) part-skim ricotta cheese
- ¾ cup grated Parmesan cheese
- 2 large eggs, lightly beaten
- ¼ cup chopped fresh basil
- 2 tablespoons chopped fresh parsley

ARRABBIATA SAUCE
- 2 tablespoons olive oil
- 6 ounces sliced pancetta, coarsely chopped
- 2 teaspoons crushed red pepper flakes
- 2 garlic cloves, minced
- 2 jars (24 ounces each) marinara sauce
- 1½ cups shredded part-skim mozzarella cheese

1. Preheat oven to 400°. Cook pasta according to the package directions for al dente. Drain and rinse in cold water.
2. In a skillet, cook and crumble beef and chorizo with onion and garlic over medium heat until meat is no longer pink and vegetables are tender, 6-8 minutes; drain. Stir in the spinach, ½ teaspoon salt and ¼ teaspoon pepper. Transfer to a bowl; cool.
3. Stir ricotta and Parmesan cheeses, eggs, basil, parsley and remaining salt and pepper into meat mixture.
4. For sauce, in a saucepan, heat oil over medium heat. Add pancetta; cook and stir until golden brown, 6-8 minutes. Add the pepper flakes and garlic; cook and stir for 1 minute. Add the marinara sauce; bring to a simmer.

5. Spread 1 cup sauce into a greased 13x9-in. baking dish. Fill pasta shells with the meat mixture; place in baking dish, overlapping ends slightly. Top with the remaining sauce. Sprinkle with mozzarella cheese. Bake until heated through and cheese is melted, 20-25 minutes.

CHEESE & SAUSAGE BREAD BOWL DIP

Guests can't resist this creamy, cheesy goodness presented in a sourdough bowl. I guarantee that the warm sausage and cheese dip will be the first appetizer to disappear at your next party.
—Nadine Mesch, Mount Healthy, OH

Prep: 20 min. • **Bake:** 30 min.
Makes: 8 servings

- 1 loaf (1 pound) sourdough bread
- 1 pound bulk pork sausage
- 1 small onion, chopped
- ½ cup chopped sweet red pepper
- 1 package (8 ounces) cream cheese, softened
- 1 cup (8 ounces) sour cream
- 1 teaspoon Worcestershire sauce
- 1 cup shredded cheddar cheese
- 1 cup shredded part-skim mozzarella cheese
- 2 tablespoons minced fresh basil
  Baked pita chips

1. Preheat oven to 350°. Cut a thin slice off top of bread loaf. Hollow out bottom of loaf, leaving a ½-in.-thick shell. Cut removed bread into cubes; reserve.
2. In a large skillet, cook and crumble sausage with onion and pepper over medium heat until sausage is no longer pink and vegetables are tender, 6-8 minutes; drain.
3. In a bowl, beat cream cheese until smooth. Beat in sour cream and Worcestershire sauce until creamy. Stir in cheeses and basil. Add sausage mixture; pour into bread bowl. Replace top; wrap in foil. Bake until heated through, about 30 minutes.
4. Serve the dip in the bread bowl alongside bread cubes and pita chips.

STUFFED SHELLS WITH ARRABBIATA SAUCE

PARTY CHEESE BREAD

FRUIT-TOPPED CHEESE BLINTZES

My dad always requested this special dish for Father's Day; it was his favorite breakfast. You can switch up the fruit you use for the topping —warmed canned peaches are my personal favorite.
—Angela Matz, West Allis, WI

Prep: 25 min. + chilling • **Cook:** 20 min.
Makes: 6 servings

- 2 large eggs
- 1 cup 2% milk
- ¾ cup all-purpose flour
- ½ teaspoon salt

TOPPING
- 2 medium peaches, sliced
- ½ cup halved fresh sweet cherries
- 1 tablespoon sugar

FILLING
- 1½ cups (12 ounces) 2% cottage cheese, drained well
- 1 large egg, beaten
- 2 tablespoons sugar
- ½ teaspoon vanilla extract
- Dash ground cinnamon
- Sour cream, optional

1. Whisk eggs and milk. In another bowl, mix flour and salt; add to egg mixture and mix well. Refrigerate, covered, 1 hour.
2. In a bowl, toss peaches and cherries with sugar. Let stand while preparing the blintzes.
3. Heat a lightly greased 6-in. nonstick skillet over medium heat. Stir batter. Fill a ¼-cup measure halfway with batter; pour into center of pan. Quickly lift and tilt pan to coat bottom evenly. Cook until top appears dry; turn blintz over and cook 15-20 seconds longer or until bottom is cooked. Remove to a wire rack. Repeat with remaining batter, greasing pan as needed. Meanwhile, in a bowl, beat cottage cheese, egg, sugar, vanilla and cinnamon until almost smooth. Spoon about 2 tablespoons filling onto each crepe. Fold opposite sides of crepe over filling, forming a rectangular bundle.
4. On a greased griddle, cook blintzes for 3 minutes, seam side down. Turn; cook until golden brown, 3-5 minutes longer. Top with fruit and, if desired, sour cream.

PARTY CHEESE BREAD

Cheesy, buttery and finger-licking good, this bread is sinfully tasty. It's so pretty, it makes a perfect centerpiece at a party, and your guests might be reluctant to dig into it. But once they do, it won't last long!
—Karen Grant, Tulare, CA

Prep: 25 min. • **Bake:** 25 min.
Makes: 8 servings

- 1 round loaf sourdough bread (1 pound)
- 1 pound (16 ounces) Monterey Jack cheese, sliced
- ½ cup butter, melted
- 2 tablespoons lemon juice
- 2 tablespoons Dijon mustard
- 1½ teaspoons garlic powder
- ½ teaspoon onion powder
- ½ teaspoon celery salt
- Minced fresh chives, optional

1. Preheat oven to 350°. Cut bread into 1-in. slices to within ½ in. of bottom of loaf. Repeat cuts in opposite direction. Insert cheese in cuts.
2. Mix all remaining ingredients except chives; drizzle over bread. Wrap in foil; place on a baking sheet.
3. Bake 20 minutes. Unwrap; bake until cheese is melted, about 10 minutes. If desired, sprinkle with chives.

POUTINE

The ultimate in French-Canadian comfort food, poutine commonly features french fries topped with cheese curds and gravy. This side dish is quick to fix with frozen potatoes and packaged gravy, but it has all the traditional comfort you'd expect.
—Shelisa Terry, Henderson, NV

Start to Finish: 30 min.
Makes: 4 servings

- 4 cups frozen french-fried potatoes
- 1 envelope brown gravy mix
- ¼ teaspoon pepper
- ½ cup white cheddar cheese curds or cubed white cheddar cheese

1. Prepare french fries according to package directions.
2. Meanwhile, prepare the gravy mix according to package directions. Stir in pepper. Place fries on a serving plate; top with cheese curds and gravy.

BUILD A PERFECT CHEESE PLATTER

Cheese, please! It's easy to build a cheese platter guests won't be able to step away from. Try these tips for the perfect cheese tray.

- You'll need about 3-4 oz. of cheese per person (2 lbs. for 8 guests).

- Choose a variety of soft, firm, blue and aged cheeses.

- Be adventurous! Select a variety of colors and flavors. But include one familiar type of cheese in the mix.

- Arrange soft cheeses in larger pieces on a cutting board so guests can slice their own samples. For easier sampling, cut harder cheeses before serving.

- Label each selection so guests know what they're sampling. They may be inspired to shop for their favorites after the party!

- Add visual appeal and complement gourmet cheese flavors with sweet grapes, sliced apples, cured prosciutto and toasted French bread. Add a small jar of fig jam, some almonds or a few slices of pear.

- Let your cheese platter sit out for about 30 minutes before guests arrive, because most cheeses taste best when they are at room temperature.

1. CAHILL PORTER CHEESE
Characteristics: Medium texture, marbling from porter beer, cow's milk
Flavor notes: Mild, caramel, chocolaty
Beverage pairing: Guinness or dark ales

2. MIFROMA GRUYERE
Characteristics: Hard texture, aged minimum of 5 months, cow's milk
Flavor notes: Nutty, fruity, earthy
Beverage pairing: chardonnay, pinot noir, cabernet sauvignon, sparkling wine

3. ILCHESTER WHITE STILTON WITH CRANBERRIES
Characteristics: Soft texture, creamy, studded with cranberries, cow's milk
Flavor notes: Mild, fresh and milky with sweet, tangy cranberry
Beverage pairing: Riesling, zinfandel

4. PRESIDENT BRIE
Characteristics: Soft texture, creamy, cow's milk, edible rind
Flavor notes: Mild, buttery, subtle mushroom notes
Beverage pairing: sauvignon blanc, syrah, dry champagne

5. BALLYSHANNON CHEDDAR
Characteristics: Smooth yet crumbly texture, creamy, aged, cow's milk
Flavor notes: Rich, sweet, earthy
Beverage pairing: Riesling, sauvignon blanc, zinfandel

Scary Movie Night

The days are shorter, there's a chill in the air, leaves are blowing and the wind in howling. Perhaps a quiet, cozy night indoors with a few fellow aficionados of classic horror flicks is your ideal setting for a delightfully and frightfully fun Halloween.

Staging the ultimate Halloween movie night is easy with these terrifyingly good treats, including fright-night features such as Dial M for Mustard Pretzels, Bates Motel Grape Salad, and even Elm Street Cheeseburger Joes.

But never fear! The savory, warm flavors of these delicious recipes are everything you want from a fall meal—the perfect antidote to the monster under the bed or on the screen!

Chicken & Cheddar Mummy Braid (p. 241) **Dial M for Mustard Pretzels** (p. 238)
Freaky Frankenstein Cookies (p. 245)

DIAL M FOR
MUSTARD
PRETZELS

ROSEMARY'S BABY APPETIZER MEATBALLS

This recipe was created as an hors d'oeuvre for a friend's wedding and became an instant hit and family treasure. Enjoy!
—Steve Hansen
Redmond, WA

Prep: 20 min. • **Bake:** 25 min.
Makes: about 2 dozen

- 2 tablespoons olive oil
- 4 garlic cloves, minced
- 1 teaspoon curry powder
- 1 large egg, lightly beaten
- 1 jar (4 ounces) diced pimientos, drained
- ¼ cup dry bread crumbs
- ¼ cup minced fresh parsley
- 2 tablespoons minced fresh rosemary
- 2 pounds bulk pork sausage
  Pretzel sticks or toothpicks, optional

1. Preheat oven to 350°. In a small skillet, heat the oil over medium heat; saute the garlic with curry powder until tender, 1-2 minutes. Cool slightly.
2. In a bowl, combine egg, pimentos, bread crumbs, parsley, rosemary and the garlic mixture. Add sausage; mix lightly but thoroughly.
3. Shape into 1¼-in. balls. Place on a greased rack in a 15x10x1-in. pan. Bake until cooked through, 25-30 minutes. If desired, serve with pretzels.

DIAL M FOR MUSTARD PRETZELS

This quick and fun snack is similar to the mustard pretzels you can buy at the store, but you can make it for a fraction of the price. It's a killer recipe for all kinds of parties and football gatherings.
—Sarah Mathews, Ava, MO

Prep: 10 min. • **Bake:** 15 min. + cooling
Makes: 6 cups

- 6 cups sourdough pretzel nuggets
- ⅓ cup prepared mustard
- 2 tablespoons honey
- 1 tablespoon cider vinegar
- ½ teaspoon onion powder
- ½ teaspoon garlic powder
- ½ teaspoon ground mustard

1. Preheat oven to 350°. Place pretzels in a bowl. In another bowl, mix remaining ingredients. Drizzle over the pretzels; toss to coat.
2. Spread in a greased 15x10-in. pan. Bake until lightly browned and crisp, 15-20 minutes, stirring every 5 minutes. Cool completely in pan on a wire rack. Store in an airtight container.

TOP TIP

Making Meatballs of Equal Size

For meatballs to cook evenly, it's important for them to be the same size. Try one of these easy methods to make a batch of perfectly sized meatballs.

Use a 1½- or 1¾-in.-diameter scoop to scoop the mixture into equal portions. Gently roll each into a ball.

Or lightly pat meat mixture into a 1-in.-thick rectangle. Cut the rectangle into the same number of squares as meatballs in the recipe (Image). Gently roll each square into a ball.

DIAL M FOR MURDER, ROSEMARY'S BABY POSTERS:

ROSEMARY'S BABY
APPETIZER MEATBALLS

CHICKEN & CHEDDAR
MUMMY BRAID

CHICKEN & CHEDDAR MUMMY BRAID

A hearty chicken filling is the spooky surprise inside this yummy mummy braid. Each slice is like a hot sandwich with flavors reminiscent of a classic pot pie.

—Lily Rose, Ogden, UT

Prep: 20 min.
Bake: 25 min.
Makes: 12 servings

- 1 medium sweet red pepper
- 1 large garlic clove
- 2 cups chopped cooked chicken
- 1 cup shredded sharp cheddar cheese
- ¾ cup frozen peas
- ½ cup mayonnaise
- ½ teaspoon dried thyme
- ¼ teaspoon salt
- 2 tubes (8 ounces each) refrigerated crescent rolls
- 1 large egg white, lightly beaten

1. Preheat oven to 375°. For mummy eyes, cut two 1-in. circles and two ¼-in. circles from pepper; chop the remaining pepper for filling. Cut garlic crosswise into slices. Reserve two center slices for eyes; mince the remaining garlic for filling.
2. Place the chopped pepper and minced garlic in a bowl. Stir in chicken, cheese, peas, mayonnaise and seasonings.
3. Unroll both tubes of crescent dough onto a lightly floured 15x12-in. sheet of parchment paper. Press dough into a 15x12-in. rectangle, pressing perforations to seal. Spoon the filling lengthwise down the center third of the rectangle.
4. On each long side, cut eight strips, extending about 3½ in. into the center. Fold one strip from each side over the filling, twisting each strip once. Repeat with the remaining strips, leaving an opening at one end for the mummy's face. Transfer to a 15x10x1-in. pan.
5. For eyes, alternately stack pepper and garlic pieces and place in the opening. Brush egg white over dough. Bake until golden brown and filling is heated through, 25-28 minutes.

BATES MOTEL GRAPE SALAD

BATES MOTEL GRAPE SALAD

Cool and tangy flavors of vanilla yogurt and cream cheese are brightened with the sweetness and crunch of red grapes in this refreshing salad. And just for scary movie night, they might look like eyeballs...

—Geraldine Saucier, Albuquerque, NM

Start to Finish: 10 min.
Makes: 8 servings

- 1 cup (8 ounces) vanilla yogurt
- 2 ounces cream cheese, softened
- 1 tablespoon honey
- ½ teaspoon ground cinnamon
- ½ teaspoon minced fresh mint
- 6 cups seedless red grapes

Process the first five ingredients in a food processor until smooth. Place grapes and the yogurt mixture in a bowl; toss to coat. Refrigerate until serving.

APPLE & BROCCOLI GHOST SALAD

Crunchy veggies, creamy dressing, and sweet fruit come together in this fabulous salad. Serve it immediately or chill until serving—it stays fresh and crisp for hours!

—Shelly Bevington, Hermiston, OR

Start to Finish: 10 min.
Makes: 14 servings (¾ cup each)

- 1 small bunch broccoli, cut into florets
- 1 small head cauliflower, cut into florets
- 2 medium apples, chopped
- ½ large sweet onion, chopped
- ½ cup chopped walnuts, toasted
- ⅓ cup dried cherries
- 1 cup coleslaw salad dressing

Combine the first six ingredients. Drizzle dressing over the salad; toss to coat. Refrigerate until serving.

ELM STREET CHEESEBURGER JOES

Turkey and bacon give the classic sloppy joe a frightfully tasty new spin. Freddy Krueger may invite himself to dinner!
—Janine Smith, Columbia, SC

Start to Finish: 25 min.
Makes: 8 servings

- 1½ pounds ground turkey
- 1 large red onion, finely chopped
- 12 bacon strips, cooked and crumbled
- 2 medium tomatoes, chopped
- ¾ cup ketchup
- ½ cup chopped dill pickle
- 2 tablespoons yellow mustard
- 1½ cups shredded cheddar cheese
- 8 hamburger buns, split

1. In a large skillet, cook and crumble turkey with onion over medium heat until turkey is no longer pink, 6-8 minutes. Stir in bacon, tomatoes, ketchup, pickle and mustard; heat through.
2. Stir in cheese until melted. Spoon meat onto bun bottoms. Replace tops.

TOP TIP

Sloppy Joe Redux

Have leftover sloppy joe meat? Put it to good use with one of these quick-to-fix variations. You may find yourself making extra just to be able enjoy these fun retakes the next day!

- Spread leftover meat in a casserole dish. Place sliced process cheese over the meat; top with homemade or refrigerator biscuits. Bake until biscuits are done.
- Stir leftover meat into cooked egg noodles. Place in a baking dish and sprinkle with shredded cheddar cheese. Bake until heated through.
- For a homemade calzone, cut store-bought pizza dough into quarters; stretch each piece into an 8-inch round. Spoon leftover meat onto dough rounds and top with shredded mozzarella. Fold dough over, pinch to seal and bake until golden.
- Add leftover meat to an omelet, a quesadilla or a grilled cheese sandwich.

SPICED STEAK POTATO FINGERS WITH DRACULA DIPPING SAUCE

These oven-roasted potatoes are a fantastic alternative to deep-fried french fries. The sauce is also great on burgers.
—Dana Alexander, Lebanon, MO

Prep: 15 min. + soaking • **Bake:** 55 min.
Makes: 10 servings

- 6 medium potatoes
- ¼ cup olive oil
- 2 tablespoons plus 1 teaspoon chili powder, divided
- 1 tablespoon dried parsley flakes
- ½ teaspoon cayenne pepper, divided
- ½ teaspoon onion powder
- ¼ teaspoon salt
- ¼ teaspoon pepper
- ¼ cup grated Parmesan cheese
- ¾ cup Miracle Whip
- ¼ cup hickory smoke-flavored barbecue sauce

1. Cut potatoes into ¼-in. strips; soak in cold water for 30 minutes. Drain; pat potatoes dry with paper towels.
2. Preheat oven to 400°. Toss potatoes with oil, 2 tablespoons chili powder, parsley, ¼ teaspoon cayenne, onion powder, salt and pepper. Arrange the potatoes in a single layer in a greased 15x10-in. pan. Bake 45 minutes.
3. Sprinkle with cheese. Bake until the potatoes are dark golden brown, about 10 minutes longer. Meanwhile, mix Miracle Whip, barbecue sauce and remaining chili powder and cayenne. Serve with potatoes.

ELM STREET
CHEESEBURGER JOES

APPLE
SCREAM
BARS

APPLE SCREAM BARS

I made these delicious bars for a friend's birthday once and now he requests them every year! They have a tasty tartness with a cinnamony kick. Be sure to chop the apples into small cubes—if the apple pieces are too big, the bars will fall apart.

—Danielle Miller, Tonawanda, NY

Prep: 30 min. • **Bake:** 30 min. + cooling
Makes: 2 dozen

- 1¼ cups all-purpose flour
- ¾ cup graham cracker crumbs
- ¾ cup quick-cooking oats
- ¾ cup packed brown sugar, divided
- ¼ cup sugar
- ¾ cup butter, melted
- 2 large Granny Smith apples, peeled and chopped
- 1 teaspoon ground cinnamon
- ¼ teaspoon ground ginger
- ⅛ teaspoon ground cloves

GLAZE
- ½ cup confectioners' sugar
- 1 tablespoon 2% milk

1. Preheat oven to 350°. Mix flour, cracker crumbs, oats, ½ cup brown sugar and the sugar. Stir in butter. Reserve 1 cup crumb mixture for topping; press the rest onto the bottom of a greased 13x9-in. pan. Bake until set, 8-10 minutes. Cool on a wire rack.
2. Mix apples, spices and the remaining brown sugar. Spread over crust; sprinkle with the reserved topping. Bake until the apples are tender, 30-35 minutes. Cool completely in pan on a wire rack.
3. Mix confectioners' sugar and milk; drizzle over top. Cut into bars.

TOP TIP

All About Apples

Although apples are available all year, each variety has its own peak season. Select apples that are firm, crisp and have smooth, unblemished skin that is free from bruises. Store unwashed apples in the refrigerator away from vegetables with strong aromas. You can store refrigerated apples for up to 6 weeks. One pound of apples (about 3 medium) yields 2¾ cups sliced apples.

FREAKY FRANKENSTEIN COOKIES

FREAKY FRANKENSTEIN COOKIES

They're alive! Each year when the Halloween invitations start coming my way, I create a little treat to contribute. These cute cookies bring every party to life .

—Philia Kelnhofer, West Allis, WI

Prep: 30 min. + chilling
Bake: 10 min. + cooling
Makes: 2 dozen

- 1 package (17½ ounces) sugar cookie mix
- ¼ cup all-purpose flour
- ½ cup butter, melted
- 1 large egg
- 1 teaspoon vanilla extract
- ¼ teaspoon peppermint extract
- 12 drops food coloring
- 24 Andes mint candies
  Black and white jimmies
  Decorating icing and candy eyeballs, optional

1. Mix cookie mix and flour; stir in melted butter, egg, extracts and food coloring until blended. Divide dough in half. Shape each half into a 1-in.-thick square; wrap each square in plastic. Refrigerate until firm enough to roll, about 1 hour.
2. Preheat oven to 350°. On a lightly floured surface, roll each portion of dough to an 8x6-in. rectangle. Cut each rectangle into twelve 2-in. squares. Place 1 in. apart on ungreased baking sheets.
3. Bake until the edges begin to brown, 7-9 minutes. Remove from oven; place a mint candy at the top of each square. Return to oven; bake until chocolate begins to melt, 1-2 minutes.
4. Using a spatula, spread mint candies to cover top end of cookies; sprinkle with jimmies for hair. Remove to wire racks to cool completely. Decorate faces as desired, using icing and eyeballs.

Alphabetical Index

A complete listing of all recipes in this book.

A

All-Star Muffin Mix, 86
Almond-Herb Bread Dressing, 97
Amazing Mac & Cheese Pizza, 228
Andrea's Stuffed Mushrooms, 93
Antipasto Skewers, 218
Appetizer Tortilla Pinwheels, 31
Apple & Broccoli Ghost Salad, 241
Apple-Celery Salad, 208
Apple Cider Doughnut Holes, 84
Apple Pecan Salad, 114
Apple Scream Bars, 245
Apricot-Chipotle Cheese Spread, 137
Apricot Cooler, 152
Apricot White Fudge, 36
Apricot Wraps, 14
Artichoke Shrimp Pasta Salad, 138
Aunt Dorothy's Russian Tea, 98

B

Bacon Beef Tenderloin with Cranberry
    Glaze, 25
Bacon-Gruyere Smashed Potatoes, 25
Baked Crab Wontons, 147
Banana Crumb Pudding, 215
Banana Nut Bread, 86
Bananas Foster Sundaes, 127
Barley, Greens & Sweet Potato Salad, 47
Basil Parmesan Bread, 80
Bates Motel Grape Salad, 241
BBQ Chicken Grits Bites, 208
BBQ Turkey Meatballs, 104
Beer-Cheese Velvet Soup, 228
Beet Salad with Orange Vinaigrette, 178
Best Cinnamon Rolls, 80
Bittersweet Chocolate Cheesecake, 66
Black Bean Chicken Nachos, 110
Black-Eyed Pea Tomato Salad, 212
Black Raspberry Bars, 151
Blue Ribbon Red Velvet Cake, 184
Bourbon-Spiced Glazed Ham, 160
Brown Sugar Pecan Cake, 98
Browned Butter Red Potatoes, 160
Brussels Sprouts with Bacon
    Vinaigrette, 22
Butter Cookies, 184
Buttery Carrots, 159

C

Candy Cane Shortbread Bars, 71
Cantina Pinto Beans, 51

Cape Cod Bay Brown Bread, 93
Caramel Apple & Brie Skewers, 9
Caraway Bread, 20
Cardamom Cookies, 128
Cardamom Crumb Cake, 131
Carrot-Parsnip Soup, 166
Cashew Clusters, 60
Cauliflower with White Cheddar
    Sauce, 118
Chai Tea Cupcakes, 124
Champagne Sipper, 190
Cheese & Sausage Bread Bowl Dip, 232
Cheese Ball Roll-Ups, 94
Cheese Grape Appetizers, 13
Cherry Dessert Lasagna, 183
Cherry Pull-Apart Bread, 83
Chicken & Cheddar Mummy Braid, 241
Chicken & Swiss Casserole, 141
Chicken Tamales, 55
Chicken with Red Pepper Sauce
    & Spinach, 178
Chickpea Salad, 201
Chile Relleno Squares, 51
Chocolate Caramel Turkey Legs, 120
Chocolate-Coconut Layer Bars, 142
Chocolate-Dipped Ice Cream Cone
    Cupcakes, 181
Chocolate-Dipped Macaroons, 66
Chocolate Molten Cakes, 62
Chocolate Pistachio Biscotti, 60
Chocolate Salted Caramel Bars, 204
Chocolate-Strawberry Pretzel
    Cookies, 77
Chocolate Tart with Cranberry
    Raspberry Sauce, 182
Chocolate Truffles, 65
Cinnamon Almond Brittle, 131
Citrus Herb Turkey, 97
Classic Tres Leches Cake, 56
Coconut-Rum Cake Pops, 14
Country White Bread, 32
Crab Cake Lettuce Wraps, 190
Cranberry Eggnog Cheesecake Bars, 71
Cranberry-Nut Couscous Salad, 43
Cranberry Roasted Squash, 19
Creamy Strawberry Cheesecake, 178
Crescent Chicken Bundles, 117

D

Deep-Fried Candy Bars on a Stick, 10
Deluxe Pizza Casserole, 118

Dial M for Mustard Pretzels, 238
Double Cheese Artichoke Frittata, 188
Double Chocolate Fudge, 62

E

Easy Biscuit Muffins, 160
Easy Strawberry Salsa, 218
Eggnog Molded Salad, 43
Elegant White Chocolate Mousse, 65
Elm Street Cheeseburger Joes, 242

F

Fava Bean & Pea Salad, 159
Favorite Chocolate-Bourbon Pecan
    Tart, 215
Feta-Cucumber Cheese Balls, 222
Fluffy Sweet Potato Custard Pie, 100
Freaky Frankenstein Cookies, 245
Freeze & Bake Rolls, 47
Fresh Artichokes with Lemon-Yogurt
    Dip, 22
Fresh Herb Vegetable Dip, 218
Fried Ice Cream, 56
Frogmore Stew, 212
Frosted Carrot Cake Cookies, 142
Fruit-Topped Cheese Blintzes, 234
Fruit with Poppy Seed Dressing, 138
Fruitcake Christmas Cookies, 72
Fruity Chicken Salad Mini
    Sandwiches, 151

G

Garden Green Bean Salad, 202
Garden Green Beans & Potatoes, 104
Garlic-Dill Deviled Eggs, 137
Ginger Apple-Pear Crisp, 124
Ginger Berry Compote, 163
Ginger-Tuna Kabobs, 9
Glazed Chocolate Angel Food Cake, 152
Green Pea Casserole, 117
Grilled Cherry-Glazed Chicken
    Wings, 218
Grilled Tomato-Peach Pizza, 221

H

Ham & Cheese Biscuit Stacks, 10
Ham & Swiss Braids, 148
Ham Biscuits with White Cheddar, 211
Hazelnut Chocolate Chip Scones, 87
Hearty Vegetable Soup, 44
Heavenly Cheese Danish, 84

Herb-Vinaigrette Potato Salad, 166
Herbed Dip for Veggies, 31
Herbed Lamb Chops with Crispy
    Potatoes, 171
Herby Pea Salad, 190
Holiday Cranberry Salad, 94
Homemade Eggnog, 35
Homemade Guacamole, 51
Homemade Sage Sausage Patties, 189
Honey Pecan Triangles, 73
Horseradish Meatballs, 13

J

Jalapeno Cheese Bread, 80
Jicama Romaine Salad, 52

K

Key Lime Trifle, 203

L

Layered Candy Cane Dessert, 35
Leek Prosciutto Pizza, 166
Lemon Basil Mojito Mocktails, 224
Lemon-Dill Cucumber Dip, 156
Lemon-Herb Salmon Toasts, 19
Lemon Layer Cake, 143
Lemon Rice Salad, 46
Lemon Ricotta Fritters, 193
Lemony Shrimp & Snow Pea Pasta, 169
Lime Chicken with Blackberry Salsa, 201
Lime Chiffon Jello, 120
Lime-Raspberry Pie with Coconut
    Cream, 194

M

Make-Ahead Mashed Potatoes, 40
Make-Ahead Veggie Salad, 141
Maple-Almond Butternut Squash, 44
Maple Butterscotch Brownies, 74
Maple-Glazed Cinnamon Chip Bars, 73
Marinated Mozzarella, 10
Marinated Steak with Grilled
    Onions, 202
Marshmallow Pops, 13
Merry Grinchmas Cookies, 74
Mexican Stuffed Peppers, 52
Minty Pineapple Rum, 224
Mocha Shortbread, 65
Molasses Spice Cake, 124
Moscow Mule, 20
Mushroom & Spinach Eggs
    Benedict, 171
Mushroom Shrimp Bisque, 19
Mushroom-Stuffed Baked Brie, 231

N

New York Cheesecake with Shortbread
    Crust, 228

O

Onion & Garlic Soda Bread, 138
Onion-Garlic Hash Browns, 193
Orange Biscuits with Honey Butter, 84
Orange Chocolate Fondue, 62
Oven-Fried Corn Bread, 210

P

Parmesan Snap Pea Pasta, 148
Party Cheese Bread, 234
Peach Champagne, 198
Pepper Mango Salsa, 148
Peppermint Brownies, 77
Perfect Winter Salad, 40
Pesto-Goat Cheese Toasts, 156
Pineapple & Coconut Carrot Salad, 148
Pistachio Brownie Toffee Bars, 74
Pork & Vegetable Spring Rolls, 168
Poutine, 234
Prosciutto Honeydew with Balsamic
    Reduction, 202
Pumpkin Cake with Whipped Cinnamon
    Frosting, 127
Pumpkin Cranberry Bread, 84
Pumpkin Cupcakes with Spiced
    Frosting, 120
Pumpkin Pie Pudding, 109

Q

Quick Tomato Soup, 178

R

Razzy Jazzy Berry Tarts, 222
Rhubarb-Buttermilk Coffee Cake, 172
Rhubarb Lemonade Slush, 163
Roasted Pepper Pimiento-Style
    Cheese, 211
Rosemary-Lemon Shortbread Sandwich
    Cookies, 163
Rosemary's Baby Appetizer
    Meatballs, 238
Rosy Apple Dumplings, 183

S

Salmon Patties with Garlic-Dill
    Sauce, 171
Sauteed Radishes, 159
Seasoned Garlic Gravy, 40
Shrimp & Garlic Bruschetta, 198
Shrimp Pomodoro, 181
Six-Bean Chili, 107
Slaw-Topped Beef Sliders, 109
Slow-Cooked Sausage Dressing, 44
Slow-Cooked White Bean Chili, 32
Slow Cooker Crab Dip, 104
Slow Cooker Pineapple Sweet
    Potatoes, 43
Smoked Sausage Appetizers, 14

Smooth & Creamy Pumpkin Soup, 94
S'mores Monkey Bread Muffins, 83
Snickerdoodle Cheesecake, 128
Snow-Topped White Chocolate
    Macadamia Cookies, 35
Sour Cream & Chives Mashed
    Potatoes, 97
South-of-the-Border Bruschetta, 222
Southwestern Rice, 52
Sparkling Peach Punch, 215
Special Occasion Cutout Cookies, 204
Spiced Brownie Bites, 131
Spiced Cranberry-Apple Punch, 107
Spiced Steak Potato Fingers with
    Dracula Dipping Sauce, 242
Spicy Chocolate Bark, 60
Spinach-Orzo Salad with Chickpeas, 147
Strawberry & Cream Bruschetta, 193
Strawberry Ladyfinger Icebox Cake, 172
Strawberry Shortcake Stacks, 163
Stuffed Jalapeno Grilled Cheese, 231
Stuffed Shells with Arrabbiata
    Sauce, 232
Sugared Raisin Pear Diamonds, 77
Sweet Onion Creamed Corn, 108
Sweet Tea Boysenberry Shandy, 208

T

Tangy Lemon Tart, 172
Thanksgiving Green Beans, 94
Three-Herb Popcorn, 32
Three-Layer Chocolate Ganache
    Cake, 26
Tomato-Goat Cheese Spread, 198
Topsy-Turvy Sangria, 56
Tortellini & Shrimp Skewers with
    Sun-Dried Tomato Sauce, 9
Triple Cheese Potato Cake with
    Ham, 141
Tropical Tabbouleh, 201
Turkey Sliders with Sesame Slaw, 221
Two-Bean Hummus, 114
Two-Berry Fluff Salad, 152

V

Vanilla Cupcakes with Rhubarb
    Compote, 189

W

Warm Cinnamon-Apple Topping, 110
Watermelon Margaritas, 224
White Cheddar Mac & Cheese, 31
White Chocolate Cheesecake with
    Cranberry-Orange Compote, 26
White Christmas Cake, 36
Wine-Poached Pears, 20

General Index

Find every recipe by food category and major ingredient.

APPETIZERS & SNACKS

Andrea's Stuffed Mushrooms, 93
Antipasto Skewers, 218
Appetizer Tortilla Pinwheels, 31
Apricot-Chipotle Cheese Spread, 137
Apricot Wraps, 14
Baked Crab Wontons, 147
BBQ Chicken Grits Bites, 208
BBQ Turkey Meatballs, 104
Black Bean Chicken Nachos, 110
Caramel Apple & Brie Skewers, 9
Cheese & Sausage Bread Bowl Dip, 232
Cheese Ball Roll-Ups, 94
Cheese Grape Appetizers, 13
Chocolate Caramel Turkey Legs, 120
Coconut-Rum Cake Pops, 14
Crab Cake Lettuce Wraps, 190
Deep-Fried Candy Bars on a Stick, 10
Dial M for Mustard Pretzels, 238
Easy Strawberry Salsa, 218
Feta-Cucumber Cheese Balls, 222
Fresh Herb Vegetable Dip, 218
Garlic-Dill Deviled Eggs, 137
Ginger-Tuna Kabobs, 9
Grilled Cherry-Glazed Chicken
    Wings, 218
Grilled Tomato-Peach Pizza, 221
Ham & Cheese Biscuit Stacks, 10
Herbed Dip for Veggies, 31
Homemade Guacamole, 51
Horseradish Meatballs, 13
Lemon-Dill Cucumber Dip, 156
Lemon-Herb Salmon Toasts, 19
Marinated Mozzarella, 10
Marshmallow Pops, 13
Mushroom-Stuffed Baked Brie, 231
Party Cheese Bread, 234
Pepper Mango Salsa, 148
Pesto-Goat Cheese Toasts, 156
Poutine, 234
Prosciutto Honeydew with Balsamic
    Reduction, 202
Roasted Pepper Pimiento-Style
    Cheese, 211
Rosemary's Baby Appetizer
    Meatballs, 238
Shrimp & Garlic Bruschetta, 198
Slow Cooker Crab Dip, 104
Smoked Sausage Appetizers, 14
South-of-the-Border Bruschetta, 222
Strawberry & Cream Bruschetta, 193
Three-Herb Popcorn, 32
Tomato-Goat Cheese Spread, 198
Tortellini & Shrimp Skewers with
    Sun-Dried Tomato Sauce, 9
Turkey Sliders with Sesame Slaw, 221
Two-Bean Hummus, 114

APPLES

Apple & Broccoli Ghost Salad, 241
Apple-Celery Salad, 208
Apple Cider Doughnut Holes, 84
Apple Pecan Salad, 114
Apple Scream Bars, 245
Brussels Sprouts with Bacon
    Vinaigrette, 22
Caramel Apple & Brie Skewers, 9
Citrus Herb Turkey, 97
Ginger Apple-Pear Crisp, 124
Ham Biscuits with White Cheddar, 211
Rosy Apple Dumplings, 183
Spiced Cranberry-Apple Punch, 107
Warm Cinnamon-Apple Topping, 110

APRICOTS

Apricot-Chipotle Cheese Spread, 137
Apricot Cooler, 152
Apricot White Fudge, 36
Apricot Wraps, 14
BBQ Chicken Grits Bites, 208

ARTICHOKES

Artichoke Shrimp Pasta Salad, 138
Double Cheese Artichoke Frittata, 188
Fresh Artichokes with Lemon-Yogurt
    Dip, 22

ASPARAGUS

Herb-Vinaigrette Potato Salad, 166
Herby Pea Salad, 190

AVOCADOS

Fresh Herb Vegetable Dip, 218
Homemade Guacamole, 51
South-of-the-Border Bruschetta, 222

BACON & PANCETTA

Amazing Mac & Cheese Pizza, 228
Apricot Wraps, 14
Bacon Beef Tenderloin with Cranberry
    Glaze, 25
Bacon-Gruyere Smashed Potatoes, 25

Black-Eyed Pea Tomato Salad, 212
Brussels Sprouts with Bacon
    Vinaigrette, 22
Elm Street Cheeseburger Joes, 242
Fava Bean & Pea Salad, 159
Mushroom & Spinach Eggs
    Benedict, 171
Stuffed Jalapeno Grilled Cheese, 231
Stuffed Shells with Arrabbiata
    Sauce, 232
Sweet Onion Creamed Corn, 108
Thanksgiving Green Beans, 94

BANANAS

Banana Crumb Pudding, 215
Banana Nut Bread, 86
Bananas Foster Sundaes, 127

BARLEY & BULGUR

Barley, Greens & Sweet Potato Salad, 47
Tropical Tabbouleh, 201

BEANS

Black Bean Chicken Nachos, 110
Black-Eyed Pea Tomato Salad, 212
Cantina Pinto Beans, 51
Chickpea Salad, 201
Fava Bean & Pea Salad, 159
Hearty Vegetable Soup, 44
Six-Bean Chili, 107
Slow-Cooked White Bean Chili, 32
Southwestern Rice, 52
Spinach-Orzo Salad with Chickpeas, 147
Two-Bean Hummus, 114

BEEF & GROUND BEEF

Bacon Beef Tenderloin with Cranberry
    Glaze, 25
Deluxe Pizza Casserole, 118
Horseradish Meatballs, 13
Marinated Steak with Grilled
    Onions, 202
Mexican Stuffed Peppers, 52
Slaw-Topped Beef Sliders, 109
Stuffed Shells with Arrabbiata
    Sauce, 232

BEER, WINE, LIQUOR & LIQUEURS

Bacon Beef Tenderloin with Cranberry
    Glaze, 25

Bananas Foster Sundaes, 127
Beer-Cheese Velvet Soup, 228
Bourbon-Spiced Glazed Ham, 160
Champagne Sipper, 190
Chocolate Tart with Cranberry
    Raspberry Sauce, 182
Coconut-Rum Cake Pops, 14
Favorite Chocolate-Bourbon Pecan
    Tart, 215
Minty Pineapple Rum, 224
Moscow Mule, 20
Peach Champagne, 198
Sweet Tea Boysenberry Shandy, 208
Topsy-Turvy Sangria, 56
Watermelon Margaritas, 224
Wine-Poached Pears, 20

BELL PEPPERS
(also see Chilies & Hot Peppers)
Black Bean Chicken Nachos, 110
Chicken with Red Pepper Sauce
    & Spinach, 178
Easy Strawberry Salsa, 218
Hearty Vegetable Soup, 44
Make-Ahead Veggie Salad, 141
Mexican Stuffed Peppers, 52
Onion-Garlic Hash Browns, 193
Pepper Mango Salsa, 148
Roasted Pepper Pimiento-Style
    Cheese, 211

BEVERAGES
Apricot Cooler, 152
Aunt Dorothy's Russian Tea, 98
Champagne Sipper, 190
Homemade Eggnog, 35
Lemon Basil Mojito Mocktails, 224
Minty Pineapple Rum, 224
Moscow Mule, 20
Peach Champagne, 198
Rhubarb Lemonade Slush, 163
Sparkling Peach Punch, 215
Spiced Cranberry-Apple Punch, 107
Sweet Tea Boysenberry Shandy, 208
Watermelon Margaritas, 224

BISCUITS & BISCUIT MIX
Easy Biscuit Muffins, 160
Ham & Cheese Biscuit Stacks, 10
Ham Biscuits with White Cheddar, 211
Orange Biscuits with Honey Butter, 84
Pumpkin Pie Pudding, 109

BLACKBERRIES & BOYSENBERRIES
Lime Chicken with Blackberry
    Salsa, 201
Sweet Tea Boysenberry Shandy, 208

BLUEBERRIES
Razzy Jazzy Berry Tarts, 222
Two-Berry Fluff Salad, 152

BREAKFAST RECIPES
All-Star Muffin Mix, 86
Apple Cider Doughnut Holes, 84
Best Cinnamon Rolls, 80
Double Cheese Artichoke Frittata, 188
Fruit-Topped Cheese Blintzes, 234
Fruit with Poppy Seed Dressing, 138
Ham Biscuits with White Cheddar, 211
Heavenly Cheese Danish, 84
Homemade Sage Sausage Patties, 189
Lemon Ricotta Fritters, 193
Mushroom & Spinach Eggs
    Benedict, 171
Onion-Garlic Hash Browns, 193
Orange Biscuits with Honey Butter, 84
Rhubarb-Buttermilk Coffee Cake, 172
S'mores Monkey Bread Muffins, 83
Strawberry & Cream Bruschetta, 193
Triple Cheese Potato Cake with
    Ham, 141

BROCCOLI & CAULIFLOWER
Apple & Broccoli Ghost Salad, 241
Cauliflower with White Cheddar
    Sauce, 118
Ham & Swiss Braids, 148

BROWNIES & BARS
Apple Scream Bars, 245
Black Raspberry Bars, 151
Candy Cane Shortbread Bars, 71
Chocolate-Coconut Layer Bars, 142
Chocolate Salted Caramel Bars, 204
Cranberry Eggnog Cheesecake
    Bars, 71
Honey Pecan Triangles, 73
Maple Butterscotch Brownies, 74
Maple-Glazed Cinnamon Chip Bars, 73
Peppermint Brownies, 77
Pistachio Brownie Toffee Bars, 74
Spiced Brownie Bites, 131
Sugared Raisin Pear Diamonds, 77

CABBAGE & COLESLAW
Apple & Broccoli Ghost Salad, 241
Hearty Vegetable Soup, 44
Slaw-Topped Beef Sliders, 109

CAKES, CUPCAKES & CAKE POPS
Blue Ribbon Red Velvet Cake, 184
Brown Sugar Pecan Cake, 98
Cardamom Crumb Cake, 131
Chai Tea Cupcakes, 124

Chocolate-Dipped Ice Cream Cone
    Cupcakes, 181
Chocolate Molten Cakes, 62
Classic Tres Leches Cake, 56
Coconut-Rum Cake Pops, 14
Glazed Chocolate Angel Food Cake, 152
Lemon Layer Cake, 143
Molasses Spice Cake, 124
Pumpkin Cake with Whipped Cinnamon
    Frosting, 127
Pumpkin Cupcakes with Spiced
    Frosting, 120
Strawberry Ladyfinger Icebox Cake, 172
Three-Layer Chocolate Ganache
    Cake, 26
Vanilla Cupcakes with Rhubarb
    Compote, 189
White Christmas Cake, 36

CANDIES & CONFECTIONS
Cashew Clusters, 60
Chocolate Caramel Turkey Legs, 120
Chocolate Truffles, 65
Cinnamon Almond Brittle, 131
Coconut-Rum Cake Pops, 14
Deep-Fried Candy Bars on a Stick, 10
Double Chocolate Fudge, 62
Marshmallow Pops, 13
Spicy Chocolate Bark, 60

CARAMEL
Caramel Apple & Brie Skewers, 9
Chocolate Caramel Turkey Legs, 120
Chocolate Salted Caramel Bars, 204
Favorite Chocolate-Bourbon Pecan
    Tart, 215

CARROTS
Buttery Carrots, 159
Carrot-Parsnip Soup, 166
Frosted Carrot Cake Cookies, 142
Hearty Vegetable Soup, 44
Make-Ahead Veggie Salad, 141
Pineapple & Coconut Carrot Salad, 148
Pork & Vegetable Spring Rolls, 168
Turkey Sliders with Sesame Slaw, 221

CASSEROLES
Chicken & Swiss Casserole, 141
Chile Relleno Squares, 51
Deluxe Pizza Casserole, 118
Green Pea Casserole, 117
Stuffed Shells with Arrabbiata
    Sauce, 232

CELERY
Almond-Herb Bread Dressing, 97
Apple-Celery Salad, 208

CELERY

(continued)
Fruity Chicken Salad Mini
Sandwiches, 151
Hearty Vegetable Soup, 44
Make-Ahead Veggie Salad, 141
Pork & Vegetable Spring Rolls, 168

CHEESE

*(also see Cream Cheese, Ricotta
Cheese & Mascarpone Cheese)*
Amazing Mac & Cheese Pizza, 228
Antipasto Skewers, 218
Apricot-Chipotle Cheese Spread, 137
Artichoke Shrimp Pasta Salad, 138
Bacon-Gruyere Smashed Potatoes, 25
Basil Parmesan Bread, 80
BBQ Chicken Grits Bites, 208
Beer-Cheese Velvet Soup, 228
Beet Salad with Orange Vinaigrette, 178
Black Bean Chicken Nachos, 110
Caramel Apple & Brie Skewers, 9
Cauliflower with White Cheddar
Sauce, 118
Cheese & Sausage Bread Bowl Dip, 232
Cheese Ball Roll-Ups, 94
Cheese Grape Appetizers, 13
Chicken & Cheddar Mummy Braid, 241
Chicken & Swiss Casserole, 141
Chicken with Red Pepper Sauce
& Spinach, 178
Chickpea Salad, 201
Chile Relleno Squares, 51
Deluxe Pizza Casserole, 118
Double Cheese Artichoke Frittata, 188
Elm Street Cheeseburger Joes, 242
Feta-Cucumber Cheese Balls, 222
Fruit-Topped Cheese Blintzes, 234
Grilled Tomato-Peach Pizza, 221
Ham & Cheese Biscuit Stacks, 10
Ham & Swiss Braids, 148
Ham Biscuits with White Cheddar, 211
Jalapeno Cheese Bread, 80
Leek Prosciutto Pizza, 166
Marinated Mozzarella, 10
Mexican Stuffed Peppers, 52
Mushroom-Stuffed Baked Brie, 231
Parmesan Snap Pea Pasta, 148
Party Cheese Bread, 234
Pesto-Goat Cheese Toasts, 156
Poutine, 234
Roasted Pepper Pimiento-Style
Cheese, 211
Slow-Cooked White Bean Chili, 32
Stuffed Jalapeno Grilled Cheese, 231
Stuffed Shells with Arrabbiata
Sauce, 232
Tomato-Goat Cheese Spread, 198

Triple Cheese Potato Cake with
Ham, 141
White Cheddar Mac & Cheese, 31

CHEESECAKES

Bittersweet Chocolate Cheesecake, 66
Creamy Strawberry Cheesecake, 178
New York Cheesecake with Shortbread
Crust, 228
Snickerdoodle Cheesecake, 128
White Chocolate Cheesecake with
Cranberry-Orange Compote, 26

CHERRIES

Apple & Broccoli Ghost Salad, 241
Cherry Dessert Lasagna, 183
Cherry Pull-Apart Bread, 83
Fruit-Topped Cheese Blintzes, 234
Grilled Cherry-Glazed Chicken
Wings, 218
Perfect Winter Salad, 40
Pork & Vegetable Spring Rolls, 168

CHICKEN

BBQ Chicken Grits Bites, 208
Black Bean Chicken Nachos, 110
Chicken & Cheddar Mummy Braid, 241
Chicken & Swiss Casserole, 141
Chicken Tamales, 55
Chicken with Red Pepper Sauce
& Spinach, 178
Crescent Chicken Bundles, 117
Fruity Chicken Salad Mini
Sandwiches, 151
Grilled Cherry-Glazed Chicken
Wings, 218
Lime Chicken with Blackberry Salsa, 201
Slow-Cooked White Bean Chili, 32

CHILIES & HOT PEPPERS

Apricot-Chipotle Cheese Spread, 137
Bacon Beef Tenderloin with Cranberry
Glaze, 25
Chile Relleno Squares, 51
Easy Strawberry Salsa, 218
Jalapeno Cheese Bread, 80
Pepper Mango Salsa, 148
Roasted Pepper Pimiento-Style
Cheese, 211
South-of-the-Border Bruschetta, 222
Stuffed Jalapeno Grilled Cheese, 231

CHOCOLATE

(also see White Chocolate)
Bittersweet Chocolate Cheesecake, 66
Cashew Clusters, 60
Chocolate Caramel Turkey Legs, 120
Chocolate-Coconut Layer Bars, 142

Chocolate-Dipped Ice Cream Cone
Cupcakes, 181
Chocolate-Dipped Macaroons, 66
Chocolate Molten Cakes, 62
Chocolate Pistachio Biscotti, 60
Chocolate Salted Caramel Bars, 204
Chocolate-Strawberry Pretzel
Cookies, 77
Chocolate Tart with Cranberry
Raspberry Sauce, 182
Chocolate Truffles, 65
Double Chocolate Fudge, 62
Favorite Chocolate-Bourbon Pecan
Tart, 215
Glazed Chocolate Angel Food Cake, 152
Hazelnut Chocolate Chip Scones, 87
Marshmallow Pops, 13
Mocha Shortbread, 65
Orange Chocolate Fondue, 62
Peppermint Brownies, 77
Pistachio Brownie Toffee Bars, 74
S'mores Monkey Bread Muffins, 83
Spiced Brownie Bites, 131
Spicy Chocolate Bark, 60
Three-Layer Chocolate Ganache
Cake, 26

CINNAMON

Apple Cider Doughnut Holes, 84
Apple Scream Bars, 245
Best Cinnamon Rolls, 80
Chai Tea Cupcakes, 124
Cinnamon Almond Brittle, 131
Ginger Apple-Pear Crisp, 124
Maple-Glazed Cinnamon Chip Bars, 73
Pumpkin Cake with Whipped Cinnamon
Frosting, 127
Rosy Apple Dumplings, 183
Snickerdoodle Cheesecake, 128
Spiced Cranberry-Apple Punch, 107
Warm Cinnamon-Apple Topping, 110

COCONUT

Black Raspberry Bars, 151
Chocolate-Coconut Layer Bars, 142
Chocolate-Dipped Macaroons, 66
Coconut-Rum Cake Pops, 14
Lime-Raspberry Pie with Coconut
Cream, 194
Pineapple & Coconut Carrot Salad, 148
Snow-Topped White Chocolate
Macadamia Cookies, 35
White Christmas Cake, 36

COFFEE & TEA

Aunt Dorothy's Russian Tea, 98
Bacon Beef Tenderloin with Cranberry
Glaze, 25

Chai Tea Cupcakes, 124
Mocha Shortbread, 65
Molasses Spice Cake, 124
Sweet Tea Boysenberry Shandy, 208
Three-Layer Chocolate Ganache
    Cake, 26

COOKIES & BISCOTTI
Butter Cookies, 184
Cardamom Cookies, 128
Chocolate-Dipped Macaroons, 66
Chocolate Pistachio Biscotti, 60
Chocolate-Strawberry Pretzel
    Cookies, 77
Freaky Frankenstein Cookies, 245
Frosted Carrot Cake Cookies, 142
Fruitcake Christmas Cookies, 72
Merry Grinchmas Cookies, 74
Mocha Shortbread, 65
Rosemary-Lemon Shortbread Sandwich
    Cookies, 163
Snow-Topped White Chocolate
    Macadamia Cookies, 35
Special Occasion Cutout Cookies, 204

CORN BREAD & CORNMEAL
Caraway Bread, 20
Grilled Tomato-Peach Pizza, 221
Oven-Fried Corn Bread, 210

CORN, CORN HUSKS
& POPCORN
Chicken Tamales, 55
Frogmore Stew, 212
Hearty Vegetable Soup, 44
Make-Ahead Veggie Salad, 141
Slow-Cooked White Bean Chili, 32
Southwestern Rice, 52
Sweet Onion Creamed Corn, 108
Three-Herb Popcorn, 32

CRANBERRIES
Bacon Beef Tenderloin with Cranberry
    Glaze, 25
Cape Cod Bay Brown Bread, 93
Caramel Apple & Brie Skewers, 9
Chocolate Pistachio Biscotti, 60
Chocolate Tart with Cranberry
    Raspberry Sauce, 182
Cranberry Eggnog Cheesecake
    Bars, 71
Cranberry-Nut Couscous Salad, 43
Cranberry Roasted Squash, 19
Holiday Cranberry Salad, 94
Pumpkin Cranberry Bread, 84
Spiced Cranberry-Apple Punch, 107
White Chocolate Cheesecake with
    Cranberry-Orange Compote, 26

CREAM CHEESE, RICOTTA
CHEESE & MASCARPONE
CHEESE
Appetizer Tortilla Pinwheels, 31
Apricot-Chipotle Cheese Spread, 137
Bates Motel Grape Salad, 241
Bittersweet Chocolate Cheesecake, 66
Blue Ribbon Red Velvet Cake, 184
Cheese & Sausage Bread Bowl Dip, 232
Cheese Ball Roll-Ups, 94
Cheese Grape Appetizers, 13
Cherry Dessert Lasagna, 183
Cranberry Eggnog Cheesecake Bars, 71
Creamy Strawberry Cheesecake, 178
Crescent Chicken Bundles, 117
Frosted Carrot Cake Cookies, 142
Heavenly Cheese Danish, 84
Key Lime Trifle, 203
Layered Candy Cane Dessert, 35
Lemon-Herb Salmon Toasts, 19
Lemon Layer Cake, 143
Lemon Ricotta Fritters, 193
Merry Grinchmas Cookies, 74
New York Cheesecake with Shortbread
    Crust, 228
Razzy Jazzy Berry Tarts, 222
Roasted Pepper Pimiento-Style
    Cheese, 211
Slow Cooker Crab Dip, 104
Snickerdoodle Cheesecake, 128
Sour Cream & Chives Mashed
    Potatoes, 97
Strawberry & Cream Bruschetta, 193
Strawberry Ladyfinger Icebox Cake, 172
Stuffed Jalapeno Grilled Cheese, 231
Stuffed Shells with Arrabbiata
    Sauce, 232
Sweet Onion Creamed Corn, 108
Tangy Lemon Tart, 172
Tortellini & Shrimp Skewers with
    Sun-Dried Tomato Sauce, 9
Two-Berry Fluff Salad, 152
Vanilla Cupcakes with Rhubarb
    Compote, 189
White Chocolate Cheesecake with
    Cranberry-Orange Compote, 26

CUCUMBERS
Chickpea Salad, 201
Feta-Cucumber Cheese Balls, 222
Lemon-Dill Cucumber Dip, 156
Lemon Rice Salad, 46

CURRY
Herbed Dip for Veggies, 31
Quick Tomato Soup, 178
Rosemary's Baby Appetizer
    Meatballs, 238

DESSERTS
*(also see Brownies & Bars; Cakes,
Cupcakes & Cake Pops; Candies &
Confections; Cheesecakes; Cookies
& Biscotti; Gelatin; Ice Cream; Pies
& Tarts; Pudding & Mousse)*
Cherry Dessert Lasagna, 183
Ginger Apple-Pear Crisp, 124
Ginger Berry Compote, 163
Key Lime Trifle, 203
Layered Candy Cane Dessert, 35
Rosy Apple Dumplings, 183
Strawberry Shortcake Stacks, 163
Two-Berry Fluff Salad, 152
Warm Cinnamon-Apple Topping, 110

DIPS & SPREADS
Apricot-Chipotle Cheese Spread, 137
Cheese & Sausage Bread Bowl Dip, 232
Easy Strawberry Salsa, 218
Fresh Artichokes with Lemon-Yogurt
    Dip, 22
Fresh Herb Vegetable Dip, 218
Herbed Dip for Veggies, 31
Homemade Guacamole, 51
Lemon-Dill Cucumber Dip, 156
Pepper Mango Salsa, 148
Roasted Pepper Pimiento-Style
    Cheese, 211
Slow Cooker Crab Dip, 104
Tomato-Goat Cheese Spread, 198
Two-Bean Hummus, 114

DOUGHNUTS & BREAKFAST
PASTRIES
Apple Cider Doughnut Holes, 84
Best Cinnamon Rolls, 80
Fruit-Topped Cheese Blintzes, 234
Heavenly Cheese Danish, 84
Lemon Ricotta Fritters, 193
Rhubarb-Buttermilk Coffee Cake, 172

DRESSING & STUFFING MIX
Almond-Herb Bread Dressing, 97
Green Pea Casserole, 117
Slow-Cooked Sausage Dressing, 44

EGGS
Double Cheese Artichoke Frittata, 188
Garlic-Dill Deviled Eggs, 137
Homemade Eggnog, 35
Mushroom & Spinach Eggs
    Benedict, 171

FALL SPICES
All-Star Muffin Mix, 86
Apple Cider Doughnut Holes, 84
Apple Scream Bars, 245

FALL SPICES
(continued)
Bananas Foster Sundaes, 127
Cardamom Cookies, 128
Cardamom Crumb Cake, 131
Chai Tea Cupcakes, 124
Fluffy Sweet Potato Custard Pie, 100
Ginger Apple-Pear Crisp, 124
Maple-Glazed Cinnamon Chip Bars, 73
Molasses Spice Cake, 124
Pumpkin Cake with Whipped Cinnamon
    Frosting, 127
Pumpkin Cranberry Bread, 84
Pumpkin Cupcakes with Spiced
    Frosting, 120
Pumpkin Pie Pudding, 109
Slow Cooker Pineapple Sweet
    Potatoes, 43
Spiced Brownie Bites, 131
Spiced Cranberry-Apple Punch, 107
Warm Cinnamon-Apple Topping, 110

FISH & SEAFOOD
Artichoke Shrimp Pasta Salad, 138
Baked Crab Wontons, 147
Crab Cake Lettuce Wraps, 190
Frogmore Stew, 212
Ginger-Tuna Kabobs, 9
Lemon-Herb Salmon Toasts, 19
Lemony Shrimp & Snow Pea Pasta, 169
Mushroom Shrimp Bisque, 19
Salmon Patties with Garlic-Dill
    Sauce, 171
Shrimp & Garlic Bruschetta, 198
Shrimp Pomodoro, 181
Slow Cooker Crab Dip, 104
Tortellini & Shrimp Skewers with
    Sun-Dried Tomato Sauce, 9

FRUIT
(also see specific kinds)
Fruit-Topped Cheese Blintzes, 234
Fruit with Poppy Seed Dressing, 138
Fruitcake Christmas Cookies, 72
Fruity Chicken Salad Mini
    Sandwiches, 151
Ginger Berry Compote, 163
Prosciutto Honeydew with Balsamic
    Reduction, 202
Spiced Cranberry-Apple Punch, 107
Topsy-Turvy Sangria, 56
Watermelon Margaritas, 224

GARLIC
Browned Butter Red Potatoes, 160
Garlic-Dill Deviled Eggs, 137
Onion & Garlic Soda Bread, 138
Onion-Garlic Hash Browns, 193

Salmon Patties with Garlic-Dill
    Sauce, 171
Seasoned Garlic Gravy, 40
Shrimp & Garlic Bruschetta, 198
Smooth & Creamy Pumpkin Soup, 94
Thanksgiving Green Beans, 94

GELATIN
Holiday Cranberry Salad, 94
Lime Chiffon Jello, 120

GINGER
Chai Tea Cupcakes, 124
Ginger Apple-Pear Crisp, 124
Ginger Berry Compote, 163
Ginger-Tuna Kabobs, 9
Pineapple & Coconut Carrot Salad, 148
Turkey Sliders with Sesame Slaw, 221

GRAPES
Apple Pecan Salad, 114
Bates Motel Grape Salad, 241
Cheese Grape Appetizers, 13
Fruity Chicken Salad Mini
    Sandwiches, 151

GREEN BEANS
Garden Green Bean Salad, 202
Garden Green Beans & Potatoes, 104
Hearty Vegetable Soup, 44
Make-Ahead Veggie Salad, 141
Thanksgiving Green Beans, 94

GREENS
(also see Spinach)
Barley, Greens & Sweet Potato Salad, 47
Beet Salad with Orange Vinaigrette, 178
Crab Cake Lettuce Wraps, 190
Jicama Romaine Salad, 52
Perfect Winter Salad, 40

GRILLED RECIPES
Grilled Cherry-Glazed Chicken
    Wings, 218
Grilled Tomato-Peach Pizza, 221
Herbed Lamb Chops with Crispy
    Potatoes, 171
Lime Chicken with Blackberry Salsa, 201
Marinated Steak with Grilled
    Onions, 202
Turkey Sliders with Sesame Slaw, 221

HAM & PROSCIUTTO
Bourbon-Spiced Glazed Ham, 160
Ham & Cheese Biscuit Stacks, 10
Ham & Swiss Braids, 148
Ham Biscuits with White Cheddar, 211
Leek Prosciutto Pizza, 166

Prosciutto Honeydew with Balsamic
    Reduction, 202
Sweet Onion Creamed Corn, 108
Triple Cheese Potato Cake with
    Ham, 141

HERBS
Almond-Herb Bread Dressing, 97
Amazing Mac & Cheese Pizza, 228
Basil Parmesan Bread, 80
Citrus Herb Turkey, 97
Feta-Cucumber Cheese Balls, 222
Fresh Herb Vegetable Dip, 218
Garden Green Bean Salad, 202
Grilled Tomato-Peach Pizza, 221
Hearty Vegetable Soup, 44
Herb-Vinaigrette Potato Salad, 166
Herbed Dip for Veggies, 31
Herbed Lamb Chops with Crispy
    Potatoes, 171
Herby Pea Salad, 190
Homemade Sage Sausage Patties, 189
Lemon Basil Mojito Mocktails, 224
Lemon-Herb Salmon Toasts, 19
Lemon Rice Salad, 46
Marinated Mozzarella, 10
Mushroom-Stuffed Baked Brie, 231
Rosemary-Lemon Shortbread Sandwich
    Cookies, 163
Rosemary's Baby Appetizer
    Meatballs, 238
Salmon Patties with Garlic-Dill
    Sauce, 171
Stuffed Shells with Arrabbiata
    Sauce, 232
Three-Herb Popcorn, 32

HONEY
Fried Ice Cream, 56
Fruit with Poppy Seed Dressing, 138
Honey Pecan Triangles, 73
Orange Biscuits with Honey Butter, 84
Pineapple & Coconut Carrot Salad, 148

ICE CREAM
Bananas Foster Sundaes, 127
Fried Ice Cream, 56

LAMB
Herbed Lamb Chops with Crispy
    Potatoes, 171

LEMONS & LIMES
Apricot Cooler, 152
Fresh Artichokes with Lemon-Yogurt
    Dip, 22
Key Lime Trifle, 203
Lemon-Dill Cucumber Dip, 156

Lemon-Herb Salmon Toasts, 19
Lemon Layer Cake, 143
Lemon Rice Salad, 46
Lemon Ricotta Fritters, 193
Lemony Shrimp & Snow Pea Pasta, 169
Lime Chicken with Blackberry
    Salsa, 201
Lime Chiffon Jello, 120
Lime-Raspberry Pie with Coconut
    Cream, 194
Minty Pineapple Rum, 224
Moscow Mule, 20
New York Cheesecake with Shortbread
    Crust, 228
Pepper Mango Salsa, 148
Pineapple & Coconut Carrot Salad, 148
Rhubarb Lemonade Slush, 163
Rosemary-Lemon Shortbread Sandwich
    Cookies, 163
South-of-the-Border Bruschetta, 222
Tangy Lemon Tart, 172
Topsy-Turvy Sangria, 56
Tropical Tabbouleh, 201
Watermelon Margaritas, 224

MAIN ENTREES
Amazing Mac & Cheese Pizza, 228
Bacon Beef Tenderloin with Cranberry
    Glaze, 25
Chicken & Swiss Casserole, 141
Chicken Tamales, 55
Chicken with Red Pepper Sauce
    & Spinach, 178
Citrus Herb Turkey, 97
Crescent Chicken Bundles, 117
Deluxe Pizza Casserole, 118
Elm Street Cheeseburger Joes, 242
Frogmore Stew, 212
Fruity Chicken Salad Mini
    Sandwiches, 151
Herbed Lamb Chops with Crispy
    Potatoes, 171
Leek Prosciutto Pizza, 166
Lemony Shrimp & Snow Pea Pasta, 169
Marinated Steak with Grilled
    Onions, 202
Mexican Stuffed Peppers, 52
Pork & Vegetable Spring Rolls, 168
Salmon Patties with Garlic-Dill
    Sauce, 171
Six-Bean Chili, 107
Shrimp Pomodoro, 181
Slow-Cooked White Bean Chili, 32
Stuffed Shells with Arrabbiata
    Sauce, 232
Triple Cheese Potato Cake with
    Ham, 141
White Cheddar Mac & Cheese, 31

MANGOES & PAPAYA
Pepper Mango Salsa, 148
Tropical Tabbouleh, 201

MAPLE
Maple-Almond Butternut Squash, 44
Maple Butterscotch Brownies, 74
Maple-Glazed Cinnamon Chip Bars, 73
Warm Cinnamon-Apple Topping, 110

**MARSHMALLOWS &
MARSHMALLOW CREME**
Apple Pecan Salad, 114
Apricot White Fudge, 36
Double Chocolate Fudge, 62
Marshmallow Pops, 13
S'mores Monkey Bread Muffins, 83

MEATBALLS
BBQ Turkey Meatballs, 104
Horseradish Meatballs, 13
Rosemary's Baby Appetizer
    Meatballs, 238

MINT & PEPPERMINT
Candy Cane Shortbread Bars, 71
Freaky Frankenstein Cookies, 245
Layered Candy Cane Dessert, 35
Minty Pineapple Rum, 224
Peppermint Brownies, 77

MUSHROOMS
Andrea's Stuffed Mushrooms, 93
Make-Ahead Veggie Salad, 141
Mushroom & Spinach Eggs
    Benedict, 171
Mushroom Shrimp Bisque, 19
Mushroom-Stuffed Baked Brie, 231
Thanksgiving Green Beans, 94

NUTS
Almond-Herb Bread Dressing, 97
Apple & Broccoli Ghost Salad, 241
Apple Pecan Salad, 114
Apricot White Fudge, 36
Banana Nut Bread, 86
Bananas Foster Sundaes, 127
Barley, Greens & Sweet Potato
    Salad, 47
Beet Salad with Orange
    Vinaigrette, 178
Bittersweet Chocolate Cheesecake, 66
Black Raspberry Bars, 151
Brown Sugar Pecan Cake, 98
Cardamom Cookies, 128
Cashew Clusters, 60
Cheese Grape Appetizers, 13
Cherry Pull-Apart Bread, 83

Chocolate Pistachio Biscotti, 60
Chocolate Tart with Cranberry
    Raspberry Sauce, 182
Cinnamon Almond Brittle, 131
Cranberry-Nut Couscous Salad, 43
Double Chocolate Fudge, 62
Favorite Chocolate-Bourbon Pecan
    Tart, 215
Frosted Carrot Cake Cookies, 142
Fruitcake Christmas Cookies, 72
Fruity Chicken Salad Mini
    Sandwiches, 151
Garden Green Bean Salad, 202
Hazelnut Chocolate Chip Scones, 87
Honey Pecan Triangles, 73
Key Lime Trifle, 203
Lemon Rice Salad, 46
Lime-Raspberry Pie with Coconut
    Cream, 194
Maple-Almond Butternut Squash, 44
Maple Butterscotch Brownies, 74
Perfect Winter Salad, 40
Pistachio Brownie Toffee Bars, 74
Pork & Vegetable Spring Rolls, 168
Slow Cooker Pineapple Sweet
    Potatoes, 43
Snow-Topped White Chocolate
    Macadamia Cookies, 35
Spicy Chocolate Bark, 60
Strawberry & Cream Bruschetta, 193
Warm Cinnamon-Apple Topping, 110
White Christmas Cake, 36

OATS
Apple Scream Bars, 245
Cape Cod Bay Brown Bread, 93
Cherry Dessert Lasagna, 183
Chocolate Tart with Cranberry
    Raspberry Sauce, 182
Cranberry Eggnog Cheesecake
    Bars, 71
Ginger Apple-Pear Crisp, 124

OLIVES
Antipasto Skewers, 218
Appetizer Tortilla Pinwheels, 31
Chicken Tamales, 55
Ham & Cheese Biscuit Stacks, 10

ONIONS & LEEKS
Buttery Carrots, 159
Herby Pea Salad, 190
Leek Prosciutto Pizza, 166
Marinated Steak with Grilled
    Onions, 202
Onion & Garlic Soda Bread, 138
Onion-Garlic Hash Browns, 193
Sweet Onion Creamed Corn, 108

ORANGES
Bacon Beef Tenderloin with Cranberry Glaze, 25
Beet Salad with Orange Vinaigrette, 178
Citrus Herb Turkey, 97
Eggnog Molded Salad, 43
Orange Biscuits with Honey Butter, 84
Orange Chocolate Fondue, 62
Topsy-Turvy Sangria, 56
Tropical Tabbouleh, 201
White Chocolate Cheesecake with Cranberry-Orange Compote, 26

PASTA & NOODLES
Amazing Mac & Cheese Pizza, 228
Artichoke Shrimp Pasta Salad, 138
Cherry Dessert Lasagna, 183
Chicken & Swiss Casserole, 141
Deluxe Pizza Casserole, 118
Lemony Shrimp & Snow Pea Pasta, 169
Parmesan Snap Pea Pasta, 148
Shrimp Pomodoro, 181
Spinach-Orzo Salad with Chickpeas, 147
Stuffed Shells with Arrabbiata Sauce, 232
Tortellini & Shrimp Skewers with Sun-Dried Tomato Sauce, 9
White Cheddar Mac & Cheese, 31

PEACHES
Fruit-Topped Cheese Blintzes, 234
Grilled Tomato-Peach Pizza, 221
Peach Champagne, 198
Sparkling Peach Punch, 215
Topsy-Turvy Sangria, 56

PEARS
Eggnog Molded Salad, 43
Ginger Apple-Pear Crisp, 124
Sugared Raisin Pear Diamonds, 77
Warm Cinnamon-Apple Topping, 110
Wine-Poached Pears, 20

PEAS
Barley, Greens & Sweet Potato Salad, 47
Chicken & Cheddar Mummy Braid, 241
Chicken & Swiss Casserole, 141
Fava Bean & Pea Salad, 159
Green Pea Casserole, 117
Hearty Vegetable Soup, 44
Herby Pea Salad, 190
Lemony Shrimp & Snow Pea Pasta, 169
Make-Ahead Veggie Salad, 141
Parmesan Snap Pea Pasta, 148
Pork & Vegetable Spring Rolls, 168

PIES & TARTS
Chocolate Tart with Cranberry Raspberry Sauce, 182
Favorite Chocolate-Bourbon Pecan Tart, 215
Fluffy Sweet Potato Custard Pie, 100
Lime-Raspberry Pie with Coconut Cream, 194
Razzy Jazzy Berry Tarts, 222
Tangy Lemon Tart, 172

PINEAPPLE
Apricot Cooler, 152
Frosted Carrot Cake Cookies, 142
Fruit with Poppy Seed Dressing, 138
Holiday Cranberry Salad, 94
Minty Pineapple Rum, 224
Pineapple & Coconut Carrot Salad, 148
Slow Cooker Pineapple Sweet Potatoes, 43
Spiced Cranberry-Apple Punch, 107

PIZZA
Amazing Mac & Cheese Pizza, 228
Grilled Tomato-Peach Pizza, 221
Leek Prosciutto Pizza, 166

PORK
(also see Bacon & Pancetta; Ham & Prosciutto; Sausage, Salami & Pepperoni)
Frogmore Stew, 212
Horseradish Meatballs, 13
Pork & Vegetable Spring Rolls, 168

POTATOES
(also see Sweet Potatoes)
Bacon-Gruyere Smashed Potatoes, 25
Browned Butter Red Potatoes, 160
Frogmore Stew, 212
Garden Green Beans & Potatoes, 104
Herb-Vinaigrette Potato Salad, 166
Herbed Lamb Chops with Crispy Potatoes, 171
Make-Ahead Mashed Potatoes, 40
Onion-Garlic Hash Browns, 193
Poutine, 234
Sour Cream & Chives Mashed Potatoes, 97
Spiced Steak Potato Fingers with Dracula Dipping Sauce, 242
Triple Cheese Potato Cake with Ham, 141

PRETZELS
Chocolate Caramel Turkey Legs, 120
Chocolate-Strawberry Pretzel Cookies, 77
Dial M for Mustard Pretzels, 238

PUDDING & MOUSSE
Banana Crumb Pudding, 215
Elegant White Chocolate Mousse, 65
Layered Candy Cane Dessert, 35
Pumpkin Pie Pudding, 109

PUMPKIN
Pumpkin Cake with Whipped Cinnamon Frosting, 127
Pumpkin Cranberry Bread, 84
Pumpkin Cupcakes with Spiced Frosting, 120
Pumpkin Pie Pudding, 109
Smooth & Creamy Pumpkin Soup, 94

QUICK BREADS, MUFFINS & SCONES
All-Star Muffin Mix, 86
Banana Nut Bread, 86
Cherry Pull-Apart Bread, 83
Hazelnut Chocolate Chip Scones, 87
Pumpkin Cranberry Bread, 84
Rhubarb-Buttermilk Coffee Cake, 172
S'mores Monkey Bread Muffins, 83

RAISINS
Frosted Carrot Cake Cookies, 142
Pineapple & Coconut Carrot Salad, 148
Sugared Raisin Pear Diamonds, 77
Warm Cinnamon-Apple Topping, 110

RASPBERRIES
Black Raspberry Bars, 151
Chocolate Tart with Cranberry Raspberry Sauce, 182
Lime-Raspberry Pie with Coconut Cream, 194
Razzy Jazzy Berry Tarts, 222

RHUBARB
Rhubarb-Buttermilk Coffee Cake, 172
Rhubarb Lemonade Slush, 163
Vanilla Cupcakes with Rhubarb Compote, 189

RICE
Lemon Rice Salad, 46
Mexican Stuffed Peppers, 52
Southwestern Rice, 52

ROOT VEGETABLES
Carrot-Parsnip Soup, 166
Jicama Romaine Salad, 52
Sauteed Radishes, 159

SALADS
Apple & Broccoli Ghost Salad, 241
Apple-Celery Salad, 208

Apple Pecan Salad, 114
Artichoke Shrimp Pasta Salad, 138
Barley, Greens & Sweet Potato
   Salad, 47
Beet Salad with Orange Vinaigrette, 178
Black-Eyed Pea Tomato Salad, 212
Chickpea Salad, 201
Cranberry-Nut Couscous Salad, 43
Eggnog Molded Salad, 43
Fava Bean & Pea Salad, 159
Garden Green Bean Salad, 202
Herb-Vinaigrette Potato Salad, 166
Herby Pea Salad, 190
Holiday Cranberry Salad, 94
Jicama Romaine Salad, 52
Lemon Rice Salad, 46
Make-Ahead Veggie Salad, 141
Perfect Winter Salad, 40
Pineapple & Coconut Carrot Salad, 148
Spinach-Orzo Salad with Chickpeas, 147

SALSA
Easy Strawberry Salsa, 218
Lime Chicken with Blackberry Salsa, 201
Pepper Mango Salsa, 148

SANDWICHES, WRAPS & BRAIDS
Chicken & Cheddar Mummy Braid, 241
Elm Street Cheeseburger Joes, 242
Fruity Chicken Salad Mini
   Sandwiches, 151
Ham & Swiss Braids, 148
Ham Biscuits with White Cheddar, 211
Pork & Vegetable Spring Rolls, 168
Slaw-Topped Beef Sliders, 109
Stuffed Jalapeno Grilled Cheese, 231
Turkey Sliders with Sesame Slaw, 221

SAUSAGE, SALAMI & PEPPERONI
Antipasto Skewers, 218
Cheese & Sausage Bread Bowl Dip, 232
Deluxe Pizza Casserole, 118
Homemade Sage Sausage Patties, 189
Rosemary's Baby Appetizer
   Meatballs, 238
Slow-Cooked Sausage Dressing, 44
Stuffed Shells with Arrabbiata
   Sauce, 232

SIDE DISHES
Almond-Herb Bread Dressing, 97
Apple & Broccoli Ghost Salad, 241
Apple-Celery Salad, 208
Apple Pecan Salad, 114
Artichoke Shrimp Pasta Salad, 138
Bacon-Gruyere Smashed Potatoes, 25

Barley, Greens & Sweet Potato
   Salad, 47
Black-Eyed Pea Tomato Salad, 212
Browned Butter Red Potatoes, 160
Brussels Sprouts with Bacon
   Vinaigrette, 22
Buttery Carrots, 159
Cantina Pinto Beans, 51
Cauliflower with White Cheddar
   Sauce, 118
Chickpea Salad, 201
Cranberry-Nut Couscous Salad, 43
Cranberry Roasted Squash, 19
Eggnog Molded Salad, 43
Fava Bean & Pea Salad, 159
Fresh Artichokes with Lemon-Yogurt
   Dip, 22
Garden Green Bean Salad, 202
Garden Green Beans & Potatoes, 104
Green Pea Casserole, 117
Herb-Vinaigrette Potato Salad, 166
Herby Pea Salad, 190
Holiday Cranberry Salad, 94
Lemon Rice Salad, 46
Make-Ahead Mashed Potatoes, 40
Make-Ahead Veggie Salad, 141
Maple-Almond Butternut Squash, 44
Parmesan Snap Pea Pasta, 148
Pineapple & Coconut Carrot Salad, 148
Sauteed Radishes, 159
Slow-Cooked Sausage Dressing, 44
Slow Cooker Pineapple Sweet
   Potatoes, 43
Sour Cream & Chives Mashed
   Potatoes, 97
Southwestern Rice, 52
Spiced Steak Potato Fingers with
   Dracula Dipping Sauce, 242
Spinach-Orzo Salad with
   Chickpeas, 147
Sweet Onion Creamed Corn, 108
Thanksgiving Green Beans, 94

SKEWERS & KABOBS
Antipasto Skewers, 218
Caramel Apple & Brie Skewers, 9
Ginger-Tuna Kabobs, 9
Tortellini & Shrimp Skewers with
   Sun-Dried Tomato Sauce, 9

SLOW COOKER RECIPES
BBQ Turkey Meatballs, 104
Black Bean Chicken Nachos, 110
Garden Green Beans & Potatoes, 104
Maple-Almond Butternut Squash, 44
Onion-Garlic Hash Browns, 193
Pumpkin Pie Pudding, 109
Six-Bean Chili, 107

Slaw-Topped Beef Sliders, 109
Slow-Cooked Sausage Dressing, 44
Slow-Cooked White Bean Chili, 32
Slow Cooker Crab Dip, 104
Slow Cooker Pineapple Sweet
   Potatoes, 43
Spiced Cranberry-Apple Punch, 107
Sweet Onion Creamed Corn, 108
Warm Cinnamon-Apple Topping, 110
Wine-Poached Pears, 20

SOUPS, STEWS & CHILI
Beer-Cheese Velvet Soup, 228
Carrot-Parsnip Soup, 166
Frogmore Stew, 212
Hearty Vegetable Soup, 44
Mushroom Shrimp Bisque, 19
Quick Tomato Soup, 178
Six-Bean Chili, 107
Slow-Cooked White Bean Chili, 32
Smooth & Creamy Pumpkin Soup, 94

SPINACH
Chicken with Red Pepper Sauce
   & Spinach, 178
Ham & Swiss Braids, 148
Herbed Lamb Chops with Crispy
   Potatoes, 171
Mushroom & Spinach Eggs
   Benedict, 171
Pork & Vegetable Spring Rolls, 168
Spinach-Orzo Salad with
   Chickpeas, 147
Stuffed Shells with Arrabbiata
   Sauce, 232

SQUASH & ZUCCHINI
Cranberry Roasted Squash, 19
Herby Pea Salad, 190
Maple-Almond Butternut Squash, 44

STRAWBERRIES
Chocolate-Strawberry Pretzel
   Cookies, 77
Creamy Strawberry Cheesecake, 178
Easy Strawberry Salsa, 218
Fruit with Poppy Seed Dressing, 138
Fruity Chicken Salad Mini
   Sandwiches, 151
Peach Champagne, 198
Strawberry & Cream Bruschetta, 193
Strawberry Ladyfinger Icebox
   Cake, 172
Strawberry Shortcake Stacks, 163
Topsy-Turvy Sangria, 56
Two-Berry Fluff Salad, 152
Vanilla Cupcakes with Rhubarb
   Compote, 189

SWEET POTATOES
Barley, Greens & Sweet Potato Salad, 47
Fluffy Sweet Potato Custard Pie, 100
Slow Cooker Pineapple Sweet
    Potatoes, 43

TOMATOES
Antipasto Skewers, 218
Black-Eyed Pea Tomato Salad, 212
Easy Strawberry Salsa, 218
Grilled Tomato-Peach Pizza, 221
Jicama Romaine Salad, 52
Lemony Shrimp & Snow Pea Pasta, 169
Lime Chicken with Blackberry Salsa, 201
Quick Tomato Soup, 178
Shrimp & Garlic Bruschetta, 198
Shrimp Pomodoro, 181
Spinach-Orzo Salad with Chickpeas, 147
Tomato-Goat Cheese Spread, 198
Tortellini & Shrimp Skewers with
    Sun-Dried Tomato Sauce, 9
Tropical Tabbouleh, 201

TURKEY
BBQ Turkey Meatballs, 104
Citrus Herb Turkey, 97
Elm Street Cheeseburger Joes, 242
Turkey Sliders with Sesame Slaw, 221

VEGETABLES
(also see specific kinds)
Beet Salad with Orange Vinaigrette, 178
Brussels Sprouts with Bacon
    Vinaigrette, 22
Fresh Herb Vegetable Dip, 218
Hearty Vegetable Soup, 44
Make-Ahead Veggie Salad, 141
Pork & Vegetable Spring Rolls, 168
Two-Bean Hummus, 114

WHITE CHOCOLATE
Apricot White Fudge, 36
Candy Cane Shortbread Bars, 71
Cashew Clusters, 60
Coconut-Rum Cake Pops, 14

Elegant White Chocolate Mousse, 65
Snow-Topped White Chocolate
    Macadamia Cookies, 35
White Chocolate Cheesecake with
    Cranberry-Orange Compote, 26
White Christmas Cake, 36

**YEAST BREADS
& YEAST ROLLS**
Basil Parmesan Bread, 80
Best Cinnamon Rolls, 80
Cape Cod Bay Brown Bread, 93
Caraway Bread, 20
Country White Bread, 32
Freeze & Bake Rolls, 47
Jalapeno Cheese Bread, 80

SHARE YOUR **MOST-LOVED RECIPES**

Do you have a recipe that's become part of your family's holiday tradition? Are homemade gifts included in your celebrations? We want to hear from you! Visit **tasteofhome.com/submit** to submit a recipe or craft for consideration.

PAGE 194

PAGE 83

PAGE 172

PAGE 118